Studies in Eighteenth-Century Culture

Volume 43

Studies in Eighteenth-Century Culture

Volume 43

Studies in Eighteenth-Century Culture

Volume 43

Published by The Johns Hopkins University Press for the
American Society for Eighteenth-Century Studies

The Johns Hopkins University Press
Baltimore and London
2014

Printed in the United States of America on acid-free paper.
9 8 7 6 5 4 3 2 1

The Johns Hopkins University Press
2715 North Charles Street
Baltimore, Maryland 21218-4363
www.press.jhu.edu

ISBN 978-1-4214-1376-1
1-4214-1376-0
ISSN 0360-2370

Articles appearing in this annual series are abstracted and indexed in *Historical Abstracts* and *America: History and Life*.

Contents

Editor's Note

The Pageant of Enlightenment

Although mythic tradition has obscured the origins of the cornucopia, with some saying that it owes to the strength of the infant Zeus and others ascribing the icon to a struggle between Hercules and a river god, the symbolic link between the horn of plenty and the earth goddess Demeter, that giver of splendid gifts as the Homeric hymn calls her, remains perfectly clear. Prompted by the joyful return of her daughter Persephone, so goes the myth, Demeter displays her generosity by providing an abundant harvest. Ancient Greece celebrated her yearly bounty with a vast annual procession followed by weeklong rituals of regeneration and renewal. The cornucopia becomes her special attribute as a result, and it also seems an appropriate symbol for the gathering of essays that follow, representing the best work of members of the American Society for Eighteenth-Century Studies as read before the various meetings of the society and its affiliates from 2010 to 2012. Published in the spring to coincide with the annual conference, the collection typically offers a wealth of learning sifted and winnowed by an expert team of editorial readers and overseen by an able editorial board.

Several essays share an interest in popular culture, whether centered in Berkeley's tar-water panacea, the narrative uses of personal anecdote, the *chanson populaire* as a focus of crowd consciousness, or contemporary film adaptations of period classics. The opening contribution of Paula R. Backscheider asks readers to entertain a certain continuity between popular pageantry and theatrical stagecraft, much as in the comic print accompanying her essay that shows John Rich entering Covent Garden theatre. The repeated use of sets and machinery in the London playhouses, she argues, provided women playwrights with an unexpected means of calling patriarchal authority into question. Backscheider's article ranges across a full century of theatrical farce from Aphra Behn, who uses the same scenery earlier employed by Dryden to radically different ends, to Elizabeth Inchbald, who will often stage a mini-procession to launch a political point. The feature is one among many others that the author calls "genre jolts" (22), theatrical moments that suddenly alert an audience to pay particular attention. Other essays share the aim of rescuing neglected authors from hasty critical assessment. In

Sarah B. Stein's recuperative study of John Dennis, for example, the act of biblical translation is understood to bridge a gap between the classical sublime of Longinus and Christian belief. Mediated by passion and reason, Dennis's theory and practice of translation becomes an interpretive guide to his entire critical program. Ann Campbell next takes up the surrogate family structures of *Moll Flanders*, where the mercenary adhockery of the heroine stands markedly at odds with the spiritual advice that Defoe gives in *The Family Instructor* and elsewhere. Campbell goes on to argue that the accumulation of personal capital largely determines the affective arc of the novel. Drawing upon the imaginative pleasures described by Addison in the *Spectator*, Patricia Comitini addresses the interplay of ideology and aesthetics in Eliza Haywood's *Fantomina.* The claim is that the novella activates forms of imaginative pleasure by aligning the senses with the understanding, and textuality with desire, in newly emergent ways, so that Haywood gives us a rare opportunity to catch aesthetic ideology on the rise.

In her essay on Jean-Jacques Rousseau, Rebecca Dowd Geoffroy-Schwinden records a popular festival that Rousseau describes in some detail before turning to Robert Darnton's *Poetry and the Police*: *Communication Networks in Eighteenth-Century Paris*, with its influential treatment of the mid-century Affair of the Fourteen. The arrest of ordinary citizens for ridiculing the royal court in song and verse not only reveals popular networks of collaborative composition, she suggests, but also recalls those demotic occasions through which seditious songs would circulate, occasions that in turn inform Rousseau's writing about music in society. In another treatment of authorial recuperation, Joanne E. Myers invites us to think about Bishop Berkeley's promotion of tar water in *Siris* as a complex sign of the bodily mediation of the divine rather than as an aberrant fit of enthusiasm in an otherwise orthodox rationalist. For Berkeley the animal spirit of the human body is analogized to the universal aether of the cosmos as microcosm to macrocosm, and his insistence upon our perception of the chains of connection forms a consistent epistemology of belief. In the essay that follows, April London takes up the generic status of the anecdote in Sarah Fielding. During the early decades of the century anecdote was linked to secret (and often scandalous) history in the practice of personal defamation sponsored by Whig and Tory party alike. By Fielding's day the anecdote had largely left behind secret history and found didactic use in the ethical comparison of character, a turn that would prove pivotal. As an important hybrid form, according to London, anecdote by mid-century has begun taking the measure of the fictive or documentary forms that increasingly play host to it.

Rori Bloom's essay on Restif de la Bretonne complicates our view of the revolutionary figure as a proponent of large-scale institutional reform. His 1789 *Le Palais Royal* recounts interviews with prostitutes that often trace the etiology of crime back to some disturbance in the family. Instead of recommending the systemic state reform he had urged two decades before in *Le Pornographe*, however, Restif now endorses a sentimental return to the family through bourgeois marriage, a reactionary solution that Bloom ascribes to Restif's own psychology and also to revolutionary fatigue. Sabrina Ferri turns our attention to the humanist, naturalist, and *filosofo* Lazarro Spallanzani in developing a hybrid sense of the ancient ruin as a human creation subject to natural decay. Combining a keen antiquarian imagination with modern empirical skepticism, Spallanzani was able to peer into the deep geological time of archaeological sites across the Mediterranean, shaping a polychronic view that would prove influential for the disciplinary formation of nineteen-century science. In her survey of female characterization in the drama of Arthur Murphy, Barbara Mackey King draws parallels between Murphy's early life and journalism on one hand, and the intelligent and lifelike characters he created for the stage on the other, characters played by some of the leading actresses of the day. Among the female roles that Murphy's mistress the celebrated Ann Elliott made her own, according to King, the witty, forceful, and much admired Lady Bell of Murphy's *Know Your Own Mind* best exemplifies his ideal. In her closing contribution to these pages, Karen Gevirtz revisits the question of film adaptation to look at three recent films, *Becoming Jane* (2007), *Gulliver's Travels* (2010), and *Crusoe* (2008–09), and suggests that while they all simplify the complexity of the past—Austen's fictional gift is implausibly attributed to a broken romance; the cinematic *Gulliver's Travels* diffuses satire to the point of negation; and *Crusoe* elevates consumerism alongside technology—their present-minded failures nonetheless foreground the value of attending to the ideological elements of inter-contextual critique.

Let me say that it has been a great pleasure to return to the task of editing *Studies in Eighteenth-Century Culture* after a dozen years and to see that the deeply collaborative nature of the publication, as well its willingness to feature the longer, more detailed study, continues strong. Let me also formally thank my co-editor Michelle Burnham and editorial assistant Garland Beasley for their kind encouragement, critical acumen, and unfailing dedication.

Editorial Readers for Volume Forty-three

From *The Emperor of the Moon* to the Sultan's Prison

PAULA R. BACKSCHEIDER

Eighteenth-century people loved processions. They crowded the streets for Lord Mayor's Day, royal progresses, and parades of prisoners to be transported, and they lucratively rewarded theatre managers for staging reenactments of coronations and all manner of grand processions from the serious to the ridiculous. Accompanied by opulent music, kings from every continent marched across the stages with a magnitude of attendees. Priests from every religion, armies in every uniform, various animals, shepherdesses nearly obscured by masses of flowers, and prisoners or beggars in grungy rags—audiences could see them all. Even the opening of theatres became performance occasions (fig. 1). Processions were but one kind of spectacle, and from the time Sir William Davenant had to overcome handicaps built into his patent at the Restoration they became a source of reliable revenue. In addition to their entertainment value, they were major ways that playwrights incorporated political commentary. Many of them began as though they were royal, even patriotic, events celebrating national values or merely calculated attempts to keep audiences coming. Suddenly a wildly ridiculous element interrupts and a serious, often angry point is disclosed.

Figure 1. John Rich's entry into the Covent Garden Theatre, 1732. William Hogarth, Thomas Cooke, Samuel Davenport, and John Trusler, *The Works of William Hogarth*, vol. 2 (London: Printed for J. Sharpe, King-Street, Covent-Garden; R. Griffin and Co. Glasgow, 1821).

Characters, costumes, sets, music, gestures, and mimicry provided means of commentary although only a few big productions with tableaux and processions had new sets and trappings. In fact, the most notable spectacular productions were the work of manager-playwrights or special alliances between managers and playwrights. Examples are the William Davenant-John Dryden-Henry Purcell *Tempest* (1674), the Thomas Betterton-Thomas Shadwell *Psyche* (1675), the John Rich-Lewis Theobald-Johann Galliard *The Necromancer; or Harlequin Dr. Faustus* 1723) and *The Rape of Proserpine with the Birth of Harlequin* (1727),[1] the David Garrick-Charles Dibdin-Isaac Bickerstaff *Maid of the Mill* (1765), and the George Colman-William Shield-Alexander Johnstone (machinist) *Blue-Beard* (1798). There is an obvious break between the seventeenth-century productions, the pantomimes of the second quarter of the eighteenth century, and the spectacular farces later in the century. In fact, farce became the genre that made a home for the seventeenth-century dramatic spectaculars. I want to work with two examples of women's uniting of spectacle and farce in times of crises as a way of beginning to explore mixed form plays as means of participation in public debate and of carrying out individual political agendas (domestic and national). My emphasis here will be popular culture formulas that are especially prevalent and long-lived in farce and spectacle.

I will begin with Aphra Behn's farce *Emperor of the Moon* with special attention to its relationship to John Dryden's *Albion and Albanius*, both elaborate spectacle plays produced during the troubled reign of King James II. Both are magnificent examples of their theatrical times. I will conclude with a few of Elizabeth Inchbald's plays. *Mogul Tale* is the farce that launched her career as a playwright, and another, *Wives as They Were, Maids as They Are*, about which she said that she could not "sustain true comedy" but "had recourse at the end of her second act to farce,"[2] is recognized as one of her most important plays. Produced nearly 100 years later, her plays are also representative of the plays of their time, of an equally tumultuous political time, and of playwrights' understanding of the work spectacle and processions can do when employed within farces.

The World of Farce and Spectacle

The standard for spectacular productions was set by Dorset Garden 1673–1692, and episodes from them continued to be performed as afterpieces and interludes throughout the eighteenth century. For example, Thomas Augustine Arne used the entire finale and Juno's Peacock machine from *Albion and Albanius* in 1771 in his *The Fairy Prince*, and *Emperor of the Moon* and pieces of it continued to be performed until 1748.[3] As the demand for afterpieces skyrocketed, farces were increasingly mined from other plays and remarkably, many of these earlier plays were spectacle or machine plays.[4] Scenery alone for *Psyche* cost more than £800, and *Albion and Albanius*, a collaboration of Dryden, Betterton, Louis Grabu, and Henry Purcell, an astonishing £4000. Psyche had nine different elaborate sets and also a cloud machine.[5] *Blue-Beard*'s £2000 sets included the panoramas of Blue-Beard-Abomelique's procession and then the liberating army's advances and the amazing mechanics of the Blue Chamber. Hiring an entire orchestra, singers, and dancers added to the cost, but the music was at least as important as the plot and its cast. In a production with a composer like Purcell or Shield, it could comprise 30–45 minutes of the performance time, and *Albion*, which reenacted the Restoration and reign of Charles II, was all song, like Italian opera. Playwrights often thanked the manager, as Dryden did Betterton, "who has spar'd neither for industry, nor cost, to make this Entertainment perfect, nor for Invention of the Ornaments to beautify it" (Preface to *Albion and Albanius* {1685}).

The only ways that a company could make such plays cover their expenses was by attracting large audiences and by mounting smaller but also spectacular productions using their engines, sets, machines, and costumes. ("Engines" were the ropes, pulleys, counterweights, etc., that moved the "machines," the chariots and scenes.)[6] Dryden, who had gone into debt with the other principals to produce *Albion*, wrote "that the playhouses were 'Like Monarchs, ruin'd with expensive War'."[7] More immediately, the machinery, special effects, and growing stock of sets and costumes made other kinds of plays, including "machine farces," possible.[8] One of the differences between spectacle plays and the great majority of long eighteenth-century plays is the wealth of stage directions. Because managers were necessary collaborators, beginning with Betterton, they wrote them and they were published with the texts of the plays.[9] These plays, thus, are an important source of information about the resources and experience of theatre in the long eighteenth century. In a time when the unities were highly respected, these plays that balanced singing, story, dancing, visuals, orchestral music, and acting opened the way for experimentation and new forms.

Richard Brinsley Sheridan's concluding scene in *The Critic* (1779) is one of the most familiar examples of the blending of farce and spectacle as political commentary. Following the crisis-ridden summer during which both France and Spain declared war on Britain, Sheridan set his play at the time of the defeat of the Spanish Armada in 1588, another time when invasion threatened. In Sheridan's final scene, after the English fleet destroys the Spanish one, a procession of all the English rivers and tributaries follows. As another example of the incompetence of the 1770s, both banks of the Thames have appeared on only one side of the river. This incident may be an allusion to *Albion and Albanius*, whose second act includes a parade of rivers, tritons, and sea nymphs attending Neptune as the scene shifts from Hell to the final act with the apotheosis of Charles II. Both Dryden and Sheridan might have remembered the wedding of the Thames and Medway in Edmund Spenser's *Faerie Queen*. In the *Faerie Queen*, while Proteus has Florimell, who is searching for the wounded Marinell, imprisoned in his dungeon, he hosts the wedding. All of the sea and river gods are present, and they are followed by all of the important continental rivers and then by English and Irish rivers. The magnificent procession is described in detail: "First came great Neptune with his threeforkt mace, / That rules the Seas, and makes them rise or fall."[10] By long tradition, the Thames is a male river-God,[11] and the Medway, a tributary of the Thames that ran through Kent, has an eloquent history, as the Battle of Medway was lost in the Roman invasion in June of 43 AD and Chatham on the Medway was the site of one of the worst defeats in the history of the Royal Navy in June 1667 during the Second Dutch War. After the *Faerie Queen* and *Albion*, personifications of rivers had become commonplace symbols of the rivers' mythic power to represent the nation and to be a gauge of Britain's power. As ridiculous as Sheridan makes his river procession, their appearance underscores his profoundly serious statement, as the parade is framed, on one side, by the plot's very strong political critique of Lord North and the response to the invasion threat and, on the other, by the music accompanying the rivers, each bringing to mind one major military victory after another in times that contrast sharply to current dithering and vulnerability.

As is probably obvious, women playwrights had to use what was left over for their tableaux and spectacles. Even *The Critic* used some from performances of other plays, and Drury Lane by 1779 was Sheridan's theatre. Limited access to the means to stage spectacles did not mean that women (and most male playwrights) did not see the benefits of staging them and using spectacular scenes. They also saw that such scenes are about power, its display and its ways of maintaining itself. Spectacles are means of subordinating and controlling people. Therefore, they offer extraordinary access to commentary on class and gender as well as national politics. Aphra Behn once wrote that plays and public "Divertisements" "are secret instructions to the People, in things that 'tis impossible to insinuate into them any other Way" (dedication of *The Luckey Chance*, 7:213). The same is true regarding Inchbald's self-conscious art and strategies. "Farce" is notoriously difficult to define, but in addition to the physicality of the action and the absurdity of situations and discoveries, a constituent element is that farces deliver topical satisfactions as those upon which Behn's and Inchbald's plays depend.

Aphra Behn's *Forced Marriage* (1670) had been pushed off the stage after only six nights by a new production of the spectacular Davenant-Dryden *Tempest* (1667), and she learned from that and her long association with Betterton's management preferences. Unlike most managers, he liked new plays and over the years he mounted a number of notably spectacular plays. His theatre developed new special effects and machines, better engines, and stunning sets, and, although only a few plays received expensive new trappings, these things were available to enhance other plays and attract bigger audiences. Behn developed considerable skill in taking advantage of Dorset Garden; the third act of *Sir Patient Fancy*, first produced in 1678, for instance, had ten changes of scene. Painted curtains, side wings, borders, and back scenes were routine. Pairs of wings ran between backscenes that were spaced far enough apart for the bedchamber and for groups of characters to appear. Successive shutters, painted canvas mounted on wooden frames and running in grooves behind the wings, allowed rapid transition from scene to scene.[12] People, properties, machines, and even scenes could be raised and lowered from traps, and some scholars have surmised that as many as six could be operated in a single production.[13] In addition to the delight in the different scenes, these possibilities provided multiple ways of unveiling dazzling spectacles and surprising combinations of characters. Behn said that she began writing *The Emperor of the Moon* in 1684 to please the beleaguered and ill Charles II, who had tried to bring a commedia dell'arte troop back to court in 1683. It was the most imaginative example of the voyage-to-the-moon and the machine farce fads. The play used twelve of the eighteen kinds of stage machinery that Dawn Lewcock identified as available, "more than any other production of the United Company."[14] (*Albion* used seven.) Because of the union of companies, Behn also benefitted from the very large cast available and in need of earning their weekly salaries.[15]

Also in 1684, Dryden began writing an all-music prologue intended, he tells us, as the prologue for a play like the Dryden-Davenant-Purcell *Tempest* but more probably for his in-progress *King Arthur*. A number of events intervened, and he expanded it to the three-act *Albion and Albanius*.[16] Charles saw a few rehearsals before his death on 6 February 1685. The opera was an allegorical history representing "the double restoration of his Sacred Majesty," specifically his return in 1660 and the royalist victory over the Rye House Plot. By 1684, "Parliament's efforts to exclude James from the line of succession had been defeated, along with a series of plots threatening Charles's authority and occasionally threatening his life."[17] Behn and Dryden, then, after extraordinary service during a time when Civil War was again an imaginable possibility, were writing elaborate, happy, extravagant plays to entertain their king and a more relaxed court. The contrast between Dryden's *Absalom and Achitophel* and Behn's *Love Letters between a Nobleman and his Sister* and these plays testify to their varied tonal talents, to their willingness to create sophisticated propaganda, and to their changed sense of what their art could be allowed to do.

Memories of the Popish Plot, Whig supremacy in the City, Monmouth's campaigns in the West, and the Exclusion Crisis that had created rapid partisanship and moments of hysteria in the general population faded. Dryden wrote *Albion* in the brief period when relations between the King and the City were better following the election of Sir John Moore, a moderate Lord Mayor, and Sir William Pritchard, a Tory one. He knew that the death of the king would likely renew Whig and Protestant opposition, but with James's coronation and the first parliamentary elections in four years there was a short period of quiet. In this short period Dryden prepared *Albion* for performance by writing thirty lines to make the play appropriate for the changed situation with the triumphant succession of James

(3.1.201–32). To "the double restoration of his Sacred Majesty," he added the triumphant succession of James. The production, however, was delayed until June 1685 to take advantage of the people returning to London for the opening of Parliament. In that delay Monmouth sailed for England. The City revealed itself again as historians have styled it, "conspiratorial and traitorous." It was again a breeding ground for maneuvers and plots against the monarchy, a home for Whigs, and a sanctuary for illegal presses that sprung up and produced mountains of pamphlets, broadsides, and newspapers. James had begun taking extraordinary measures, such as searching homes, seizing arms, horses, and wagons, and increasing guards at every City gate as support for Monmouth was no secret.[18]

The memories of past events and plots flowed anew into the unease aroused by actions James took after the crushing of Monmouth's rebellion, actions that were revealing the new king to be a devious plot master. Thus, *Albion* and *Emperor* actually mark two different periods of British history.

Albion and *The Emperor*

Unlike other texts by Dryden, the opera gestured throughout toward the special providences that had marked Charles's life from the escape at Worcester in 1651 to the fire that sabotaged the assassination attempt and that had been the subject of numerous sermons after the discovery of the Rye House Plot.[19] With the staging of Charles's rising to Heaven in the manner of Elijah (2 Kings: 2, 11), he maintained the divine right of kings. Dryden's opera opens with a new Frontispiece, an unusual and expensive addition. The majestic, highly symbolic scene was attached to one of the three sets of great pilasters, which stood on both sides of the proscenium opening, flat against the side-walls.[20] The inclusion of Peace, Plenty, Poetry, and the King's and Queen's Cyphers prepare the audience for *Albion*'s elaborate allegorical history of the highpoints of Charles II's reign and the hopes Dryden projects onto James's ascension to the throne. The curtain opens between the pilaster scenes with a replica of one of the statues of Charles standing at Charing Cross and the one of James at Windsor. Between them are the dejected and inert Augusta (London) and Thamesis (the River Thames) in poses recalling Satan's collapsed and defeated forces in *Paradise Lost*. Mercury descends in a Chariot drawn by Ravens, the birds Charles had declared guardians of the kingdom.[21] Augusta and Thamesis confess their disloyalty to Charles, and Dryden, thus, establishes the polar choices: loyalty to the King or evil. Mercury urges Thamesis to wash away their crimes against their good king.[22] Democracy and Zelota

(Zeal), the seducers and now would-be rapists of Augusta, and Archon (General Monck) demand financial tribute from Augusta and Thamesis. The opera is punctuated by dramatic conflicts, and the chorus of rivers urges Thamesis, first, to cleanse Augusta and himself and, second, to resist paying the tribute. Archon changes sides and rescues Augusta from being gang raped by Democracy and Zeal. Mercury announces that the 1660 Restoration of Charles is near. He, Archon, Augusta, and Thamesis joined by a representation of the "Four parts of the World" and the chorus sing a hopeful reprisal of the Restoration with a call to arms ("Hark! the Peales the People ring, / Peace and freedom and a King," 24).[23] Juno appears and announces that the gods have agreed that "*Albion* shall his love renew" (1.1.209). Albion's arrival is greeted by "Crowd's of People" and "*Welcome* rang like Peals of Thunder; *Welcome* rent the Skies assunder" (1.1.226–27). The four triumphal arches that had been erected at Charles's coronation are revealed, and Albion and Albanius arrive with a large procession.

Act 2 is set in classical hell with elements recalling Dante's *Divine Comedy* and Milton's Hell. Because Prometheus, Sisiphus, and other recognizable mythical figures are there, the audience easily recognizes the location. Democracy and Zelota identify themselves as Pluto's children and recite some of their evil deeds. Pluto needs a larger, steadier supply of damned souls and offers "A bravely bold design/. . . / In borrow'd shapes to Earth return" (2.1.67–68). This act, then, traces the Popish Plot, the Exclusion Crisis, and the decision to calm unrest by sending James away from London, which is presented as an "exile." In an especially pointed move, Dryden has Pluto send Commonwealth disguised as Patriot; "patriot," as it so often would in the long eighteenth century, had become a site of struggle with differing groups claiming it and accusing others of claiming it while acting as traitors to their country.[24] In *Absalom and Achitophel* Dryden sardonically calls it "All-atoning Name" and launches a full-blown attack: "Gull'd with a Patriots *name*, whose Modern sense/ Is one that would by Law supplant his Prince" (ll. 965–66). Alecto, the Fury of unceasing anger, accompanies them and infects Augusta. The second scene shifts back to London, and Augusta appears with a snake in her bosom for her repentance was "writ in Sand." A stronghold of Whigs who were largely safe from prosecution because of the allegiances of elected officials and juries, London seemed always on the edge of resistance if not rebellion.[25] Augusta proves an easy mark again for Democracy and Zeal's seduction. References in *Albion* to the suspension of London's ancient Charter in an important King's Bench decision in June 1683 provide evidence of the strife and distrust between Augusta and the King. The prologue had concluded with an admonishment: "Voices may help your

Charter to restoring;/ And get by singing, what you lost by roaring" (15).

The rest of the opera presents in real detail one threat after another to the royal pair and entertaining rescues and acts of courage. The allegory often assumes specific knowledge, as of Lord Grey greeting Monmouth with "100 Batchellors all in white. . . with white wands."[26] In *Albion*, "Boys in White," associated with the Saints and called Property Boys in a masque staged by Zelota, perform dances that end in fights with Sectaries with Protestant flails. Venus escorts Albanius back to Albion and proclaims, "Take a Warlike Loyal Brother; / Never Prince had such another" (3.1.6–7). The London audience loved fire, and a blast of flame protects Albion from the one-ey'd Archer hired to kill him; it was an allegorical depiction of Richard Rumbold, who had a blemished eye and was the renter of the farm from which the assassination of Charles and James was to be staged and of the fortuitous fire in Newmarket that led to the royals' early departure. Albion and Acacia (Catherine of Braganza as Innocence) have captured Proteus in his cave. Proteus, emblem of the political qualities needed in a successful king, changes himself into a lion, crocodile, dragon, and back and delivers the prophecy Albion and Albanius are seeking.[27] These historical dangers are punctuated by rallying, joyous choruses such as the call to arms and, at the end of Act 2, Neptune, the Tritons, Thamesis, and all the other characters joining in a grand chorus led by Apollo beginning, "All Hail yee Royal pair!" (39).

The production used the full, enormous space and resources of Dorset Garden (fig. 2). In Act 1 alone, Mercury descends in a chariot drawn by ravens, Juno among clouds drawn by peacocks, and Iris in a machine large enough to carry three people. Unlike the other theatres, individuals, groups, and vehicles could descend, ascend, move across the stage or from up- to downstage, or even swoop higher or lower while moving across the stage.[28] The clouds, frequently deployed in the opera, were of varying sizes and tints and could be lowered from various places and at differing speeds and opened to reveal heavenly arrivals.[29] Juno's machine, for instance, appears from behind clouds and moves slowly forward to the front of the stage where it descends. "While a Symphony is playing, . . . it opens and discovers the Tail of a Peacock, which is so Large, that it almost fills the opening of the Stage between Scene and Scene" (26). Pedestals large enough for sleeping men rise and then are lowered again. In Acts 2 and 3 using large traps, Apollo's chariot drawn by mechanical horses rises and disappears; Neptune, the Nereids, and Proteus rise and, with their followers, put on a magnificent show. Finally Albion is taken away to become a star in Apollo's machine. "Renown, assume thy trumpet" began a solo by Fame and then is taken up by the chorus with full orchestra accompaniment as the final song.

Figure 2. Dorset Garden Theatre. Undated print.

Using sliding flats, Betterton constructed a feast for the eyes that was at almost every moment deeply symbolic. For example, one vista is a walk between "very high Trees" with receding views of part of Windsor, Castlehill, St. George's Chapel, and the King's Lodgings (52). In a highly unusual and expensive decision, Act 2 opened to an entirely new set described as "The change is Total," a rendering of classical Hell. Grabu, widely recognized as the best composer of orchestral dance music working in London at the time, provided an unusual variety of kinds of dances. In Act 3, a near-civil war is acted out by six Sectaries (the "saints," those wishing the restoration of the Commonwealth) who "begin a formal affected Dance" and mime a plot with libels, and then the White Boys (Monmouth's followers) dance around them, falling "into a confus'd Dance, imitating fighting" (47).

Behn's play took place in the same city that Dryden portrayed in his first two acts, a city now more dangerous than during Charles's reign. That Monmouth's invasion occurred during the first performances of *Albion* certainly makes the point. Behn's revision of the play begun to amuse Charles in that peaceful interval, then, is marked not only by what Monmouth's rebellion taught her but by the reactions to James's retention of a standing army of 14,000 that included commissioned Catholic officers who had not conformed to the Test Act, dispensations that allowed the appointment of many Catholics to administrative offices, the trials of bishops who refused to distribute the second Declaration of Indulgence and forced the king to send them to the Tower, and efforts to pack parliament that "involved an intrusion by the central government into the affairs of the localities on an unprecedented scale."[30]

Behn used sets and machines that Dryden had, and, like so many of the plays after *Albion*, is somewhat in dialogue with it. Both of the plays take up a major issue, how the middle terms of the patriarchal triad God-ruler-father should be performed, and both are critical, although in radically different ways. After all, Charles I's extreme sovereign behavior had led to the Civil War and his execution, and Behn was watching James's shockingly obvious power plays aimed at undermining the influence of both the Church of England and Parliament. Inseparable from this discussion were the implications for fathers and, as is well known, the conduct of fathers became, perhaps, the major subject of novels for decades. As in *Absalom and Achitophel*, Dryden portrays Charles as too lenient, too easy on his beloved people; in Act 2, Charles says,

> I thought their love by mildness might be gain'd,
> By Peace I was restor'd, in Peace I Reign'd:
> But Tumults, Seditions,
> And haughty Petitions,
> Are all the effects of a merciful Nature (2.2.67–71)

Dryden continues to say that James will be "Ador'd and fear'd" and be more "Warlike." Charles, Dryden's "indulgent David," had left some participants in the Rye House Plot unpunished and pardoned Monmouth for his part in it in 1683 and even excused him from giving evidence against the other conspirators.[31]

One of the remarkable things about Dryden's and Behn's plays were how backward looking they were within the repertory of 1684–87. The machines and allegorical elements, the percentage of singing and dancing, and the mix of realistic and mythical characters in Dryden's play clearly claimed the legacy of court masques while Behn used some of the oldest conventions of intrigue comedy and commedia dell'arte and then transformed them into the symbolic representations of the court masque in her final scene. Although Drury Lane was used for most of the plays produced by the United Company, both *Emperor* and *Albion* were performed at Dorset Garden, which was used chiefly for spectacles.[32] The stage depth at Dorset Garden was at least 48' deeper than Lincoln's Inn Fields and the forestage a striking 12' deeper; the proscenium width was 10'6" larger, and the height 5' greater. With almost twice the space, the use of more wings and shutters, much more machinery, and more lavish spectacular effects could be optimized.[33]

Emperor begins modestly with scenes in rooms in a house, a garden, and an ordinary street provided by shutters, and Behn provides her usual comic scenes with characters bumping into each other in darkness and being forced to hide in closets in bedchambers. The antics of Harlequin and Scaramouch with tricks played on the serious characters, mock fights, and tumbling stunts add original and delightful diversions. The new scene in Act 2 was a drop curtain, and in it and Act 3, Behn employs drop, side, and hanging curtains for double discovery scenes, for unusual entertaining scenes as well as continuing to use shutters. Dorset Garden provided nine shutters and four curtains. In one scene, the characters, directed by Scaramouch, disguise themselves by standing as if they were painted on a hanging. The posing of Bellemante and Elaria becomes an important part of the theme of deception and gullibility, and there is a moment like a freeze-frame as Baliardo enters. In the final act, the parody of scenes like Dryden's is emphasized as, instead of "Timbrils, Kettle-Drums and Trumpets," the lovers' music is "Brass Kettles, and Pans, and Bells, and many tinkling things" (7:198). Staged in the gallery, thereby occupying the entire stage, the last scene expands to use the full resources of spectacular plays. As the scene in the front is drawn off, a long walk leading to Parnassus appears with symbolic figures and "machine of the Zodiack." Chariots fly, descend, and rise, and action, such as fighting at "Barriers," entertains the audience.

Emperor of the Moon is a fine example of political commentary and of an influential use of spectacle by women playwrights to admonish fathers, often through insisting upon similarities between them regardless of their level of governing. Although Emperor is part of the most overtly political decade of Behn's dramatic output, it is also an important example of women's sustained awareness of the patriarchal concept of God-ruler-father, and their exploration of the influence of the second term, ruler, on the third, father. Throughout the century, the difficulty of the middle term, to be justly sovereign as God is and in command without crossing into tyranny, as many thought King James did, becomes a new topic of exploration. It features Baliardo, a mock-patriarch keeping his daughter and niece captive in order to marry them to his advantage. A stock commedia character and perhaps a salvo at her Whig rival Thomas Shadwell, he is a spectacle whenever on stage. He enters wearing mathematical instruments hanging from a tool belt and with Scaramouch carrying his twenty-foot long telescope. Baliardo has timed his viewing with the hope that the Emperor will be in his closet, and he can steal his secrets. He admits that this is "flat Treason," and the fact that he is aiming at the closet shows that he hopes he will see a scheming, clandestine meeting. In 1686, King James had "initiated the process known as 'closeting', canvassing peers and MPs to agree to repeal the tests and penal laws that discriminated against the catholics." One of James's most resented initiatives, it has been described as "the most intensive process of . . . questioning that has ever been attempted in English history, bringing pressure to bear directly on virtually every individual within, or on the fringes of, the political nation."[34] Charmante, one of the lovers, enters and greets him, "Hail from the great Caballa," an obvious play on cabal (7:165). He claims that their intelligence, then the word for information or news, often about an enemy, is "more secret and sublime" than any other nation's. He tricks him into thinking that he has seen the Emperor, who is very sad because he loves a mortal, through his telescope. And so the plot begins, and Baliardo imagines the power he will have with such an alliance, his daughter married to the Emperor.

A stunning combining of English farce, opera, and court masque, the kinds of songs and dances common in comedy and commedia dell'arte especially as it had evolved on the French stage, it was an adaptation of a popular French play, *Arlequin empereur dans la lune*, and therefore was "news" from a prestige source. It had run fifteen consecutive days until the Easter break, and "it made an uproar which goes beyond everything that can be imagined. All Paris ran there and at every performance the place was found to be too small."[35] Behn could have seen the scenario for the production in March 1684 in Paris, and it was printed that year.[36] As in commedia dell'arte pieces, the servants Scaramouch and Harlequin lead the plots, which in this play are aimed at helping the daughter and niece marry their lovers. Behn has Scaramouch promise that the audience will see a farce embedded in the main play, which is his and Harlequin's.[37] He reports to Elaria that Cinthio and Charmante are "laying their heads together for a Farce" and it will be acted "Here, here, in this very House." The plot labeled "farce" is what is usually the main story, and the most common used in comedies, the attempts of young lovers to outwit an old guardian and marry. By having the father aim at marrying his daughter to the Emperor of the Moon, Behn is, of course, hugely exaggerating the obstacles to a happy conclusion.[38] Thus Behn slips in a comment on the state of London theatre and is, rightly, claiming the originality of her production. The romantic plot becomes the competition between Scaramouch and Harlequin for Mopsophil, the governante who doesn't even want to get married. What seems to persuade her is her desire not to "lye alone to Night" (204), a bawdy comment in harmony with the prioritizing of physicality in commedia. By styling this the romantic plot, Behn makes Baliardo's a political one, a story of scheming.

Scaramouch exclaims at the beginning, "There are such stratagems abrewing . . . ; Such a plot" (7:162). The action is farcical and physical, and such language gestures toward the culture of plotting in which the audience lived. Performed just before James issued the Declaration of Indulgence for Liberty of Conscience in April, a trick in its own right intended to undermine Anglican authority, the play turned schemers into fools like Baliardo or, more frequently, into tricksters working toward a happy ending. In a powerful scene Behn equates the desires of the gullible with voyeuristic, incestuous sex. Baliardo creeps into Elaria and Bellemante's room and finds them in nightgowns feigning sleep. They mumble as though they are being courted by the invisible Emperor and Prince, and Baliardo exclaims, "I am Ravish'd!" "I am Transported, Over-joy'd, and Ecstacy'd." He leaps and jumps around the room in physical demonstrations of his transport. His conclusion is that, indeed, the Emperor of the Moon is in love with a mortal: "Heaven keep me moderate! Least excess of Joy shou'd make my Vertue less.... How this agrees with what the learned Caballist inform'd me of last Night!" (182–83). The representation of ambitious political passion as sexual passion was common in plays of this period, as it was in *Albion and Albanius* when Democracy and Zelota, first, intend to rape Augusta and then to seduce her deceitfully.[39]

Behn's play moves from one deceiving performance to another. Desire is at the heart of deceptions; characters want and other characters want to believe. Even in so light and delightful a scene as when Harlequin writes alternate lines of Bellemante's poem, she persuades herself "some Divinity of Love" rather than a devil is writing the lines she wants to believe (7:171). The entry of the lovers Charmante and Cinthio disguised as the Emperor of the Moon and the Prince of Thunderland is both masterful entertainment and a satire of the attempts being used to dazzle the gullible. As other critics have demonstrated, Behn's political attitude at this time is complex, and exactly how the audience was to take Charmante and Cinthro's finale in the chariot is unclear.[40] Especially for those who saw *Albion* or had read the lavish new edition, it would have recalled the royal brothers. The opera portrays them as exceptionally close, united in virtue, purpose, and love for each other. Grabu's preface to the 1687 edition of the full score asserted, "Never were two Princes united more straightly together in common Sufferings for ungrateful and Rebellious Subjects" (*Works of Dryden*, 15:324). Unlike many comedies in Behn's time, her lovers are almost indistinguishable with none of the common elements such as different sensibilities.

Plot, characters, music, setting, props, favorite commedia dell'arte touches, low action, and a final spectacular procession kept entertainment high from beginning to end. Mini-processions develop themes and have satiric bite. One of the best involves a procession through a checkpoint, which includes an apothecary's cart with a real horse, and other vehicles. One of the many *lazzi* taken directly from the French source, Harlequin's game with the calash is a wonderful example of Behn's adaptation for political partisanship. He enters riding grandly and dressed as a gentleman. The officer dressed like a London constable stops him and demands the City's custom fees. Harlequin says he is a baker with a cart, therefore exempt, and when the Constable goes to get help to seize the horse, Harlequin quickly puts the back of the chariot down to create a cart and puts on a baker's coat. The Constable is accused of being drunk, the switch is played twice more. The episode with a mock fight and the farcical dialogue is characteristic of commedia, showcases the theatre's machinery, but also pokes fun at the City of London's petty and (to Behn and the court set) laughable and mercenary government.

This action is another comic illustration of the difficulty ordinary people have detecting deception. Chariots fly about the sky, and the people are depicted as easy to dazzle and enthrall. Behn situates this desire and gullibility in Beliardo, and the well-honed practices of Betterton's theatre take on symbolic significance in her hands as they had in Dryden's opera. Parodying the openly English operas that included Dryden's *King Arthur* and *Albion and Albanius* (1685), the play concludes as political musicals including Richard Sheridan's *Critic* did. In contrast to Dryden, Behn and Sheridan use pantomime and mimicry to avoid censorship and thrilled the audience with a grand but completely nonsensical procession. By massing the special effects that were, in fact, readily available at the theatre, Behn moves away from the more overtly political depiction of gullible people during the Popish Plot in her *Luckey Chance* (1686) and creates a series of surprises and delights for the audience. At that time, part of the entertainment was watching scene changes.[41] Unlike today's closing curtains, the curtain remained open throughout almost all plays, and, in plays like Behn's, the audience's view of scene changes provided a kind of dramatic irony—characters might be taken in but audiences watched the preparations for deceptions. The conversion to an exuberance of parody, satire, and individual episodes in Emperor is remarkable. Behn's finale is in a gallery "richly adorned, with scenes and lights" that quickly opens to show "the hill of Parnassus; a noble large walk of trees leading to it, with eight or ten negroes upon pedestals, ranged on each side of the walks." It had a full symphonic orchestra, the entire zodiac, a chorus, and finally a chariot bearing Cinthro and Charmante disguised as the Emperor of the Moon and the Prince of Thunderland. Kepler and Galileo descend in chariots and talk with Baliardo. Behn's play replaces special providences with human ingenuity openly creating what an ambitious and hopeful man wants to believe. Yet more than in *Albion* the charioteers rescue the "nation," and the vision of the union of king and prince is equally strong although less programmatic. From a gullible, conspiratorial milieu emerges a fantasy of harmony and union.

Overloading the audience with presentations of the escapes and illusions they enjoyed in the theatre of their time, Behn dramatizes the desire to be dazzled and fooled, then she provides the procession, and it stages the deepest purposes of spectacular parades. The finales of her play and Dryden's actualize the allusions to spectacular plays and their serious political allegories. Like all rulers attempting to impress their subjects with their power and might, Cinthro and Charmante have put together an imperial vision. The Negroes on pedestals are majestic signs of Empire, replicating the iconography of continents on map corners, but also pointing to Behn's unusual knowledge of British colonial slavery. At this sight, "Doctor falls on his Face." Dazzled by show, wanting to believe, and deceived, the Doctor is like the gullible people who are the dupes of spectacle, self-serving reportage, and naïve faith in government. Claiming literature (Parnassus) and science (Kepler and Galileo) as well as Empire, the lovers demonstrate their right to colonize the women and gullible, feminized men.[42] Significantly, *Arlequin empereur* had a richer plot for the doctor and his wards and no large procession. Virginia Scott, who has researched the plot, concludes, "in fact the spectacle is confined primarily to verbal descriptions."[43]

Clifford Geertz wrote, "Chiefs are changed to rajahs by the aesthetics of their rule," and the processions were aesthetic triumphs loaded with iconographic images.[44] In a time of ugly plots and public fear, the spectacle seemed omnipotent, "positive, indisputable, and inaccessible"—therefore, conferring invulnerability upon those who had the means and imagination to stage it.[45] The tableaux, like the final scene of Dryden's *All for Love* and other plays, imprinted allegorical meanings.

Mini-Processions

One hundred years after Behn's play, another woman playwright, Elizabeth Inchbald, was fascinated by the effects of imperial thinking and colonial governance, and she had a remarkable gift for staging miniature processions with shocking revelations of her acute insights. Rather than constructing full-scale spectacle plays, which by her time had become a separate genre more likely to be an afterpiece than a main piece, Inchbald's gift was the insertion of spectacle and processions in unexpected places. In *Wives as They Were, and Maids as They Are* (1797), Lord Priory arrives for a visit with Mr. Norberry with a grand procession very much symbolic of his opinion of his rights. Two heavily laden porters enter with trunks "from an upper Entrance," then Lord Priory, then Norberry's servant Oliver co-opted to carry small boxes, and finally Lady Priory, who, at her husband's signal, curtsies to her host. Priory announces grandly, "I have literally accepted Mr. Norberry's invitation, and am come to him with all my luggage."[46] Like the English governors entering Indian cities, his boxes and trunks testify to his wealth and importance. The action halts and everyone who is not in the procession becomes a spectator, perhaps "astonished" as Geertz describes the peasants who watch "an archaic traffic jam."[47] One has to wonder if Norberry was prepared for such an invasion of material goods and a rigidly governed "family."

In fact, the colonization of women is the theme of *Wives as they Were*, and it is a sign of a progression in the depiction of this concept in Inchbald's plays. Her first successful play, *The Mogul Tale* (1784), was a spectacle play with more in common with *Emperor of the Moon* than first meets the eye. First produced at George Colman's Haymarket Theatre, it was a huge, lasting hit, and it was clear she understood the combination of spectacle, comic threat, eccentric, original characters, and timely allusions. It, too, is a fantasy about space travel, and the commedia dell'arte doctor is a leading character. He, Johnny, a cobbler from Wapping, and his wife have gone on a balloon ride and crash-landed in a harem, which can be seen as a colony of imprisoned women. With spectacular backdrop and exotic costumes and locale, *Mogul Tale* opens with the harem women discussing the benefits of being the Mogul's favorite. The visitors are told immediately that they are guarded by eunuchs and that no one but the Great Mogul and "our wretched sex" can visit them. Johnny tells the eunuchs that Fanny "is my property" (1:17). The doctor displays the kind of thought that imagines England at the center of the universe. He explains that the balloon "is a Machine of French invention, founded on English Philosophy," "a method of Navigation in the Clouds," a distinction that awards hierarchy to theory over "mere application."[48] He is dazzled by the trappings the monarchy can award and uses a fake parchment roll to impress the Mogul:

> The King his master, is by the Grace of God, King of Great Britain, France, Ireland, Scotland, Northumberland, Lincolnshire, Sheffield, and Birmingham; giver of all Green, Blue, Red, and pale Blue Ribbons . . .—Grand master of every Mason Lodge in Christendom, Prince of the River Thames, Trent, Severn, . . . Fleet-Ditch, and the Tweed . . . husband of one good wife, and father of eighteen fine children. (1:9–10)

Plays were quite intertextual, and the gesture toward Sheridan's procession of rivers instantly allies her play with political commentary that stripped ceremony away to reveal the masking of a lack of substance. In fact, Inchbald's doctor's speech is a description of a procession in Dryden's *Albion and Albanius*. The stage direction reads, "In the Air is a Vision of the Honors of the Garter, the Knights in Procession, and the King under a Canopy." The next stage direction instructs, "A full Chorus of all the Voices and Instruments . . . and Twenty four Dancers all the time in a Chorus."[49]

Both Behn and Inchbald display "a foolish—yet operative—patriarchy" in which household management and state government are mirror images.[50] The phrase is Susan Carlson's description of the situation of the women in *Emperor of the Moon*, but its application to the other texts converts it into a powerful tool for explication. "Foolish—yet operative": the entertainment and satire of the foolish raise the question of whether the experience of them trumps the fact that the patriarchy is clearly "operative," and the women "dwindle into wives" who often cease even to speak. In *Wives as They Were*, Inchbald most clearly dramatizes the absorption of the assumption of patriarchal privilege into male characters. Lord Priory's despotic control of his wife with her rigid schedule (up at five and in bed by ten) and her duties as a servant (including serving as his valet) is an obvious example. He and Sir William agree that "indulgence [is] the bane of female happiness" (2:7). The most revealing scene is a "point," a theatrical technique used to call attention to a climactic, revealing moment in a role or situation. Sir William Dorrillon, who has been in India making his fortune for many years, has returned disguised as Mr. Mandred in order to observe his daughter and gauge her character. In a tense scene, his daughter begins a compliment in a light tone, one that has developed as they have sparred with each other: "Indeed, my rigid monitor, I cannot but express admiration, that, under those austere looks . . . , there still should lurk—" Suddenly he thunders,

> Have a care—don't proceed—stop where you—dare not you complete a sentence that is meant to mock me. I have borne the impertinence of this whole company with patience, with contempt; but dare you to breathe an accent suspicious of my conduct, and I will instantly teach you how to respect me, and to shrink with horror from yourself. [She stands motionless in surprise.]
>
> Miss Dorrillon [rallying]: "I protest, Mr Mandred—"
>
> Sir William: Silence [Raising his voice.] Dare not to address yourself to me. (2:50)

The audience knows he is her father, but this sudden assumption of the right to exercise authority and absolute power as a mere guest in Norberry's house is a striking moment, one followed up by his allowing a bailiff to seize her and take her to prison for her debts (fig. 3). Once again, like the harem women and Fanny, another Inchbald leading lady is confined, the victim of patriarchal power that creates a position for her as a colonial subject under an obviously "operative" patriarchy. Inchbald's plays, written at the time when the multiplication of kinds of subject people and the rising self-consciousness of women and the lower-classes, further complicate the middle term of the patriarchal concept. All these texts end with a marriage, which is clearly presented as accomplishing the colonial project: to put subjects in a highly controlled situation and to set up the conditions in which the governor (the father-ruler) can expect no further trouble of any kind from them. Miss Dorrillon is denied the opportunity of refusing or accepting Sir George; her father pronounces, "You will not be surprised, if the first command I lay upon my daughter," is to marry Sir George and "become the subject of a milder government" (2:94). Sir William with the wealth and experience of India and with lines that thundered authority is another father-ruler, one who can make mistakes and even become an object of ridicule, but the conclusion reveals the operative patriarchy, the master fictions by which that social order lives.

Inchbald knows the insignias and formalities of power well. Many of her plays, both comedies and sentimental ones, include a procession leading to an execution. As the execution of the doctor in *Mogul Tale* approaches, the first eunuch invites Johnny and the rest to watch. Then the second eunuch arrives with a paper with, significantly, a seal on it. The next scene begins with the curtain opening to reveal the Mogul on his throne. Wallace Stevens once wrote, "Women understand this. / One is not duchess / A hundred yards from a carriage," and there is no royalty without

Figure 3. Miss Dorrillon begging not to be turned over to the Bailiff. Elizabeth Inchbald, *Wives as They Were, Maids as They Are* (Longman, 1817).

a throne. Before the Mogul are the guards and executioners beside the "Apparatus for Execution" and the fettered doctor. He has been sentenced after the discovery of his plan to kidnap a woman "as I want to try an experiment, which can live longest in the air, the women of this country, or our own" (1:12). Naturally it is women on which he intends to experiment. Commedia dell'arte featured men, not women, and Inchbald's doctor is part of the tradition. At one point Baliardo says, "I am of that opinion, sir; man was not made for woman." Charmante responds with Rosicrucian philosophy from *The Count of Gabalis*, which associates women with gnomes and salamanders.[51]

Inchbald would have been familiar with the characters and, more significantly, with the sets and machinery easily available to her. *The Mogul Tale* took advantage of them, and in a more serious play she used some of them again. Harris, the producer of many of Inchbald's plays, was a notoriously business-oriented manager, but he kept a large cast to staff the many pantomimes. What he would finance is illustrated by the production of John O'Keeffe's pantomime, *Omai; or, a Trip round the World* (1785), which included music and sets designed by a collaboration of Shield, Philippe Jacques de Loutherbourg, and John Webber, the chief illustrator on Captain Cook's voyage.[52] *Such Things Are* (1787), set in Sumatra, included a dungeon that held Arabella, a beautiful English woman, and a small but carefully devised procession toward another execution. Twineall, a fop who has unapologetically stated that he is there only to seek a lucrative position, asks a friend whom he has not seen for six years to "inform me of the secret dispositions, and propensities of every one in this family, and of all their connections." Like Baliardo, he believes secrets to be the path to advancement, and Inchbald conjures up another age of unprecedented scrutiny of people even on the fringes of politics, another time of "closeting." But Twineall's blunders in using the information lead to his arrest and conviction as a revolutionary. An exotic Eastern potentate again has a pretentious, foolish Englishman in his power. One of the great masters of mixed form plays, Inchbald stretched the boundaries of genre by, for instance, effectively combining the sentimental plots popular in her time with all kinds of comedy, including the great traditions of English farce and political spectacle.[53]

Conclusion

In times of crises with the monarchy, playwrights deploy the patriarchal link between ruler and father. Not only is it a protection from censorship but it also emphasizes the importance for ordinary citizens who historically and without thinking model their concept of parent and master on that of ruler and especially king. "Father" can be depicted in myriad ways and specific gestures toward the sovereign made with biting acuity. In a dramatic tradition like London's in which playwrights hold a strong sense of national responsibility, they take up the "solemn duty of exposing and contending with those [master] fictions."[54] In a time when new fictions by which new generations would live were being created as in the 1680s and the 1780s and 90s, the responsibility is greater. The sultan in *Mogul Tale* lectures the English travelers: "I am an Indian, a Mahometan, my laws are cruel and my nature savage—You have imposed upon me, and attempted to defraud me, but know that I have been taught mercy and compassion for the sufferings of human nature" (1:20). He sends them back to England. Contrasting starkly to the pompous exaggeration of the trivia in the Doctor's summary of the British king's power (minor rivers, ribbons, "countries" including Lincolnshire), he is a majestic figure. Surrounded by the scruffy English characters, he regally takes center stage physically and morally, thereby dramatizing what was becoming a frequent challenge to the British people to live up to their ideals of liberty and humanity.

It is telling that Dryden moved back to employ masque techniques known to create "a settled system of values . . . divinely ordained,"[55] while Behn and Inchbald wrote innovative mixed form plays that built in genre jolts. From the pen of a skilled writer, no genre shift is accidental or even neutral, especially when the shift involves the evocation of something as exceptional and expensive as spectacles and tableaux or as different from the dominant category of the play, as Inchbald's moments of farce are. These jolts move audiences out of comfortable expectations and force interpretation. They are, indeed, examples of Behn's "secret instructions to the People, in things that 'tis impossible to insinuate into them any other Way." As women, Behn and Inchbald left considerable evidence that they were aware of the "operative patriarchy" and its effects. "Dryden said he was 'only the historian' and not the 'inventor' of [*Absalom and Achitophel*], and an historian was obliged to be impartial."[56] In this poem and in *Albion* his gift is allegory. In contrast, Behn uses spectacle to tap into allegorical potential, but relies upon farce to exploit that form's potential for topical allusions and messages. Inchbald does the same. In fact, in her most farcical moments, Inchbald parodies the upper ranks of society and lays bare the destructive and undeniable links between the assumed privileges and practices of rulers and the conduct of fathers and those, like the doctors, who believe they have special rights.

Unlike the gullible characters and largely dazzled audiences, we as theatre historians need to reach toward these secret instructions and consider how they were received in their first appearances when they were often covert interpretations and advice on immediate political situations and how they forge sustained commentary on the most important concepts in English government.

NOTES

1. Marc Martinez notes that Rich's pantomimes played 777 nights between 1723 and 1760, in "The Tricks of Lun: Mimesis and Mimicry in John Rich's Performance and Conception of Pantomimes," *Theatre History Studies* 29 (2009): 148–70. His article makes clear the importance of the Dorset Garden operas and commedia dell'arte. On the collaboration, see Roger Fiske, *English Theatre Music in the Eighteenth Century* (London: Oxford University Press, 1973), 72–87. I want to thank my research assistant, Pamela Frank, for her contributions.

2. Elizabeth Inchbald, *Remarks on Wives as They Were, Maids as They Are* in *Remarks for The British Theatre (1806–1809)* (Delmar, NY: Scholar's Facsimiles & Reprints, 1990), 1.

3. Tanya Caldwell, *Popular Plays by Women in the Restoration and Eighteenth Century* (Peterborough, Ontario: Broadview Press, 2011), 22. She also notes a production at the Patagonian Theatre in London in 1776; this theatre primarily performed puppet shows and pantomimes, 22 n. 6.

4. See Tonya Howe, "Abject, Delude, Create: The Aesthetic Self-Consciousness of Early Eighteenth-Century Farce," *Restoration and Eighteenth-Century Theatre Research*, 25, no. 1 (2010): 26, 32–33.

5. Judith Milhous, "The Multimedia Spectacular on the Restoration Stage," in *British Theatre and the Other Arts, 1660–1800*, ed. Shirley Strum Kenny (Washington: Folger Books, 1984), 47–48, 55, 61.

6. Dawn Lewcock, "Computer Analysis of Restoration Staging, III, 1682–1694," *Theatre Notebook*, 48, no. 2 (1994): 111.

7. Quoted in James A. Winn, *John Dryden and His World* (New Haven: Yale University Press, 1987), 443 and see 416–17.

8. Among these plays were Dryden's *Amphitryon* (1690) and Thomas Shadwell's *Lancashire Witches* (1681), Milhous, "Multimedia Spectacular," 43–44. Todd Gilman appends "A New Register of First Performances of English Operas and Related Genres, 1660–1719" to "London Theatre Music, 1660–1719" in *A Companion to Restoration Drama*, ed. Susan J. Owen (Oxford: Blackwell, 2001), 269–73. He does not include Behn's play.

9. David Roberts, *Thomas Betterton: The Greatest Actor of the Restoration Stage* (Cambridge: Cambridge University Press, 2010), 143–50; Frans and Julie Muller, "Completing the Picture: the Importance of Reconstructing Early Opera," *Early Music*, 33, no. 4 (2005): 673; see importance of Betterton's large collection of illustrated books, 667–81.

10. Edmund Spenser, *The Faerie Queene*, ed. A.C. Hamilton (London: Longman, 1977), Book 4, canto 11, verse 11, p. 509. Earl Miner points out that Ben Jonson's *Neptunes Triumph for the Returne of Albion* was intended to celebrate Charles I's return from Spain in 1624, *The Works of John Dryden*, ed. Earl Miner (Berkeley: University of California Press, 1976), 15:327. All references to *Albion and Albanius* and Miner's scholarship are from this source.

11. On Dryden's association with Spenser, see *Works of John Dryden*, 15:327–29 and 370.

12. See Richard Southern's elaborate description in *Changeable Scenery: Its Origin and Development in the British Theatre* (London: Faber and Faber Limited, 1952), 146–51; see also 125–26, 138. His drawings show the possibilities for many scene changes, and he is illustrating Behn's *Sir Patient Fancy*, 150.

13. Colin Visser, "Scenery and Technical Design" in *The London Theatre World, 1660–1800*, ed. Robert D. Hume (Carbondale: Southern Illinois University Press, 1980), 94–99.

14. Steven Henderson records Charles's attempt to bring the troop, "'Deceptio Visus':Aphra Behn's Negotiation with Farce in *The Emperor of the Moon*," in *Aphra Behn (1640–1689): Identity, Alterity, Ambiguity*, ed. Mary Ann O'Donnell, Bernard Dhuicq, and Guyonne Leduc (Paris: L'Harmattan, 2000), 60, quotation, 63. Henderson is quoting Lewcock's study in *Theatre Notebook*, 48, no. 2 (1994): 103–15. On the popularity of moon travel literature, see Janet Todd, ed., *Works of Aphra Behn*, 7 vols. (Columbus: Ohio State University Press, 1992–96), 7:155, and Al Coppola, "Retraining the Virtuoso's Gaze: Behn's *Emperor of the Moon*, the Royal Society, and the Spectacles of Science and Politics," *Eighteenth-Century Studies*, 41, no.4 (2008): 481–506, and on machine farces, Coppola, 495–96, and Milhous, "Multimedia Spectacular," 55–57. Derek Hughes gives a good summary of the resources available to Behn, "Aphra Behn and the Restoration Theatre" in *The Cambridge Companion to Aphra Behn*, ed. Derek Hughes and Janet Todd (Cambridge: Cambridge University Press, 2004), 37–38. Coppola's important article also compares *Albion* and *Emperor* and discusses many of the same points that I do. He sees a different relationship between the two plays, interpreting Behn's as a satire of Dryden's, and is also analyzing a different thematic drive. All references to Behn's *Emperor of the Moon* are to Todd's edition.

15. Roberts notes that immediately upon union, the number of performers swelled to forty-two, while 22–28 was more routine, *Thomas Betterton*, 138–39.

16. Winn, *John Dryden and His World*, 394–95; John Dryden, "Preface" to *Albion and Albanius* in *Works of Dryden*, 15:3, 11.

17. Andrew Pinnock, "A Double Vision of Albion: Allegorical Re-Alignments in the Dryden-Purcell Semi-Opera King Arthur," *Restoration*, 34, nos.1–2 (2010–2011), 58.

18. J.R. Jones, *Country and Court: England, 1658–1714* (Cambridge: Harvard University Press, 1979), 223; Paula Backscheider, *Daniel Defoe: His Life* (Baltimore: Johns Hopkins University Press, 1989), 37–38.

19. On special providences, see Phillip Harth, *Pen for a Party: Dryden's Tory Propaganda in Its Contexts* (Princeton: Princeton University Press, 1993), 223–25, 254–61.

20. Southern, *Changeable Scenery*, 185–87.

21. In 1675, Charles had accepted a prophecy that, should all of the ravens leave the Tower of London, a great catastrophe would befall the kingdom, and he decreed that there would always be six cared for by the Raven Master.

22. On Charles II's problems with the City, see Paul Hammond, "Dryden's *Albion and Albanius*: The Apotheosis of Charles II" in *The Court Masque*, ed. David Lindley (Manchester: Manchester University Press, 1984), 171–72.

23. Archon represents General George Monck, later Duke of Albemarle, who

was thought to be marching from Scotland to bolster the Protectorate but who joined the royalist side.

24. See Ronald Knowles, "The 'All-Attoning Name': The Word *Patriot* in Seventeenth-Century England," *Modern Language Review*, 96, no.3 (2001): 624–43. He points out that Dryden reached a "revised conservative" definition by the 1690s that influenced later discourse, 641–43.

25. On the struggle between Court and City in the 1680s, see Harth, *Pen for a Party*, 206–68.

26. Winn, *Dryden and His World*, 338.

27. The specificity of the allegory suggests the small theatrical audience of the time; the One-Ey'd Archer is Richard Rumbold, who possessed the farm Rye House. Charles was to pass it when he returned from Newmarket, but a fire in Newmarket led him to return early and avoid the plot, Miner, "Commentary" in *Works of Dryden*, 15:378; I have benefitted from his careful notes throughout this discussion. On Proteus, see Hammond, "Dryden's *Albion and Albanius*," 176.

28. Visser, "Scenery and Technical Design," 101–2.

29. Visser, "Scenery and Technical Design," 94, 101–4.

30. Jones, *Country and Court*, 243.

31. Harth, *Pen for a Party*, 221, 237–38.

32. Lewcock, "Computer Analysis," 103–05.

33. Edward A. Langhans, "The Theatres" in *The London Theatre World, 1660–1800*, ed. Robert D. Hume (Carbondale: Southern Illinois University Press, 1980), 42, 61–62.

34. Jones, *Country and Court*, 231 and 241.

35. Quoted from *Mercure galant*, Virginia Scott, *The Commedia dell'Arte in Paris, 1644–1697* (Charlottesville: University Press of Virginia, 1990), 293.

36. Henderson, "'Deceptio Visus,'" 60; Todd, *Works*, 7:154; Jane Spencer questions the publication date of the French production, T*he Rover and Other Plays* (Oxford: Oxford University Press, 1995), xviii.

37. Henderson discusses what he calls the farce-within-a-farce in "'Deceptio Visus'": 59–66.

38. Robert Markley notes that this is the plot in "most comedies," "Behn and the Unstable Traditions of Social Comedy" in *The Cambridge Companion to Aphra Behn*, ed. Derek Hughes and Janet Todd (Cambridge: Cambridge University Press, 2004), 99.

39. See James A. Winn, *"When Beauty Fires the Blood": Love and the Arts in the Age of Dryden* (Ann Arbor: University of Michigan Press, 1992), 256–59, 267–68. See also George Haggerty, *Men in Love: Masculinity and Sexuality in the Eighteenth Century* (New York: Columbia University Press, 1999), 23–43.

40. Coppola sees *Emperor* as a satire targeting *Albion* and attempting "to identify, stimulate, and ultimately retrain a troubling appetite for uncritical wonder in her audience." He summarizes and cites the major studies of Behn's "ambivalence toward Toryism and the Court" in the 1680s, 481–82, 498–99 nn. 3, 4.

41. Southern, *Changeable Scenery*, 17, 20; liveried servants removed and

changed furniture and props, 261–62.

42. The frontispiece for *Albion* shows Poetry, Painting and two Muses with musical instruments, a similar identification of power with the arts.

43. Scott, *Commedia dell'Arte in Paris*, 293–97; on authorship, 280–83, 296, 328.

44. Clifford Geertz, "Centers, Kings, and Charisma: Reflections on the Symbolics of Power," in *Culture and its Creators*, ed. Joseph Ben-David and Terry Nichols Clark (Chicago: University of Chicago Press, 1977), 157.

45. Guy Debord, *Society of the Spectacle* (Detroit: Black and Red, 1983), par. 12.

46. Elizabeth Inchbald, *Wives as They Were, Maids as They Are* in *The Plays of Elizabeth Inchbald*, ed. Paula R. Backscheider, 2 vols. (New York: Garland, 1980), 2:21. Quotations from all of Inchbald's plays are from this edition.

47. Geertz, "Centers, Kings," 159.

48. Daniel Defoe is at some pains to praise England as a nation that applies discoveries (makes improvements), while he praises a list of discoveries including the compass in *A General History of Discoveries and Improvements* (London: J. Roberts, 1726). These categories presented a clear distinction to people of the time.

49. Dryden, *Albion and Albanius*, 15:52–53.

50. Susan Carlson, "Aphra Behn's *The Emperor of the Moon:* Staging Seventeenth-Century Farce for Twentieth-Century Tastes," *Essays in Theatre* 14, no.2 (1996): 124.

51. Behn, *Emperor of the Moon*, 7:166. Jane Spencer's notes to *The Emperor of the Moon*, illuminate the references to *The Count of Gabalis*, *The Rover and Other Plays*, 282–85.

52. Daniel O'Quinn, "Theatre and Empire" in *The Cambridge Companion to British Theatre*, 1730– 1830, ed. Jane Moody and Daniel O'Quinn (Cambridge: Cambridge University Press, 2007) 243–45.

53. Betsy Bolton describes Inchbald's plays this way, *Women, Nationalism, and the Romantic Stage: Theatre and Politics in Britain, 1780–1800* (Cambridge: Cambridge University Press, 2001), 42.

54. Geertz, "Centers, Kings," 171.

55. Hammond, "Dryden's *Albion and Albanius*," 179.

56. John M. Wallace, "Dryden and History: A Problem in Allegorical Reading," *ELH*, 36, no.1 (1969): 279.

Translating the Bible to Raise the Fallen: John Dennis's Psalm 18

SARAH B. STEIN

John Dennis, the influential literary critic of the early eighteenth century, is primarily read today as an important theorist of the sublime and a stock proponent of neoclassicism in poetics.[1] Throughout his critical oeuvre Dennis struggles to unite these two seemingly opposed forces through a theory of poetry which could be passionately sublime and simultaneously adhere to strict rules. As noted by numerous critics, the attempt to combine passion and rule causes Dennis considerable trouble.[2] What has not been noted before is that Dennis himself attempts to provide a solution to the contradictions in his theory: translation. Although he devotes considerable effort to the development of a theory of biblical translation in his two most influential essays, *The Advancement and Reformation of Modern Poetry* (1701) and *The Grounds of Criticism in Poetry* (1704), scholarship has paid little attention to the central role that translation plays in Dennis's work. The contribution of this article will be to present a new outlook on Dennis—as a biblical translator. Through a reading of Dennis's translation of Psalm 18 in *The Grounds*, the article will argue that the traditional reading of Dennis as a theorist of both the sublime and the neoclassical can best be understood through his attempt to harmonize these two (opposing) forces through the process of translation. The poetry that he reveals as truly sublime is based on biblical text but translated into English according to his version of neoclassical poetic rules in order to combine biblical passion with neoclassical reason and order. By means of translation, he attempts to unite contrary forces in order to return poetry to what he viewed as its original, harmonious state.

Dennis's understanding of translation developed from the work of John Denham and John Dryden. Both Denham's and later Dryden's theories of translation, based on a reading of Horace, provided the model for eighteenth-century translation. In 1656, John Denham's *The Destruction of Troy* argues for a free approach to translation. Similarly, Dryden's 1680 preface to *Ovid's Epistles* follows Denham's lead in calling for a move away from literal translation.[3] This understanding of translation as a process of domesticating imitation became the norm of translation throughout the eighteenth century.[4] In T*he Translator's Invisibility: The History of Translation* Lawrence Venuti argues that eighteenth-century translations which focused on the free hand of the translator served to erase the signification of the foreign in translated texts, changing them in order to claim them as domestic works.[5] In this narrative, the investment in free translation as a means of incorporating foreign texts continued unabated throughout the century, being taken up by both the Earl of Roscommon in his 1685 *An Essay on Translated Verse* and by Alexander Pope in his translation of Homer.[6] Dennis was certainly greatly influenced by the work of Dryden and promotes domestication in translation in his critical work. In fact, Dennis goes so far as to claim that Virgil "is now, by Mr. Dryden's Translation, to be reckon'd among our own Poets; and so comes within the compass of my Design."[7] By way of translation poetry can come into the English language, but also, in Dennis's estimation, into the English tradition.

By turning away, however, from the focus on classical translation found in Denham, Dryden, and Roscommon, and towards the Bible, Dennis also promotes a more radical understanding of translation as a means of personal and communal redemption.[8] Dennis's psalm translation serves to radicalize the neoclassical notion of translation, investing it with the religious connotation of translation as the means of moving from earth to heaven.[9] His writing reveals a passionate voice calling for the reform of literature and society through a process of biblical translation. Dennis's theory of harmonizing translation is, thus, both firmly within the conventional Denham-Dryden-Pope trajectory of eighteenth-century translation history and opposed to it in key ways. While Dennis supports the notion of translation as the reclamation of a classical or biblical tradition for England, he also sees translation as a path to personal and societal redemption and as a way to connect earthly and spiritual realms.[10]

At the same time, Dennis also uses translation as the means to overcome contradictions in his own theory. Previous critics have noted a tension in Dennis's work and a way in which his thought seems to be at odds with itself. Shaun Irlam notes: "The most palpable tension in Dennis's treatise arises from [the] wishful juxtaposition of 'rules' and 'passion.'"[11] He argues that Dennis never fully articulates the relationship between passion and rules. In "Mapping the Aesthetic Mind: John Dennis and Nicolas Boileau" Ann T. Delehanty writes, "The analogy between religion and poetry causes Dennis the most difficulties for his poetics."[12] She proposes that the difficulty stems from a tension between poetry as divine revelation on the one hand and as a craft with specific knowable rules on the other hand. John Morillo points to the same problem: "Dennis reveals how fully politicized the far-from-disinterested world of aesthetic values had become by 1701, and how difficult it could be to try to maintain simultaneous and sincere allegiance to Locke, Longinus, and Luke in one unified-field theory of poetry."[13] Morillo puts the tension in political terms; he links any apparent contradictions in Dennis's theory to a need to speak about enthusiasm and divine revelation without seeming to support political radicalism. In *The Religious Sublime*, David B. Morris locates the tension in Dennis in the meeting of the neoclassical rule of imitation, in which imitation of something knowable is the best form of art, and the need to imitate the unknowable in the form of the Christian God.[14] In short, all of these critics locate Dennis's problem at the intersection of the neoclassical and the religious. I contend that it is by means of translation into English that Dennis overcomes the contradiction between the neoclassical and the religious within his own critical writing.

The radical nature of the theory of translation as harmonization that Dennis promotes becomes apparent in the vision of purity and redemption that he sees as possible through biblical translation. For Dennis, poetry and religion are not simply complementary. They are one and the same project, and redeeming one will redeem the other. Poetry is not only a metaphor for salvation, but the actual means of salvation. Alexander Pope famously maligned Dennis for his enthusiastic embrace of sublime passion, calling him "Sir Tremendous Longinus."[15] Although in the ruin of Dennis's reputation that followed, Pope's assessment could be called cruel, his understanding that Dennis was a radical was very astute.[16] Dennis's version of translation is more than a repetition of Denham's and Dryden's neoclassical model. It calls on translation as the means of religious redemption.

In *The Advancement and Reformation of Modern Poetry* (1701) Dennis argues for the inseparability of religion and poetry based on a retelling of the story of the fall. He states that man is unhappy when his reason and passion are divided and at odds with one another, a state that he argues came about with the fall. In paradise man was completely happy, but by eating from the tree of knowledge he gave in to his animal passions, thus separating reason from passion and causing all of modern man's present unhappiness: "Man's fatal Original Sin, whether the business of the Tree of Knowledge is Literal or Allegorical, consisted in his horribly diverting his affections from his god to the Creatures. And thus the Harmony of his Intellectual and Animal powers was very miserably broke."[17] In essence, Dennis here rewrites the story of the fall as a severing of faculties, moving away from a 'literal' reading of the story and toward an 'allegorical' explanation that makes the division of passion and reason the actual event and epicenter of the fall.

The restoration of the harmony of the faculties is, for Dennis, found in both Christian religion and poetry. In the second half of *The Advancement*, entitled "That the Design of the True Religion and Poetry are the Same," Dennis asserts that by using the Christian religion modern poets can be as good as and even exceed the ancient poets, who he contends were superior due to the incorporation of religion in their poetry. He begins with the proposition of the French neo-classical theorist (and translator of Longinus) Nicolas Boileau: "that Christianity and poetry were things that were inconsistent."[18] Dennis disagrees with Boileau, who had encouraged modern poets to write "pagan poetry," and says that, on the contrary, "the true Religion" is favorable to poetry.[19] According to Dennis, philosophers have tried to answer the problem of disharmony either by taking the side of reason or passion, but they have failed to return man to a state of happiness because passion will always come to haunt reason and reason passion as long as they are placed at odds with one another.

It is the poets that Dennis contends have had the most success reconciling reason and passion.[20] Just as Christianity "restores the Harmony of the Human Faculties," poetry works to please "the Reason and Passions and Sences . . . at the same time superlatively."[21] In the end he ties poetry and Christianity together through an image of the fall and the return to paradise promised, he argues, by both Christianity and poetry: "Poetry, by restoring the Harmony of the Human Faculties, provides for the Happiness of Mankind, better than any other Human Invention whatever."[22] Poetry has the power, according to Dennis, to return people to paradise "for a time."[23] Through the figure of the fall, he thus makes poetry and Christianity the same project.[24] The radical nature of Dennis's claim cannot be overstated. Poetry and "the True Religion" do not only happen to both partake of the passions or happen to complement one another, they are the same and their "very method" is the same.

For Dennis, poetry refers specifically to translated biblical and classical texts. Almost every example of English poetry in his essays comes from a translated text. Significantly, Dennis considers Milton's work in *Paradise Lost*, his prime example of sublime English poetry, to be essentially a translation of the Bible. For Dennis, John Milton and specifically Milton's psalm 148 are *the* example of the sublime religious poetry that he is calling for.[25] In reference to Milton's "hymn" Dennis writes in *The Grounds*: "I know several Gentlemen of very good Sense, who are extremely mov'd by *Milton's Hymn*, in the fifth Book of *Paradise Lost*, and hardly at all stir'd with the Translation of the 148th Psalm, from whence that Hymn is taken."[26] Dennis finds the King James translation lacking because it provides a prose translation of what he considers poetic works, and he sees Milton's new, versified version of Psalm 148 as a truly sublime translation of the text.[27] When Dennis calls for his new religious poetry he specifically states: "What Milton has done in relation to the 148th Psalm, others may do in a less proportion to other parts of the Old Testament."[28] His call for a poetry that can reconcile reason and passion is then a call for English translation of the Bible.

Psalm 18: Reconciling Passion and Reason

It is in the context of the claim that poetry can redeem fallen man, and in emulation of Milton, that Dennis undertakes the translation of Psalm 18. Dennis gives Psalm 18 as his example of a sublime, passionate poem which could solve the crisis of English poetics, reharmonize the faculties, and provide redemption. Dennis translates what he calls the "prosaic" King James translation into a versified psalm, greatly expanding the psalm as he does so. Through the use of modern English versification, Dennis turns the psalm from biblical text to a text that is simultaneously biblical and neoclassical. And differences between Dennis's psalm and the King James Version of the psalm do not end at length and use of versification. Dennis makes key linguistic changes that reflect the simultaneous incorporation of religious passion and neoclassical grammar.[29] By bringing these elements together, Dennis provides a reinterpretation of Psalm 18 that attempts to reconcile passion and reason.

Passion, for Dennis, is the key to sublime poetry. Dennis's theory of passion divides the passions into vulgar and enthusiastic passions.[30] Enthusiastic passions are those which create sublime reactions and are the domain of religious ideas: "The strongest enthusiastic Passions, that are just and reasonably rais'd, must be rais'd by religious Idea's, that is, by Idea's which either shew attributes of the Divinity or relate to his Worship."[31] Dennis clarifies that these "religious Idea's" are sublime because their causes are unknowable. Through praise of God and the unknown a poet can return needed passion to poetry. Dennis's aim is not only to argue that religious objects, such as God and creation, create the most passionate poetry, but that poetry is essential to the most passionate religion: "Figurative Language is but a Consequence of the Enthusiasm, that being the natural Langue of the Passions."[32] He writes of the poetry of Ancient Greek authors: "The Wonders of Religion naturally threw them upon great Passions, and great passions naturally threw them upon Harmony and figurative Language."[33] For Dennis, poetic language comes 'naturally' from an encounter with sublime passions. In addition, harmony, the force that Dennis identifies as having the power to overcome the fall, comes along with passion and figurative language. Religion leads naturally to passion, which leads naturally to poetry, which makes harmony possible.

In the context of Dennis's search for religious passion in poetry, it is no surprise that he turned to Psalm 18. The psalm begins with an expression of love for God and then describes the fate of the psalmist who is trapped in a flood and snared by enemies. From this place of total despair, the psalmist calls out to God who responds by coming down from on high and shaking the foundations of the earth as described in the several verses translated by Dennis. God saves the psalmist, who goes on to praise God for rewarding his righteousness and punishing his enemies, and ends by calling for praise of God and thanksgiving. In *The Advancement*, Dennis does not translate Psalm 18 but cites verses 6–15 from the King James Bible, as follows:

> 6. In my Distress I called upon the Lord , and cryed unto my God: He heard my Voice out of his Temple, and my Cry came before him, even into his Ears.
> 7.Then the Earth shook and trembled, the Foundations of the Hills also moved and were shaken, because he was wroth.
> 8. There went up a Smoak out of his Nostrils, and Fire out of his Mouth devoured; Coals were kindled by it.
> 9. He bowed the Heavens also, and came down, and Darkness was under his Feet.
> 10. And he rode upon a Cherub, and did fly: He came flying upon the Wings of the Winds.
> 11. He made Darkness his secret Place; His Pavilion round about him were dark Waters, and thick Clouds of the Skies.
> 12. At the Brightness that was before him, his Clouds remov'd Hail-stones and Coals of Fire.
> 13. The Lord also thundered in the Heavens, and the Highest

> gave his Voice Hailstones and Coals of Fire.
> 14. Yea, he sent forth his Arrows, and scattered them, and he shot out Lightnings, and discomfited him.
> 15. Then the Channels of the Waters were seen, and the Foundations of the World were discovered, at thy Rebuke, O Lord, at the Blast of the Breath of thy Nostrils.[34]

Dennis chooses to quote and later translate, in *The Grounds*, only these lines, which reveal the sublime imagery of God descending to shake the earth and serve to raise the passions of the reader. These lines are theophanic, that is, they depict an actual appearance of God and not simply his speech or works.[35] The expansive natural imagery that defies simple understanding can easily be read as an example of the sublime. In fact, the view of the theophany of Psalm 18 as sublime became commonplace in the following decades.[36]

Thus, Dennis's choice of Psalm 18 can be seen to follow directly from his theory of poetic passion. In *The Advancement* where Dennis cites the King James version of the psalm as an example of poetic sublimity but does not translate it, Dennis writes of the theophany of Psalm 18: "That which satisfies the Reason the more here, raises the Passion more strongly, and entertains the Senses the better, because there are more and more amazing Effects of the Divine Pleasure. For how great, how lofty, how terrible, is that; *He bowed the Heavens and came down, and Darkness was under his Feet*."[37] Dennis argues that Psalm 18 meets his basic criteria for a sublime religious poem: it raises the passions with thoughts of the divine.

While *The Advancement* only quotes from the King James Version of Psalm 18, *The Grounds* provides Dennis's own translation of the psalm. The move from citation to translation takes part in a larger shift from the primarily descriptive writing in *The Advancement* to a more prescriptive writing in *The Grounds*. That is, while both essays provide a similar argument about the need for religious passion in poetry and in many ways complement each other, *The Grounds*, with its translation, performs an intervention in the narrative supported by simple citation in *The Advancement*. While *The Advancement* focuses on recounting a narrative of the fall from ancient to modern poetry, *The Grounds* assumes this narrative in order to provide a more practical explication, through the example of Longinian sublimity, of what Dennis believes should be the work of modern authors in response to this fall. It is in the context of the move from telling a narrative of creation, both biblical and poetic, to a focus on actually laying out rules that should be followed by modern, English poets that Dennis presents his translation, a translation which he hopes will provide an intervention in the trajectory of fallen, modern poetry. (I have included my own interpretation of the verse numbers that correspond to Dennis's translation in brackets):

> [6] In my Distress I call'd upon the Lord,
> And to my God I cry'd; he from his Height,
> Above all Heights, strait heard my mournful Voice,
> And to my loud Complaint inclin'd his Ear.
> [7] Strait the Earth trembled, and her Entrails shook,
> As conscious of her great Creator's Wrath:
> The Mountains from their fix'd Foundations ran,
> And frighted from their inmost Caverns roar'd.
> [8] From out his Nostrils a tempestuous Cloud
> Of pitchy Smoke in spiry Volumes flew,
> And from his Mouth there ran a raging Flood
> Of torrent Fire, devouring as it ran:
> [9] And then he bow'd the very Heaven of Heavens,
> And arm'd with fearful Majesty came down.
> Under his feet he plac'd substantial Night,
> Which aw'd the Nations with its dreadful Gloom:
> [10] Upon the flaming Cherubim he rode,
> And on the Wings of all the Winds he flew;
> [11] Still Darkness usher'd his mysterious Way,
> And a black Night of congregated Clouds
> Became the dark Pavilion of his Throne.
> [12] The Clouds his Brightness could no longer bear,
> But vanishing rever'd the sacred Source of Light;
> And as the congregated Clouds dispers'd,
> A Storm of monstrous Hail came pouring down,
> Down the red Lightning wing'd its slanting way;
> [13] But when his wrathful Voice was heard on high,
> Strait both the Poles rebellow'd to the Sound,
> In thicker Sheets the rattling Hail came down,
> [14] Down came the Lightning with repeated Flames,
> And Thunder bellowing through the boundless Space,
> Astonish'd Nature with redoubled Roars:
> [15] Earth could no longer bear the mortal Fright,
> But shook it self from its perpetual Hinge
> At thy Rebuke, O Lord, and at the Blast,
> The dreadful Blast of thy revenging Breath;
> Then upwards from the gaping Center cleav'd,
> With a prodigious Wound.
> The fix'd Foundations of the World display'd,
> Display'd the ghastful Caverns of the Deep,
> A Sight that blasted ev'n the World's great Eye,

And made the starting Sun recoil
From his eternal Way.[38]

In Dennis's translation of Psalm 18 he highlights the passion of the theophany through the personification of the natural world. In verse seven, he gives consciousness to the mountains. Whereas, originally the mountains "moved and were shaken, because he was wroth" here the earth shakes "as conscious of her great Creator's Wrath" and the mountains are "frighted from their inmost Caverns." Similarly in verse twelve of the King James Version, the clouds move due to "the Brightness that was before Him," but in Dennis's version they "rever'd the sacred Source of Light." In both examples, Dennis takes a verse that was descriptive of action, and provides a characterization that has natural phenomena (mountains or clouds) afraid of or revering God. In verse fourteen, Dennis shows nature as actually "astonished." Dennis also greatly expands verse fifteen to illustrate an earth that splits because it "could no longer bear the mortal Fright." When it finally does split, Dennis describes it as "a prodigious Wound." The earth, as personified, can both be frightened and receive wounds, as though it had both consciousness and flesh. Nature reacts in a direct and personal fashion to the creator's descent. Dennis's incorporation of fear, astonishment, and reverence into the natural world allows him to write a passionate reaction directly into the psalm. In Dennis's view, the best religious poetry, of which the psalms are the prime example, should raise the passions. The description of God's actual appearance to the psalmist is just the sort of awe inspiring moment that Dennis has called for. Yet, he cannot leave it up to the reader to be moved and have his passions raised, he must act out the raising of the passions that he seeks by writing it directly into the story.

The awe filled reaction Dennis cultivates also comes out in his verse nine and the much expanded verse fifteen. In verse nine of the King James psalm God actually begins his descent toward the earth. The verse describes the descent with darkness "under his feet." In his verse nine, God's descent "aw'd the Nations with its dreadful Gloom." Here, Dennis has added the reaction of people to the theophany, writing his reader into the psalm. Thus, he provides the reader with characters in the psalm, witnesses of God's descent, who can be identified with in their awe. In verse fifteen, the witness Dennis provides is the sun, "the World's great Eye," whose "Sight" of the unfolding events makes him "recoil." In the King James Version of verse fifteen there is the figure of sight as "the Channels of the Waters were seen, and the Foundations of the world were discovered," but the text does not provide an agent who does this seeing and witnessing. Dennis, on the other hand, has again added a figure not present in the original psalm as a witness of the event, and therefore a witness of and within the psalm. Whether mountains, clouds, nations, or sun, Dennis continues throughout his psalm to incorporate figures of the good reader, a reader who sees the psalm as a witness to God and his creation and has his passions raised through the sublimity of the text. Given Dennis's avid interest in theater, this reader can also be read as an audience member. The incorporation of an audience in the translation, then serves to bring an element of the dramatic into the psalm, making it almost a hybrid poem and theatrical work. The passionate audience of the psalm becomes the audience of a new, modern, and passionate genre of Dennis's own devising.[39]

For Dennis, however, passion alone is not enough to create sublime poetry. For true redemption poetry must also follow the rules. If the correct poetic rules can be discovered and implemented in the translation of sublime, religious poetry, poetry can become more perfect. But Dennis does not find the basis for poetic rules in the same text where he finds the basis for religious passion. While religion is inherited from the Hebraic tradition, Dennis's poetic rules are inherited from the classical tradition, specifically from the works of Longinus and Aristotle. Although the use of classic texts to derive rules for literature was a central tenet of neoclassicism, Dennis's own version of the rules does not adhere to any clear neoclassical school.[40] He derives his belief in rules from an understanding of nature as full of order and harmony and finds his specific rules for psalm translation primarily in Longinus's writing on the sublime. Dennis draws additional rules, as presented in *The Grounds*, from Aristotle's writing on rhetoric and from Hermogenes. Interestingly, Dennis does not focus primarily on Aristotle's unities, as Boileau and other neoclassical critics had, but points, rather, to Aristotle's definition of poetic language as better suited to "Methaphors, Dialects, and Epithets."[41] At times Dennis's rules, which include the need for passion and violence in poetry, even seem opposed to the very notion of neoclassical order.[42] Ideal poetry, in Dennis, emerges out of the combination of two forces: neoclassical rules and religious passions.[43] Religion provides the ideas, but classical poetics, and specifically the rules found in Aristotle and Longinus, provide the form. At its most simple, Dennis's plan for poetry is one in which the correct poetic rules must be combined with the most sublime religious ideas. By combining rule and idea correctly, Dennis sees a sublime, modern, and specifically English poetry rising from the ashes.[44]

In his translation of Psalm 18, Dennis attempts to bring neoclassical rule and order to the King James text. This can be seen primarily in the grammar he imposes on the psalm. The grammar serves to turn the psalm into a clear, ordered narrative, removing any ambiguity from the text.

The clear, narrative structure imposed on the psalm can also be read as a dramatic structure, imposing unity of time, place, and action upon the psalm. Thus, the neoclassical interpretation of Aristotle's rules for drama becomes the basis of the imposition of grammar in religious poetry. Just as Dennis's invocation of passion interpolates a theatrical audience into the poem, his use of grammar blurs the distinctions between the poetic and the dramatic. Grammar becomes the vehicle for the imposition of neoclassical, dramatic order.

Dennis's rules are based in an understanding of an ordered universe. In the second chapter of *The Grounds*, entitled "That Poetry is to be established by laying down the Rules" Dennis lays out an argument about the rules that contains a series of strikingly neoclassical equivalences:

> The Work of every reasonable Creature must derive its Beauty from Regularity; for Reason is Rule and Order, and nothing can be irregular either in our Conceptions or our Actions, any further than it swerves from Rule, that is, from Reason. As Man is the more perfect, the more he resembles his Creator; the Works of Man must needs be more perfect, the more they resemble his Maker's. Now the Works of God, tho infinitely various, are extremely regular.[45]

In his argument he first aligns reason with both beauty and regularity, then immediately turns these into rule and order. Rule is Reason which equals regularity. Man is like the Creator, and therefore man's work, when it is perfect, will be regular like God's work. In other words God's work corresponds to rules which, in man's actions become reason, beauty and regularity. Dennis also makes the argument for the regularity and rules of "the Universe" as a model of perfect, Godly order. For Dennis the problem of order returns one to creation and the fall. As he laid out in *The Advancement*, man is fallen by transgressing order and breaking God's perfect rules. According to this logic, a return to the rules could, in a sense, undo the fall. Poetry is fallen because it does not follow the rules just as man is fallen because he did not follow the rules. Poetry, by turning to God given rules, can, then redeem its fallenness and in turn redeem man's fallen state by serving as orderly instruction to man in his disorder.

Dennis describes the rule and order of poetry as coming from God's universal order, but as a neoclassical thinker he derives his rules for great writing not from the Bible but from ancient writers. In *The Grounds*, he compares modern poetry unfavorably to sublime Greek poetry, writing that he will show "what is to be done to restore Modern Tragedy first to

Innocence, and secondly to the Greatness of the Grecian Stage."[46] In his reference to the fall, Dennis presents the Grecian stage as a metaphorical Eden. Dennis takes his authority from the ancient Greeks throughout his argument: "And this we shall show by the Authority of the greatest Criticks among the Antients, *Aristotle*, *Hermogenes*, and *Longinus*."[47] These ancient writers are presented as the greatest authorities on great writing in every time and place. It is with the authority of the ancient Greek texts that an Englishman of the eighteenth century can judge universally. Dennis's focus on the Greeks as opposed to the Romans reveals his unique form of the neoclassical, a neoclassicism that draws on the ancient Greek dramatic tradition in combination with a reading of Longinus's sublime. Dennis applies these standards to Milton and by extension to his own translation in emulation of Milton.

The ancient standards, as defined by his eighteenth-century, neoclassical interpretations of them, are, therefore, those by which he judges the work of English writers. For example, Dennis compares Spenser and Milton in light of their relation to ancient rules:

> Spenser, by not following these Rules, fell so very far short of the Ancients . . . . Milton, by daring to break a little loose from them in some particulars, kept up in several others to the Nature of the Greater Poetry in general, and of the Epick Poetry in particular, better than the best of the Ancients.[48]

According to Dennis, Spenser failed because he did not take the Greek rules into consideration. Even while Dennis admits that Milton did not exactly follow the rules, he still reads Milton in light of these rules and ends by saying that he has excelled the Greeks in their own sphere. Therefore, even in a context in which Dennis appears to question the Greek norms, he finishes by reinstating their authority. The greatest compliment he can give Milton is that he is better than the best of the ancients. Dennis adds: "That great Man had a desire to give the World something like an Epick Poem; but he resolv'd at the same time to break thro' the Rules of Aristotle. Not that he was ignorant of them or contemn'd them."[49] Milton may have broken these rules, but his poem is still categorized as "Epick" based on the ancient categories and is still read in light of Aristotle's rules. Dennis is also careful to point out that Milton did not condemn the rules. In the need for a defense of Milton we can see the revered status of the ancient rules. In fact, Dennis will use the rules of Aristotle to support his point that religious ideas have the most sublime potential: "Religious Ideas are the most admirable; and what is most admirable, according to the Doctrine of

Aristotle, is most delightful."[50]

In the preface to *The Grounds*, Dennis makes clear that one of the goals of his essay will be to bring a new order, based on the rules, to the psalms. He writes in reference to the versified psalms of Hopkins and Sternhold commonly used in the liturgy of the Church of England: "the vile Meetre of Hopkins . . . suffers the most Lofty and the most Pathetick Divine Poetry to be Burlesqu'd and Ridicul'd in our Churches."[51] Dennis clearly reveals an interest in the form of the psalms by specifically noting the "vile Meetre" of the common translation. Sternhold and Hopkins have not followed the rules and for this reason the passionate poetry of the psalms has suffered. In order to bring out the "Lofty" and "Pathetick" nature of the poetry, Dennis proposes that a new form must be found.[52] He does this by imposing a sense of neoclassical order upon the biblical text through neoclassical translation.[53]

While verse six in the King James reads, "He heard my Voice out of his Temple, and my Cry came before him, even into his ears," Dennis translates "he from his Height, Above all heights, strait heard my mournful Voice, And to my loud Complaint inclin'd his Ear." The King James version gives two clauses which essentially repeat the same information in different forms; "He heard my voice out of his Temple" and "my Cry came before him, even into his ears" describe the same events. This is a classic case of biblical parallelism, in which the two clauses give the same event or image with only slight differences, a form commonly found in the psalms.[54] Dennis's version, in contrast, creates a seamless narrative out of the events in which God hears a voice and leans in to register the complaint being made by the speaker. In addition, the King James Version, in emulation of the Hebrew grammar, provides for great ambiguity. In the phrase "out of his Temple," it is unclear exactly what the preposition "out" refers to. Is the voice "out" of the Temple? Is God "out" of the Temple when he hears the voice? Is this a Temple that God inhabits or the Temple that the speaker cries from? Dennis makes it clear that the Temple is the place that God inhabits, "his Height, Above all Heights," and that God hears the voice while in the temple. From the beginning of his translation, Dennis brings rule and order to the psalm.

Dennis also adds many small clarifying conjunctions to his Psalm 18, adding a sense of continuity and causality to the verses. In verse nine "He bowed the Heavens also" becomes "And then he bowed the heavens." The "and then" more clearly links the verse to the preceding verse and provides a sense of ordered causality to the events of the psalm. Verse ten features another instance of parallelism in the King James: "And he rode upon a

Cherub, and did fly: He came flying upon the Wings of the Winds." In the King James the "Wings of the Winds" are a figure for the "Cherub." But Dennis adds the word "and" between the two phrases, turning the parallelism into the description of two separate events: "Upon the flaming Cherubim he rode, And on the Wings of all the Winds he flew." Similarly, in verse eleven Dennis uses the conjunction "and" to divide the separate phrases of the verse. In the King James, "He made Darkness his secret Place; His Pavilion round about him were dark Waters, and thick clouds of the skies," the two verses are again an example of parallelism, repeating the same image while expanding upon it and adding nuances to the description. Dennis, on the other hand, divides the phrases, making the Hebrew phrasing orderly and anglicized: "Still Darkness usher'd his mysterious Way, And a black Night of congregated Clouds Became the dark Pavilion of his Throne." In a sense, Dennis's grammar removes the nuances of Hebrew poetic structure and turns the psalm distinctly English.

In the psalms, lines that form a parallel pair are often echoes of the same event, temporally simultaneous. Dennis takes the simultaneous layers of theophany and turns them into an ordered set of events, with one line following the next chronologically in a narrative of God's descent. Dennis makes no direct reference to parallelism, and the understanding of parallelism as the defining principle of Hebrew poetry did not come into the English tradition until Bishop Lowth published his lectures on Hebrew poetry in 1753.[55] Yet, the effect of Dennis's grammar is to undermine the complexity of the parallelism found in Psalm 18. In parallelism, the paired phrases are similar in form or content, but the precise relationship between them, whether the lines are complimentary or contradictory, is not specifically given in the text. Dennis's addition of "and" and "but" predetermines the interpretation of the parallel lines and in many instances does away with the parallelism all together. Dennis exchanges a hebraicized form and grammar, as reflected in the King James translation, for proper neoclassical order.

In verse twelve and thirteen Dennis makes order out of the somewhat confusing repetition of the phrase "Hailstones and Coals of Fire." The phrase appears at the end of both verses. In verse twelve "Hailstones and Coals of Fire" adds detail to the image of God moving the clouds with his brightness and in verse thirteen it illustrates the attributes of the thundering voice of the Lord.[56] Dennis's translation does not include a repetition of any phrase. Although he does mention "hail" in both verses, he specifically marks the difference between the two invocations of the hail. In Dennis's verse twelve, "A Storm of monstrous Hail came pouring down" and in his verse thirteen "In thicker Sheets the rattling Hail came down." Dennis's repetition creates a logical link between the two invocations of hail. In the first instance hail comes down, and in the second instance the hail comes down even "thicker." The translation makes the static repetition become progressive, once again imposing a narrative structure on the psalm.

Finally, as already noted in my discussion of passion in Dennis's Psalm 18, Dennis removes the ambiguity of the passive voice from verse fifteen. Whereas in the King James "the Channels of the Waters were seen and the Foundations of the World were discovered," in Dennis the earth and the sun become the spectators of the splitting open of the world. Dennis's awed audience serves not only to illustrate the raising of passions, but also serves to bring order to the psalm. The passive construction of the verse leaves the subject of sight ambiguous. By adding a concrete subject, Dennis removes the ambiguity from the verse. By way of imposing order, Dennis also imposes an interpretation on the psalm. In verse fifteen, Dennis adds clarity and order to the psalm while simultaneously attempting to raise the passions of the reader. Thus, in the final verse of his translation, Dennis may seem to have accomplished his goal of harmonizing passion and reason.

Biblical Passion and Classical Rules in Harmony and in Conflict

In *The Grounds* Dennis lays out very specific rules to be followed when translating sublime religious poetry. He argues for a combination of neoclassical rules, based on Greek and Roman texts, with Christian religious Ideas as derived from the biblical text. It is in their combination that he sees the greatest potential for sublimity. In Psalm 18, Dennis attempts to carry out the combination of rule and idea that he calls for. He tries, in a sense, to make the reader's sight of the events of Psalm 18 perfect. He does this by adding in passionate witnesses who can stand in as the ideal readers in the psalm, and by giving narrative and grammatical clarity to the psalm. The clarified psalm provides for an unambiguous image in the reader's mind, giving better access to the sight of God's actions.[57]

In addition, the incorporation of a passionate poem, Psalm 18, as an integral piece of a reasoned, prose argument turns Dennis's essay, itself, into a performance of the very harmony of passion and reason that he seeks. The reasonable argument does not carry its full weight without being harmonized with the passionate poem which embodies its message. Dennis's theory of translation then, becomes a key to unlock the reasoning of his entire body of criticism. Not only as a poet and translator, but as a critic, Dennis attempts to harmonize passion and reason. The result of combining passion and reason, whether as an ordered translation of passionate poetry or in the form of an essay that uses poetry in its argument, should, then, be harmony and transcendent sublimity.

Yet, the relatively simple argument for rule and idea in poetry is complicated by Dennis's complex relationship to the Attic and Hebrew traditions, respectively. The argument for the sublimity of Greek and Roman rules presents several conflicts for Dennis's overall argument. First, he sets up a dichotomy between Greek rule and Divine idea. The sublime Rules come from Ancient Greek texts, but the sublime Ideas come from the Divine. And yet, the Divine Ideas, even if they are inspired by God, need the ancient pagan rules if they wish to be truly sublime. Secondly, he sets up a division between Ancient and Modern, relating them through the figure of the fall. The ancient, Grecian poetry has fallen and now we have modern poetry that is inferior. But when the Bible or biblical poetry enter into this dichotomy, the Bible disrupts the simple chronological narrative of ancient as opposed to modern. For Dennis, the Bible as the source of Divine ideas is both ancient and modern. It is ancient in the sense of being the original document, a poetic creation with divine origins. But it does not follow the rules of those other ancients, the Greeks. It is modern, according to Dennis, as a Christian text. The Bible is, in effect, both perfect and imperfect, the original source of poetry but lacking the sublime poetic rules that Dennis holds out as the example of true sublimity.

Dennis's inherently ambivalent attitude toward the biblical text comes out clearly in his omission of Longinus's own citation of the Bible as sublime. Longinus writes that, "The lawgiver of the Jews, no ordinary man, since he recognized and expressed divine power according to its worth, expressed that power clearly when he wrote at the beginning of his Laws: 'And God said' What? 'Let there be light, and there was light; let there be land, and there was land.'"[58] Here, Longinus cites the fiat lux as an example of sublime writing, but Dennis, while he takes time to show that Longinus's argument about the sublime is really an argument for the religious sublime, never once makes reference to this moment in Longinus. Dennis argues that Longinus, while never defining the sublime as religious, described a sublime that can only be found in religious texts.[59] It would seem that Longinus's own citation of the Hebrew Bible would greatly support Dennis's reading of Longinus as well as his own argument for the sublimity of the biblical text and make it all the easier for Dennis to meld the Pagan rules and the Christian tradition that he so wants to reconcile. The omission of the citation from Longinus reveals that Dennis is not arguing simply that the Bible is sublime in its own right. Rather, for Dennis, the biblical text is sublime in idea, but needs a supplement to also be sublime in form. If the Hebrew Bible is already sublime, without the supplement of modern English translation or New Testament Christian interpretation, his project to reclaim poetry for modern England loses its raison d'être.

The logical impasse presented by Dennis's attitude toward biblical text was already apparent in his complicated use of the figure of the fall. On the one hand he argues that poetry has the properties needed to restore fallen man. On the other, he presents the idea of poetry itself as fallen and needing its own redemption. He has used 'the fall' in two very different ways here in relation to poetry. Poetry is both fallen and redemptive. Similarly, biblical text in general is both the sublime creation of God and a poetry that implicitly lacks sublime form. In order to avoid a direct discussion of the ancient sublimity or lack thereof in biblical Hebrew poetry, Dennis does something very interesting; he claims biblical poetry for modern authors and English audiences. In comparing Homer to an excerpt from the prophet Habakkuk, Dennis writes "The Advantage is clearly ours."[60] With this declaration, he implicitly claims the biblical text of *Habakkuk*, as a Christian text, for modern England. "Ours" claims Habakkuk for the Christian tradition, in contrast to the pagan tradition of Homer, but also at once takes part in a larger argument that aligns Christianity with the modern. Therefore, as a 'Christian' text, Habakkuk actually becomes modern. Through the use of chronological ambiguity, Dennis avoids a discussion of his conflicting images of the Bible and of fallen poetry. He maintains his simple dichotomy between ancient and modern by putting Biblical text on the side of the modern. In *The Advancement* Dennis gives several biblical examples of sublimity, including Psalm 18, but then moves on to examples from Milton, claiming that if he gives more biblical examples people could say that these were divinely inspired writings and therefore not really examples in favor of his argument about modern Christianity's poetic potential.[61] The tone of his argument implies that while others might question him, Dennis believes that biblical texts *are* examples of modern Christian sublimity.

In support of his argument for Christian poetry Dennis brings up the example of Psalm 18. He compares the psalm to a theophanic passage in Virgil's *Georgics*: "But now let us see how the Psalmist has treated the same Subject in the Eighteenth *Psalm*, and we shall find, that the Greatness of *Virgil* is Littleness compared to his."[62] The Psalmist, then, becomes the poet who can redeem modern Christianity. Essentially, he has made David, as psalmist, a modern Englishman by giving the Psalms as the prime example of sublime Christian poetry. The Bible and its authors, for Dennis, belong to England. And yet, Dennis only displaces the original contradiction. If the biblical text is "ours" then it is also aligned with fallen modern text.

As I have already noted, numerous critics of Dennis have come to the conclusion that his theory is at odds with itself, full of irreconcilable contradictions between poetry and religion, reason and passion, Greek and Hebrew, and modern and ancient. Certainly, his anxiety about the sublimity of the biblical text points to an underlying instability in his categories. Superficially, translation into English immediately reconciles the contradiction between Greek and Hebrew language, but it does much more than this. In his translation of Psalm 18 Dennis attempts to unite poetry and religion, make the ancient modern, harmonize reason and passion, and combine what he sees as the strengths of both the biblical and classical traditions. Dennis's translation is not simply, as biographer H. G. Paul has noted, "a practical exemplification of his theory."[63] It also provides a solution to the contradictions that his theory struggles with. In the psalm, as Dennis envisions it, all contradictions break down and are recombined to make a new form that is simultaneously English, Hebrew, and Greek; reasonable and passionate; modern and ancient; poetic and religious.

Taking a step back to look at Dennis's place in the history of eighteenth-century translation, we can see Dennis's notion of translation as a harmonizing force for religious redemption as both deeply rooted in eighteenth-century notions of harmony and translation promoted by John Denham and John Dryden and simultaneously radically opposed to concepts of eighteenth-century decorum. By focusing on the importance of passion and sublimity, investing translation with spiritual powers, turning his attention to the Bible as the source for great poetry, and drawing on the theophany of Psalm 18 for his translation, Dennis's notion of translation provides a dissenting view of the role of English translation in the early eighteenth century.[64] Dennis's focus on the importance of passion in poetry and translation led to his portrayal, in his feuds with important literary figures of his day, including Addison, Pope, and Swift, as a mad-man who was obsessed with Longinus and dangerous enthusiasm. Essentially, Dennis's notion of a form of translation that could save England and Christianity simultaneously was rejected by his peers in favor of a more conventional understanding of the role of translation as a cultural necessity and means of the incorporation of foreign literature for England. But Dennis's lasting influence on English literary history remains.[65] His alternate theory of translation provides a note of complexity in the generally monolithic narrative of domesticating eighteenth-century translation. Dennis's translation of Psalm 18 also reveals a Dennis not seen before, one who views translation not simply as a means to illustrate his argument, but as the equivalent of religious redemption, with the power to harmonize the conflicts in his theory and the conflicts inherent in the world.

NOTES

1. Dennis promoted a modern, English poetics that would raise sublime passions while following neoclassical rules for poetry. Studies of the sublime in the eighteenth-century often note the important role that Dennis played in the development of an English notion of sublimity. Marjorie Hope Nicolson reads a letter Dennis wrote about his travels through the Alps as an example of early eighteenth-century sublimity (*Mountain Gloom and Mountain Glory: The Development of the Aesthetics of the Infinite* [Ithaca: Cornell University Press, 1959], 276–289.) Similarly, in *The Religious Sublime: Christian Poetry and Critical Tradition in Eighteenth-Century England* (Lexington: University Press of Kentucky, 1972), David B. Morris devotes the whole of chapter 2 to reading Dennis's theory of sublimity. At the same time, Dennis is also considered a neoclassical figure, although as editor Edward Niles Hooker notes, Dennis cannot be confined to one clear school of neoclassicism. He drew on the work of Boileau and Rymer, while deriving his own understanding of "the rules" from his reading of Aristotle and Horace and by incorporating the theories of Longinus (*The Critical Works of John Dennis,* ed. Edward Niles Hooker [Baltimore: John Hopkins Press, 1939], lxxvii.) John D. Morillo argues that Dennis specifically turns to Longinus for a model of both sublimity and the neoclassical in order to counter the neo-Aristotelian version of neoclassicism supplied by Boileau (*Uneasy Feelings: Literature, the Passions, and Class from Neoclassicism to Romanticism* [New York: AMS Press Inc., 2001], 25.) Phillip J. Donnelly notes: "In formulating his arguments, Dennis draws at length upon Longinus but takes as point of departure a set of commonplaces derived from Aristotle and Horace" ("Enthusiastic Poetry and Rationalized Christianity: The Poetic Theory of John Dennis." *Christianity and Literature* 54, no. 2 [2005]: 239.) Irène Simon reads the conflicting views of Dennis as both a theorist of the sublime and a proponent of neoclassicism and concludes that the split in criticism of Dennis reflects a split between passion and reason in Dennis's own work ("John Dennis and Neoclassical Criticism," *Revue belge de philosophie et d'historie* 56, no. 3 [1978]: 663–77.)

2. Shaun Irlam summarizes the tension found in Dennis's work as "the oxymoron of 'regulated Enthusiasm'," noting that, in Dennis, passionate poetry actually becomes the means for regulating the passions (*Elations: The Poetics of Enthusiasm in Eighteenth-Century Britain* [Stanford: Stanford University Press, 1999], 60.) Similarly, Jon Mee refers to the "regulated nature of the religious sublime" in Dennis (*Romanticism, Enthusiasm, and Regulation: Poetics and Policing of Culture in the Romantic Period* [London : Oxford University Press, 2005], 55.)

3. John Denham, *The Poetical Works of Sir John Denham* (New Haven: Yale University Press, 1969), 159–160; John Dryden, *The Works of John Dryden* (Berkeley: University of California Press, 1956), I.114–115.

4. Imitation is one of three types of translation as laid out in Dryden's "Ovid's Epistles." The three types are metaphrase—translating word for word, paraphrase—translating meaning, and imitation—translating freely based on the text (Dryden, *Works*, I.114–115.) While "paraphrase" most readily accords with current notions of translation, in the eighteenth century the free adaptation of a text through imitation was considered an equally valid, if not superior, form of translation.

5. Lawrence Venuti, *The Translator's Invisibility: A History of Translation* (London: Routledge, 1995), 53.

6. Venuti, *Translator's Invisibility,* 54–66. Roscommon, in particular, calls for English translation of Roman and Greek texts which will make them properly English, bringing "Roman Majesty" to England. (*An Essay on Translated Verse, 1685*. [Menston, Eng.: Scholar Press, 1971], 3, 26). Julie Candler Hayes's recent history of neoclassical translation does provide an alternative narrative, attempting to complicate the idea of domesticating versus foreignizing translation, but she still notes the nationalizing project in the work of Denham and Dryden and reads them as key figures of eighteenth-century translation practice in England (*Translation, Subjectivity, and Culture in France and England, 1600–1800* [Stanford: Stanford University Press, 2009], 11–16.)

7. John Dennis, *The Critical Works of John Dennis,* ed. Edward Niles Hooker (Baltimore: John Hopkins Press, 1939), 1.331.

8. While both Denham and Dryden did translate the psalms at different points, their main focus was on classical and not biblical translation. Dennis's work shifts the focus of translation toward biblical poetry.

9. *Oxford English Dictionary*, entry on "Translation."

10. Throughout the seventeenth and eighteenth centuries, John Milton, Isaac Watts, the Wesleys, and many others added their renditions to the long tradition of English psalmody.

11. Irlam, *Elations*, 66.

12. Ann T. Delehanty, "Mapping the Aesthetic Mind: John Dennis and Nicolas Boileau," *Journal of the History of Ideas* 68, no. 2 (2007): 238.

13. John D. Morillo, "John Dennis: Enthusiastic Passions, Cultural Memory, and Literary Theory," *Eighteenth-Century Studies* 34, no. 1 (2000): 22.

14. Morris, *Religious Sublime,* 73.

15. Pope lampooned Dennis as "Sir Tremendous Longinus" in the 1717 play *Three Hours After Marriage*, but their feud was already underway; in 1713 Pope published *The Narrative of Dr. Robert Norris, concerning the strange and deplorable frenzy of Dr. John Dennis, an officer in the Custom-House* in response to Dennis's attack on Joseph Addison's *Cato.* Dennis also carried out ongoing feuds with Richard Steele and Joseph Addison, and was famously made fun of in Jonathan Swift's *Tale of a Tub*.

16. In *The Dunciad*, Pope refers directly to Dennis, writing "And all the mighty Mad in Dennis rage" in the body of the poem. This is followed by a long mocking

note written in a reasonable tone, as though in his defense, while casting Dennis as "Poor Furius" whose paranoia drives him to print outrageous accusations (*Poetical Works* [London: Oxford University Press, 1966], 479–480.) Jon Mee has noted the demonization of Dennis in *The Dunciad* arguing that it was carried out precisely because Dennis's "definition of the religious sublime left the boundaries between poetry and prophecy too porous for most polite eighteenth-century readers" (Mee, *Romanticism*, 55.) In other words, it is the very tension between the neoclassical poetic rules and biblical passions in Dennis's work, which he attempted to reconcile through translation, which left him open to being cast as a radical by Pope.

17. Dennis, *Works*, 1.150.
18. Dennis, *Works,* 1.134.
19. Dennis, *Works,* 1.135.
20. Dennis, *Works,* 1.143.
21. Dennis, *Works,* 1.159.
22. Dennis, *Works,* 1.171.
23. Dennis, *Works,* 1.172.
24. Shaun Irlam has noted Dennis's "millennial aspirations. . . to accomplish nothing less than the moral rejuvenation of literature and modern society and the redemption of mankind from the consequences of the Fall" (Irlam, *Elations*, 65.)
25. Although Dennis cites many examples from Milton in *The Grounds*, the longest excerpt he provides is from what he calls Milton's "incomparable hymn" in Book Five of *Paradise Lost.* Dennis identifies it as a translation of Psalm 148, writing: "A Hymn, which tho it is intirely taken from Scripture, for it is apparently the 148th Psalm, yet will always stand alone, the Phoenix of lofty Hymns; and nothing equal to it, no nor second to it, can ever be produc'd from the *Grecian* Writers of Hymns" (Dennis, *Works,*1.351.) See Mary Ann Radzinowicz, *Milton's Epics and the Book of Psalms* (Princeton: Princeton University Press, 1989), for a detailed discussion of Milton's Hymn and his method for turning psalms into hymns.
26. Dennis, *Works,* 1.372; H.G. Paul notes Dennis's importance as an early Milton critic (*John Dennis: His Life and Criticism* [New York: Columbia University Press, 1911], 195.)
27. It should be noted here that this is translation in an eighteenth-century sense, meaning that imitation—either an English-to-English adaptation or an English domestication of a foreign-language text—is considered a genre of translation. Here, Dennis even claims imitation, as in the case of Milton's 148th psalm, as a superior form of translation.
28. Dennis, *Works,* 1.372.
29. Dennis specifically brings the neoclassical into this translation through the imposition of grammar. Through grammar he brings a sense of order to the text, mirroring a neoclassical investment in rules and standards for art. The specific school of neoclassical criticism to which Dennis belongs is difficult to assert. As noted by Hooker, he partakes of Rymer's investment in rules but cannot be said to be of the school of Rymer. He was certainly not part of the school of taste as it developed in the early eighteenth century. Hooker specifies that he believed in the division of genres and the application of rules to each genre in order that each type

could have its proper emotional impact (Hooker, *Works,* lxxvii.) In other words, the rules make the passions possible. In fact, the very contradictions in Dennis between neoclassical rules and biblical passions are already present in this conflicted notion of the neoclassical as the rules for passion.

30. For an account of Dennis's use of the word 'enthusiasm' as it related to the political and religious conditions of the time see Morillo, "Enthusiastic Passions," 21–41.

31. Dennis, *Works,* 1.339.

32. Dennis, *Works,* 1.359.

33. Dennis, *Works,* 1.364.

34. Dennis, *Works,* 1.268.

35. Donald K. Berry identifies these lines of Psalm 18 as theophanic, depicting an actual appearance of the deity. Berry separates these verses from the rest of the psalmic text, writing of its use of "mythic language:" "In the theophany, images of water and fire combine in a mysterious amalgam. . .The themes of light and darkness are combined with the fire and water imagery of the theophany, for the waters surrounding Yahweh are 'darkness', and his lightnings are 'brightness'" (*The Psalms and their Readers: Interpretive Strategies for Psalm 18* [Sheffield, England: JSOT Press, 1993], 98.)

36. David B. Morris writes that "Psalm 18 . . . became a favorite illustration of sublimity in the eighteenth century" (Morris, *Religious Sublime,* 19.) Much later in the eighteenth century, Bishop Lowth cited these same lines, writing of "the force, the grandeur and sublimity of these images" (Robert Lowth, *Lectures on the Sacred Poetry of the Hebrews* [New York: Crocker & Brewster, 1829],77.)

37. Dennis, *Works,* 1.269.

38. Dennis, *Works,* 1.367.

39. Although Dennis is remembered primarily as a critic, he also wrote for the stage and always hoped to be a successful playwright.

40. Hooker writes that Dennis's "considered himself a champion of the rules" but his rules were not taken directly either from Boileau in the French tradition or Rymer in the English tradition (Hooker, *Works,* lxxix.)

41. Dennis, *Works,* 1.340.

42. Dennis, *Works,* 1.369.

43. It is important to note here that these divisions are never absolute. That is, Dennis's rules encompass the passions from the outset and his passions are always, already defined within his understanding of the rules.

44. Dennis biographer and critic Avon Jack Murphy writes of Dennis's interest in 'the fall' and its relation to the regularity and order of rules: "Firmly convinced of the macrocosm-microcosm analogy, he sees everywhere signs of our Fall. Jugglers and Italian opera singers performing before large audiences, theatrical factions that keep sound plays off the stage, Alexander Pope's unjustified success, widespread foreign luxuries, stock-jobbers' pernicious influence upon a greedy public, Jacobite plotting against the king, treacherous High Church priests—all indicate a radical disorder throughout society. To reestablish literary, social, and political order, we must choose methods that themselves evince order. In literature, we must insist upon

rationality and regularity, upon methods and forms that mirror the reason immanent in God's planning." Through the rules, Dennis seeks to raise poetry and society from their fallen status. (*John Dennis* [Boston: Twayne, 1984], 10.)

45. Dennis, *Works,* 1.335.
46. Dennis, *Works,* 1.332.
47. Dennis, *Works,* 1.340.
48. Dennis, *Works,* 1.331.
49. Dennis, *Works,* 1.333.
50. Dennis, *Works,* 1.360.
51. Dennis, *Works,* 1.326.
52. In "The Advancement and Reformation of Modern Poetry" Dennis has defined poetry using the word "pathetick": "Poetry then is an imitation of Nature by a pathetic and numerous Speech" (Dennis, *Works,* 231.) By giving the psalms as "the most Pathetick Divine Poetry" Dennis is, then, clearly elevating the psalms and making it clear that they fit into his notion of sublime religious poetry.
53. Although the neoclassical rules that Dennis provides may seem to have little to do with meter, they do prescribe the need for a certain dramatic structure, which Dennis wants to import into his poetry. It is this need for ordered dramatic structure which then dictates a new, grammatical form of verse for Dennis.
54. In *The Idea of Biblical Poetry: Parallelism and its History* (New Haven: Yale University Press, 1981) James L. Kugel gives a detailed account of the understanding of parallelism as it developed in English literary history.
55. Lowth, *Lectures.*
56. Of course, it is likely that the repetition of the phrase at the end of both lines is due to scribal error. In other words, it originally appeared at the end of only one of the lines, but the scribe's eye wandered up or down when copying the text, writing the phrase into both verses. But in any case, the psalm as it now stands, contains the repetition.
57. The need for clarity and the fear of any ambiguity comes not only from the neoclassical focus on order but also on a post-Reformation concern that people should correctly understand and interpret the Bible.
58. Longinus, *On Great Writing (On the Sublime),* trans. G.M.A. Grube. (Indianapolis: Hackett Publishing Company, Inc., 1957), 14.
59. Dennis, *Works,* 1.360.
60. Dennis, *Works,* 1.366.
61. Dennis, *Works,* 1.191.
62. Dennis, *Works,* 1.268.
63. Paul, *John Dennis*, 38.
64. In 1712, in *Spectator* no. 465, Joseph Addison, for example, when providing his own version of psalm translation, turns to the ordered vision of creation given in Psalm 19 (*The Works of Joseph Addison: The Spectator, no. 315–635* [New York: Harper and Brothers, 1837], 211.)
65. Dennis has been credited as a major influence on Wordsworth. John D. Morillo discusses the passions in both Dennis and Wordsworth and notes that Wordsworth mention Dennis in an 1815 letter: "Poetic passion (Dennis has well observed) is of

two kinds: imaginative and enthusiastic, and merely human ordinary" and refers to an 1842 letter from De Quincey who claims that Wordsworth "had an absurd 'craze'" for Dennis at one time. (Quoted in Morillo, *Uneasy Feelings*, 16–17.) See also James A. W. Heffernan, "Wordsworth and Dennis: The Discrimination of Feelings," *PMLA* 82, no. 5 (Oct., 1967): 430–36; and Edward Niles Hooker's discussion of the relationship between Dennis and Wordsworth (Hooker, *Works*, lxxiii.)

Strictly Business: Marriage, Motherhood, and Surrogate Families as Entrepreneurial Ventures in *Moll Flanders*

ANN CAMPBELL

In Daniel Defoe's *Moll Flanders* (1722), surrogate families, or as John Richetti calls them, "small groups of friends who act as substitute families," are the norm for the novel's protagonist Moll Flanders, while families of origin and conjugal families are aberrations.[1] These surrogate families are often no more than temporary families of convenience— formed, dissolved, and forgotten in a matter of pages— although a few of them, most notably Moll's connection to her governess, are nurturing and enriching connections that sustain her for long periods of time. While this sustenance is sometimes emotional, it is most often financial. Moll discovers early, as a member of two types of what I argue are biological families— the gypsies and the parish orphanage—her intuitive entrepreneurial skills. Exercising these skills in these circumscribed arenas proves challenging, however, so Moll shrewdly seeks out other family models with greater exploitative potential. She learns over the course of the novel, having observed and experimented with marriage, motherhood, filial and sororal ties, as well as less clearly defined connections to what I call *surrogate families*, that these latter contingent relationships produce for her maximum profit with minimum risk. Husbands prove unreliable, while biological ties, which become conflated in her mind with incest itself, are stifling. Loyal attachments to spouses, fathers, mothers, and children are not merely cumbersome, but to Defoe's highly adaptable protagonist signify a deficiency of ambition. Surrogate families, on the other hand, are disposable and for-profit.

Although the structure of *Moll Flanders* is often described as episodic or picaresque, the novel follows a discernable trajectory based on Moll's evolving wariness about the impositions, such as providing for children and being assailed by economic calamities not of her making, that biological and conjugal ties often entail.[2] Her assimilation into the surrogate family she forms with the governess in the second half of the novel instructs her about the advantages of contingent ties, which are formed and dissolved based solely on whether they facilitate mutual benefit. Since profit is dear to Moll's heart, the capital she accumulates during this period becomes the basis of daughterly affection for her governess, her mother midnight. Moll's surrogate ties to the governess come to resemble the affective ideals of eighteenth-century family life far more than her previous marriages or connections to her mother, brother, nurse, and the gypsies.[3] They form a companionable unit affiliated through mutual respect, much like the nuclear families idealized by Defoe in his didactic manuals, including *The Family Instructor* (1715) and *Religious Courtship* (1722), and described by Lawrence Stone as developing during the eighteenth century in *The Family, Sex, and Marriage in England, 1500–1800*.[4] When Moll is eventually transported to the American colonies, her surrogate ties to the governess become the model she uses to revise marital and biological ties so they too can perform according to the profitable premises of surrogate families. Her relationship to her son Humphry and her husband Jemy are founded financially on money earned through her connection to the governess, and emotionally on strategies she develops as a surrogate daughter.

Although Moll shares with all Defoe's other protagonists an enterprising energy associated with individualism that, as Hal Gladfelder observes, "tends, in its pure . . . form, to set the self against all others," as a woman her ambition translates into a powerful attractive force towards others.[5] Scholars sometimes overlook or underrate Moll's connections to other people on the basis of assumptions that, as Tina Kuhlisch argues, "Moll never establishes true relationships with the many people she meets."[6] However, just because Moll's relationships are formed for financial rather than emotional enrichment does not make them any less meaningful to her, or less significant to the trajectory of the narrative itself.[7] Moll asserts that for a woman social connections are particularly important because she needs friends to "advise" and "assist" her: to help her out of "Difficulties and into Business."[8] Despite her atomistic impulses, Moll must seek through ties to others the means of making, growing, and safeguarding a fortune.

Defoe's apparent acceptance of Moll's preference for surrogate ties formed exclusively to promote her economic advancement demonstrates a moral flexibility on his part about marriage and family not only unusual for the period, but also directly contradictory to his own advice about these topics in didactic works like *The Family Instructor* and *Religious Courtship*, texts that popularized an affectionate paradigm for family life. Scholars offer numerous explanations for the contradiction between Moll's cavalier attitudes towards the ties that Defoe himself apparently held sacred, though none of their arguments is wholly satisfying.[9] I will not advocate here for the accuracy of any one of these readings. It is rather the incongruity which they attempt to explain, and which is particularly glaring in *Moll Flanders*, that interests me. This dissonance is most obvious in Moll's violation of her duties as a wife and mother. Although much less widely noted, her preference for surrogate families united by temporary financial advantages over other family models is also a significant and insufficiently understood manifestation of this discrepancy.

While she participates in her first two first families, the gypsies and the parish orphanage, Moll exhibits an entrepreneurial desire to advance herself that these biologically defined families impede. I define these two groups as families because both fit Samuel Johnson's definition of *family* as a "household," "generation" or a "race."[10] The gypsies, whom Moll also describes as "Egyptians," are racially segregated in England, and accept as members only those born into their ranks or formally adopted (28). Similarly, membership in a parish is determined by place of birth. Neither of these families allows outsiders to join them voluntarily, nor do they allow their members autonomously to decide to leave them. Authorities in both types of families police membership. The gypsies "discolor" or "blacken" their adopted children's skin, while magistrates establish formal procedures to determine who belongs to a particular parish (28). As a child of three, it is almost impossible to believe Moll capable of prevailing over legal and conventional barriers erected to keep her in one of these insular families and exclude her from the other. However, according to her recollection, or "Notion in my Head" as she calls it, she does exactly this, hiding from the gypsies and refusing to "go any farther with them" and then engaging the "Compassion" of the parish magistrates to designate her "one of their own, as much as if [she] had been born in the Place" (28–29). It is impossible to know for certain whether Moll actually abandons the gypsies intentionally, as she believes she does, or whether she imposes this interpretation retroactively based on the mature version of herself who tells the story. However, in either case her account demonstrates two significant things about Moll's conception of herself and her evolving understanding of how families affect her ability to pursue her ambitions: she aspires to improve her situation, whatever the circumstances, and is able to do so with more success if she trades up to families with increased promotional opportunities; and the inert structures of biologically defined families stymie her self-advancement.

Residing at the parish orphanage, Moll continues to hone her self-promotional skills while becoming increasingly frustrated with the checks biological family models place on them. As Moll matures, she learns to manipulate her nurse in order to increase her own status in this family. She becomes her nurse's favored child, a privileged status that ultimately allows her to avoid the magistrates' requirement that she go into service when she turns eight. Moll's greatest fear about becoming a servant, as she confides to her nurse, is being placed as a "Drudge to some Cook-Maid" and thus becoming vulnerable to beatings by "the Maids" in an unknown master's household (29). Her comments reveal that it is the prospect of social demotion in a new family that agitates her most: not so much that she will be beaten, but rather that even maids will be allowed to beat her. The primary symptom of Moll's anxiety about this transition—she is "always Crying"—is overt and tailored to exploit the tenderness of her "good Motherly Nurse" (30). Moll explicitly claims she "Ha[s] no Policy in all this [crying]" and that her response is instead "all Nature" (31).

Even if the reader believes Moll's traumatized behavior is instinctual, however, it provides strong evidence of the strategic nature of her intuition. This episode is comparable to Moll's transition from the gypsies to the parish orphanage because her success in achieving her aims, even if it is not deliberate, enables her to engage in later machinations. Moll self-consciously enacts this knowledge when she starts performing the role of aspiring gentlewoman to neighborhood ladies for tips, even parlaying the jest into a week as a quasi-companion to the daughters of one her admiring audience members. Moll states that the "Tast of Genteel living" she gets during this stay makes her "not so easie in [her] old Quarters" and wish to remain instead "among Gentlewomen" (34). I would argue that it is not just the parish orphanage to which she refers in this instance, but more broadly to the biological model of family it represents, and which she views as constraining rather than enabling. It is worth observing in this context that Moll expresses virtually no curiosity about her own mother or her other relatives despite being told that "some Relation of my Mothers took me away for a while as a Nurse" (28). It is not just the impracticality of finding her relations or making claims on them that dictates this indifference. Moll is willing to take risks of all sorts if she thinks there will be a reasonable chance of reward, and her exigent circumstances should make her desperate enough to at least make inquiries. Rather, I interpret Moll's lack of interest in her own family as recognition that there is little to be gained by anchoring herself to a lowly biological family such as her own. She is better off seeking families with better promotional opportunities, which her nurse's death gives her immediate occasion to do.

Defoe's extended attention to the next family Moll joins, a conjugal family referred to by Moll simply as a *gentlewoman's family*, illustrates how considerably it formulates her future expectations about marriage and parenthood. Not only is this one of the only intact nuclear families Defoe describes in any detail or at any length in *Moll Flanders*, but also one of the very few that merit more than passing mention in any of his novels. It also has a tremendous impact on Moll's life, providing her with both her first lover and husband. Additionally, the gentlewoman's family shapes her character and ambitions and equips her to achieve her goals. From her perch on its periphery—she acts as both companion to the daughters and an upper servant—she observes its members, studying their behavior anthropologically. It becomes for her a sort of exemplary *every family*, one that inverts all of the domestic ideals advocated by Defoe in his didactic works such as *Religious Courtship*, and especially *The Family Instructor*. In these texts Defoe explicitly rejects mercenary matches and recommends that women instead marry religious husbands who will morally guide their households. In contrast, the dysfunctional foil to these families in *Moll Flanders* inspires Moll to marry for wealth, the only apparent path to status, and to view family members as just additional competitors in the Hobbesian war of one against all.

The very name Moll uses to refer to this family—the *gentlewoman's family*—denotes its lack of guidance by a strong father, a serious fault according to Defoe's didactic writing. Moll describes the father in passing as a "man in a hurry of publick Affairs, and getting Money, seldom at Home, thoughtful of the main Chance," but unconcerned about family matters, which he delegates entirely "to his Wife" (62). It is particularly telling that the father is missing during two episodes that determine the future composition of his family, one set at the family's dinner table, when the younger son's proposals to Moll provoke an "Uproar," and another that occurs when his wife unilaterally consents to the match, informing him after the fact "by Post Letters" (53, 64). In contrast, the father in *The Family Instructor* spends so much time engaging with his wife and children that the series of dialogues between them takes up more than three hundred pages.[11] His moral directives about when they must pray, what they are allowed to read, and where they may go enforce a corporate moral as well as social identity on their family, in contrast to the laissez-faire spirit that reigns in the gentlewoman's family.

Not only the father, but also the gentlewoman, along with her daughters, model to Moll mercenary attitudes about marriage she later adopts as her own. The sisters are quarrelsome and vain, educated in social graces meant to impress suitors rather than religious principles intended to prepare them to nurture families. Their attitude towards marriage is consistent with their overall worldview: wholly pragmatic. They explicitly state that "nothing but Money now recommends a Woman" to a potential husband (37). Though largely undeveloped as characters, they resemble somewhat the frivolous elder sister in *The Family Instructor* who protests against the burning of her playbooks, novels, and ballads. Their mother, who ought in their father's absence to educate her children religiously, instead focuses only on maintaining the family's "very good" and, if the lessons in *The Family Instructor* are seriously intended, unearned reputation "for Vertue and Sobriety, and every valuable Thing" (92). Her worldly view of marriage is apparent in her mournful response, "there's one Son lost," to her son's improvident match to Moll (56).

While the parents and sisters in the gentlewoman's family stoke Moll's matrimonial aspirations, the brothers provide her with tutorials in how to achieve them. The younger brother would seem a likely matrimonial prospect for Moll since he has strong earning potential and is willing to defy his family for her sake. His idealism is not, however, the admirable sort displayed by the prophet-like younger son in *The Family Instructor*. He is not focused on higher duties to God. Instead, his romantic naivety is just another manifestation of the selfishness characteristic of his entire family. He coerces Moll into marriage by courting her so persistently and publicly that even if she turns him down she will still be ejected from the house. His aggressive courtship forces Moll to the altar "like a bear to the stake," and his lack of ready money leaves her dependent on future earnings that dry up when he dies five years later (48).[12] From this younger brother Moll learns she must assess and manipulate potential suitors before they have any opportunity to pursue her. She makes certain to scrutinize carefully their fortunes as well, understanding through experience the advantages of ready money or annual rents over contingent revenue.

From the elder brother Moll learns that to marry well, she must conduct herself strategically during courtship. The attractive, wealthy elder brother is an ideal matrimonial prospect for Moll. However, he is also a canny and experienced rake who shares Moll's worldly attitudes about marriage. Moll's poverty makes her an undesirable spouse, but a perfectly acceptable mistress. Far more depraved in fact than the elder brother in *The Family Instructor*, whose greatest fault is petulance, this brother avoids his counterpart's comeuppance by deceiving rather than defying his family. He acts parts to everyone, playing a dutiful son and brother to his family, and a passionate lover to Moll. It is ironic that this self-indulgent sensualist discontinues his affair with Moll, supposedly for the sake of family honor, when he learns she might marry his brother and "become my Sister" (62). His renunciation burlesques the family loyalty and moral probity it is supposed to signify. The more likely explanation for his sacrifice is a selfish one; he performs ardor in order to engage her affections, and then remorse in order to conveniently dispose of her. Moll learns from her apprenticeship as this brother's mistress that courtship itself is a performance, and in order to obtain an advantageous match she must occupy the stage rather than observe from the gallery. "LOVE," she determines as a discarded mistress, is a "*Cheat*" and a "Game," and in order to procure a desirable husband she must act her part based on rational self-interest rather than emotion (66).

Based on these paradigmatic relationships with the brothers and the mercenary ideals of marriage she adopts while living in the gentlewoman's family, Moll develops principles of courtship meant to maximize her marital profits and minimize the risks she takes to achieve them. Melissa Mowry interprets Moll's intentions to become "part of [this] prosperous family" by marrying the elder brother as arising not just from ambition, but also "desire to belong to a greater whole."[13] I would argue that instead this episode hones in Moll what Gladfelder describes as an "irremediable sense of apartness" expressed through the "relentless pursuit" of profit.[14] The marriage market, no less than family life, is driven by competition, and any woman who succumbs to the romantic notion of belonging to a "greater whole" is vulnerable to becoming a mistress or poor widow. The marital axioms Moll develops based on her experiences in this family constitute a sort of business plan intended to woo investors without exposing herself to the attendant risks of speculation. She begins to use explicitly commercial language to describe marriage, repeatedly conflating faulty spouses with dangerous business "ventures," good husbands to revenue or "prize[s]," and marriage to a "Lottery" (77).

Conjugal ties for Moll, who marries or pretends to marry many times, become business transactions. Her cynical views about marriage directly contradict Defoe's own advice to courting couples in *Religious Courtship*, which was published, as David Blewett notes, within a month of *Moll Flanders*.[15] In *Religious Courtship*, Defoe cautions young people not to "act an unwise Part for both Time and Eternity" by ignoring the "religious

Principles and Temper" of suitors in order to pursue anyone who is "Rich and Handsome."[16] Moll learns when her first lover spurns her not to fall prey to a handsome face, but according to Defoe's assessment of marriage she becomes shrewder rather than wiser. He states unequivocally in *Conjugal Lewdness; or Matrimonial Whoredom* "Love is the only Pilot of a married State; without it there is nothing but Danger in the Attempt; nothing but Ruin in the Consequence."[17] Moll understands *danger* and *ruin*, however, only in economic terms. She is the very definition of the "matrimonial whore" Defoe derides in his pamphlet, a figure succinctly described by Blewett as "one who uses the institution of marriage improperly for gain."[18] The affectionate companionship Defoe recommends elsewhere appears only as cessations in Moll's story when she claims she is "landed in a safe Harbour, after the Stormy Voyage of Life" (161). These periods are typically brief, though, and her safe harbors prove to be floodplains. As Mona Scheuermann observes, money, not marriage is the real "source of security for Moll."[19]

The most erotic scenes in the novel, consequently, are about accumulating money rather than having sex. Several representative scenes occur between Moll and three of her husbands or pseudo-husbands, and stand in for courtship and consummation. The most obvious of these is when Moll's married friend forces one of her hands into his "Drawer" of gold coins, demands she take a handful of them and "put them into [her] Lap" where he also "[pours] out all [her] own Money among his." The double-entendres continue as she carries the loot "into [her] own Chamber" (105). Less explicit but equally playful and significant are the series of scenes in which Moll brings gold, linen, and cash to her half-brother/husband: for Moll, this signifies marital commitment more than consummation because she considers her goods more valuable than access to her body. Even the least libidinous union, her marriage to her banker husband, commences with a flirtatious exchange about money. She comes to him for advice on how to invest her money and he responds with a proposal to become the "Steward" of Moll as well as her fortune (121). In each case, marriage or at least long-term commitment is cemented not by a ceremony or by sex, but by uniting funds. When those funds fail, Moll considers the business venture of marriage concluded, and reenters the market as a free agent. For example, her second husband, the draper, may well be alive when Moll marries many, if not all, of her future husbands, but she considers him "effectually dead in Law" because he is bankrupt and absent (91). Despite the probable bigamy she repeatedly commits, Moll continues to pursue for-profit matches because financial prospects are better for a pretended wife than an avowed mistress.

Although Moll continues as long as possible to pursue social and economic advancement through marriage, she cannot entirely avoid becoming entangled by biological ties. Most of the time, these biological connections occur in the predictable form of children. In one memorable instance, however, kin emerge unexpectedly in the persons of her husband and mother-in-law, who turn out to be her half-brother and mother. Moll's marked aversion to biological ties develops, as I mention earlier, during her childhood at the parish orphanage; it is only exacerbated by this incestuous relationship with her half-brother/husband. Incest becomes for Moll an exaggerated version of kinship itself, insular and stifling to her entrepreneurial instincts. Since Moll's hostility to biological ties only increases over the course of her lengthy marital career, she repudiates both her newborn and newfound relations with all possible expediency.

Children are the most obvious example of blood relations Moll rejects, and her refusal to raise them in adverse circumstances illustrates her especial dislike for the expensiveness of motherhood.[20] As infants and young children they are certain to be costly and troublesome. As young adults they must be educated and placed in some sort of apprenticeship or service. As adults they are far more likely to expect an inheritance than to provide one. For Moll, who is wary of acknowledging even fairly profitable blood ties, children have no charms. Although it may be argued that her decision to dispose of so many of them throughout the course of the novel is forced on her by exigent circumstances, her claims of poverty are disputable, or at least exaggerated, according to David Spielman's claims in a recent article.[21] Even when she does have enough money to keep her children, and according to Spielman's assessment she always has enough money, she declines to do so. When possible, Moll leaves her children with extended family members. Thus she escapes from membership in these families and from motherhood at the same time. When such kinship networks are unavailable, she pays a stranger to take them permanently off her hands, usually through deals brokered by her governess.

It is Moll's treatment of her children that elicits the greatest condemnation from scholars such as Michael Shinagel, who denounces her as an "unnatural mother who steadfastly rejects her moral—and natural—responsibility as a parent," and Klaus Jochum, who describes Moll as an "utter failure" as a mother.[22] Going even further, Marilyn Francus accuses Moll of "consciously choos[ing]. . . infanticide" in certain instances over the wearisome self-sacrifice associated with motherhood.[23] Though Moll never actually murders any of her children, Francus's point is well taken. Moll's experience with her own nurse aside, orphans left in group homes with professional nurses were notoriously prone to disease, neglect, and abuse. Moll's refusal to raise these children under any circumstances makes sense when it is considered as an extreme manifestation of her larger animosity towards biological ties. Unlike conjugal relationships, which she screens for profitability, children always take rather than give; they are the opposite of productive investments.

Moll's disrelish for biological ties of any sort is also evident in the deterioration of her relationships with her mother and half-brother after she discovers they are kin. Moll appreciates the financial security her position in a prominent Virginian family provides her, so she cleaves to the source of their wealth: her mother-in-law. This relationship cools significantly, however, when Moll learns her mother-in-law is actually her mother. Moll explains the alienation from her mother as a symptom of her overriding disgust with her incestuous marriage to her half-brother (87). However, it is surprising that her horror is not mitigated at all by excitement over a reunion with her family. Defoe emphasizes Moll's coldness by contrasting it with her mother's passionate display of emotion, "kiss[ing]" her daughter through her tears despite the devastating implications of this revelation (92). Lois Chaber explains Moll's unkindness towards her mother by interpreting it as a sign that Moll never fully acknowledges their kinship since her mother "seemed [to be] only a surrogate mother—a mother-in-law— for so long."[24] Rather, I would argue that far from "leveling" biological ties with other sorts of bonds, as Chaber asserts, Moll's realization that she has committed incest reinforces her privileging of marital ties over kinship.[25] Equating incest with blood ties further diminishes Moll's already dubious estimation of their value. While Moll's relationship to her mother becomes more detached after learning that they are related, her bond to her brother ruptures entirely. Her instinctive repugnance at having sex with him explains her "provoking" behavior to him while she remains in Virginia (90). However, it does not account for the enduring bitterness apparent in her pronouncement many years later when she returns to the American colonies that "the old Wretch, my Brother (Husband) was dead" (274).

This incest episode only intensifies Moll's desire to act again as a free agent. Katerina Kitsi-Mitakou argues that the ultimate "object of Moll's desire" when she commits incest "is the mother, or even [Moll's] 'self,'" since Moll and her mother have similar backgrounds and personalities.[26] I agree with Kitsi-Mitakou that discovering a biological family nested like Russian dolls inside a conjugal family is a form of self-discovery, and would expand her claims to include Moll's half-brother/husband as well. However, if Moll sees herself reflected in her newfound relations, she proves to be no Narcissus. Far from falling in love with these images of herself, she becomes "uneasie" and "restless," anxious to separate herself fully from them by returning to England (99). The forced intimacy of discovering they are connected inextricably to her is for Moll a form of entrapment. After leaving, she returns to her earlier practice of marital entrepreneurship, a "Scene of Life" she is qualified to succeed at since she is "still far from being old" (100).

While serial matrimony remains profitable for quite a long time for Moll, her governess introduces her to a more abiding and remunerative family model: the surrogate family. Moll meets her governess, or Mother Midnight (an ambiguous term meaning midwife, bawd, and abortionist) as Moll initially calls her, midway through her conjugal career. Their bond is much more immediate and emotionally intense than Moll's connection to her biological mother, so much so that it constitutes what I call *surrogate motherhood*. Inconveniently pregnant by her husband Jemy, who has now abandoned her, Moll becomes ill with worry about how to safely give birth to and then dispose of the child. By helping Moll out of her difficulties, the governess "births" Moll back into life again, or as Moll phrases it, "put[s] new Life and new Spirit into my very Heart" (141). Defoe turns what is typically a simple metaphor signifying invigoration into a literal physiological phenomenon when he writes that Moll's "Blood began to circulate immediately" upon speaking to the governess (141). Before Moll even becomes an inmate of the governess's lying-in hospital, she has already become her surrogate daughter. The unusual degree of intimacy between Moll and her governess has led other scholars to a similar conclusion about the maternal nature of their bond. Francus, for example, even views the governess as a parallel figure to Amy in *Roxana*, arguing both of these "surrogate parents . . . propagate monstrous behaviors through their 'children.'"[27]

The governess intensifies this maternal connection with Moll by redefining Moll's view of motherhood itself. In a scene that is often interpreted ironically, Moll confesses to her governess her qualms of conscience about abandoning her infant son. The episode consists of a lengthy conversation (spanning three pages) positing alternative theories of motherhood and childrearing. Moll, an admittedly unlikely proponent for her own position, argues that mothers must raise their own children because "Affection was plac'd by Nature in the Hearts of Mothers" by God (150). According to Moll, relying on paid surrogates to "take the Child off" a mother's hands for as "long as it lives" is a form of infanticide because their "Gain consists in being quit of the Charge" (152). The governess counters Moll's argument by portraying motherhood as one of many "Trades." Any woman can learn to perform a mother's duties and will perform them well *because* she is paid for them. According to this logic, foster mothers may even be superior to biological mothers because they "get their Bread by it," while biological mothers must act out of instinctual altruism (151).

Although Moll initially appears skeptical of the governess's economic vision of motherhood, over the course of the novel she comes to endorse it and to adopt it as her own. Even as Moll appears to doubt the equation between profit and conscientiousness espoused by the governess, she cannot help but respect the simple pragmatism of the governess's final defense of paid surrogates. The governess reminds Moll she cannot afford to enact the lofty ideals of motherhood she advocates, and thus must "be contented with things as they must be, tho' they are not as [she] wish[es]" (152). Despite her reservations, Moll follows the governess's advice and spends ten pounds to hire a "Country Woman" to "take the Child off our Hands entirely" (153). More importantly, the linguistic markers in the conversation suggest that Moll's acceptance of the governess's vision of motherhood is personally as well as philosophically significant. As Moll's use of *our* rather than *my* in reference to her own child indicates, Moll now sees herself as a member of the governess's economic family. Defoe clarifies the nature of this familial connection through his use of the term *mother* more than thirteen times during the course of the conversation, at least five of which are direct addresses by Moll to the governess, whom she "had now learn'd to call Mother" (151). The relationship between Moll and her new economic mother is cemented by mutual self-interest, a stronger foundation than blood in Moll's view for an enduring connection.

The surrogate mother-daughter relationship formed between Moll and the governess fulfills their mutual expectations of profitability. When Moll and the governess reconnect after the death of Moll's banker husband, they are both in reduced circumstances: Moll has no income to support herself, and the governess has become a pawnbroker. The governess assists Moll by fencing her stolen goods and acting as a liaison between Moll and other members of London's criminal underworld. The governess also arranges for Moll's education as a thief by locating an expert "School-Mistress" for Moll to apprentice under as a pickpocket "just as a Deputy attends a Midwife without any Pay" (171). The governess even masterminds one of Moll's most lucrative schemes, the mercer's cash settlement for falsely detaining and defaming Moll, and directs her to numerous profitable ventures, such as stealing from a family whose house is on fire. Over the course of her lengthy criminal career Moll accumulates £700 as well as many stolen goods, making her according to the governess the "richest of the Trade in *England*" (209). If the economic advantages Moll reaps from her connection to the governess are fairly obvious, the benefits the governess enjoys are even more overt since she takes a "Share of the Gain" of all of Moll's exploits with "no Share in the hazard" (181). Moll's surrogate mother is perfectly matched to her, as both share a spirit of entrepreneurship, delight in conning the credulous, an unscrupulous willingness to exploit any situation, and an insatiable ambition for profit.

More surprisingly, the relationship between Moll and her surrogate mother also develops many aspects of the selfless love Moll associates with biological motherhood. The favoritism the governess displays for Moll in giving her the "full value" for any stolen plate she smelts, something Moll knows the governess does not do for her other "Customers," hints early on at the increasing exclusivity of their attachment to each other (170–71). Later, the governess not only protects Moll, but also places herself at risk for her sake, hiding Moll in her house when an angry mob tries to seize her for theft. In contrast, she does nothing to intervene when numerous of her other associates hang for their crimes. The intimacy that develops between them becomes so marked that the governess actually refers to herself and Moll as a single unit, advising Moll to "[leave] off while *we* were well" and be "satisfy'd with what we had got [emphasis mine]" (216). Her sentiments as much as her phrasing signify the transformation of this relationship from economic opportunism to maternal tenderness, since she proposes to forgo any further profits merely for the sake of protecting her surrogate daughter.

The nurturing relationship between Moll and her governess becomes even more pronounced after Moll is caught stealing and sent to Newgate. The governess apparently has access to all of Moll's money and stolen goods, so it is in her self-interest to let Moll hang. Instead, she attempts repeatedly and at some expense (though the bribes she offers would be paid for with Moll's own money) to free Moll. After Moll is condemned, the governess continues to "[act] a true Mother to [her]," coming to her surrogate daughter's aid emotionally and pragmatically (231). She tends to Moll's spiritual health by encouraging her to repent. She also provides Moll with invaluable practical services, arranging Jemy's passage on the ship that transports Moll to America, purchasing the necessary items they need to settle there, and negotiating the terms of their freedom once they arrive. It is telling that the boatswain who carries a letter to the governess from Moll mistakes her for Moll's "Sister" and is surprised to learn she is "no Relation" of Moll's, but rather a "dear Friend" (250). He assumes that only a blood relation would display such empathy and offer so much help, since "there are few such Friends in the World" (250). Even though Moll ultimately reunites with her biological son and never sees her governess again, the boatswain's casual observation is far more insightful about the nature of Moll's relationship to the governess than he is capable of knowing. For Moll, this *friend* is the only *relation*, according to his understanding of the word (which mirrors Moll's in her earlier conversation about motherhood with the governess), that Moll ever really has.

Although Moll is ultimately forced to leave her governess for a new life, including a husband and child, in the American colonies, she imposes on these ties desirable aspects of her former surrogate family. Moll is accustomed, after her many years partnering with the governess in their criminal enterprises, to accumulating her own capital. Rather than depend again, as she did before she joined the governess's surrogate family, on a potentially hapless husband, Moll refashions her conjugal bonds to Jemy to continue exercising financial free will. This final marriage is the only one Moll enters into knowing she is richer than her husband. It is not mercenary motives or the desire for status that drive their union, but rather Moll's strategy of choosing a spouse who will acquiesce wholly to her management of their affairs. Since it would be difficult for Moll to transact business independently in the colonies, she marries a man who allows her to control their accounts. Jemy resembles the sort of wife Moll was formerly consigned to being. He allows her to decide which plantation to buy and how to invest their money. He reveals how little he knows about any of these transactions when the goods purchased with Moll's ill-gotten gains arrive from England. He worries Moll has run them "too deep in Debt," a response that reveals the extent of his ignorance about their finances (273). He is the matrimonial whore Moll once was, thanking providence that he "married a Fortune, and a very good Fortune too," and leaving the rest to his spouse (274). This inverted spousal relationship is the closest approximation Moll can achieve in marriage to the financial autonomy she experienced in her surrogate family.

Moll also transforms her biological ties to her son Humphry into a profitable connection founded on principles she forms and capital she accumulates as the governess's surrogate daughter. When Moll returns to the colonies she seeks out her kin in order to claim the inheritance her mother promised. The sight of her son Humphry walking around their plantation sends her into the state of emotional rapture she experienced earlier when her governess resurrected her by helping her dispose of a different child. The scene is overwrought and sentimental, recounting how Moll's "very Bowels mov'd" at the sight of him, leaving her exhausted by her paroxysm of emotion, "we[eeping], and kiss[ing]" the ground on which he stood (260). This agitation also characterizes a letter Moll sends, ostensibly to her half-brother/husband but really to her son (who Moll knows reads all the family correspondence). It is full of "Passionate" outpourings of a tormented heart to "[see] my one, and only Child" (267).[28] These two passages forge a stylistic connection between Moll's relationships with her son and her governess. Defoe further reinforces this association through Moll's gift to Humphry of a stolen watch she hopes he will "now and then kiss" (271). This relic of Moll's surrogate family embodies her connection to the governess, who funded the training that made Moll an expert watch-puller. Humphry construes the watch just as Moll would wish, as a "Debt upon him, that he would be paying, as long as [he] liv'd" (271). Typically, motherhood is conceived of as a lifelong debt to one's children, but through the watch Moll upends the conventional terms of this relationship. The watch that becomes the emblem for this unorthodox model of parenthood is best interpreted not as a gift from Moll to her son, but instead from the governess to Moll. It is a lasting memorial to surrogate parenthood, a tribute that reflects the values of the surrogate family in which it originates by paying regular dividends.

NOTES

1. John Richetti, "The Family, Sex, and Marriage in Defoe's *Moll Flanders* and *Roxana*," *Studies in the Literary Imagination* 15, no. 2 (1982): 19–35, 19. I continue to attribute *Moll Flanders* to Daniel Defoe despite Ashley Marshall's warnings in a recent article that there is no definitive evidence for his authorship of either *Moll Flanders* or *Roxana* (Ashley Marshall, "Did Defoe Write *Moll Flanders* and *Roxana*?," *Philological Quarterly* 89, nos. 2–3 [2010]: 209–241). While her argument is intriguing, I am convinced by the external and internal evidence for Defoe's authorship of both novels produced by P. N. Furbank and W. R. Owens in an article published in the same volume (P. N. Furbank and W. R. Owens, "On the Attribution of Novels to Daniel Defoe," *Philological Quarterly* 89, nos. 2–3 [2010]: 243–253). For more on this debate see also Robert J. Griffin, "Did Defoe Write *Roxana*? Does it Matter?," *Philological Quarterly* 89, nos. 2–3 (2010): 255–262.

2. A recent article by Tina Kuhlisch examines the strengths and weaknesses of arguments that *Moll Flanders* is a picaresque novel (Tina Kuhlisch, "The Ambivalent Rogue: Moll Flanders as Modern Picara," in *Rogues in Early Modern Culture*, eds. Craig Dionne and Steve Mentz [Ann Arbor: University of Michigan Press, 2004], 337–360).

3. Lawrence Stone claims that the ideal of companionate marriage, a match made for the purpose of "emotional satisfaction" rather than "ambition for increased income or status," became widely accepted over the course of the eighteenth century (Lawrence Stone, T*he Family, Sex, and Marriage in England 1500–1800* [New York: Harper and Row, 1977], 217). While Stone's claims in this

book have elicited a great deal of controversy since it was first published, and many specific aspects of his argument have been debated, his account of the increasing value accorded to love and domesticity during the period is still accepted by most scholars.

4. Defoe's didactic texts helped popularize the companionable domesticity associated with affective individualism, the definitive quality of eighteenth-century families according to Stone in *The Family, Sex, and Marriage in England 1500–1800.* As Laura Curtis observes, Defoe's families in *The Family Instructor* and *Religious Courtship* "clearly belon[g] to the category of affective individualism," though they retain an older patriarchal structure (Laura A. Curtis, "A Case Study of Defoe's Domestic Conduct Manuals Suggested by *The Family, Sex and Marriage in England, 1500–1800*," *Studies in Eighteenth-Century Culture* 10 [1981]: 409–428, 414).

5. Hal Gladfelder, "Defoe and Criminal Fiction," in *The Cambridge Companion to Daniel Defoe*, ed. John Richetti (Cambridge: Cambridge University Press, 2008): 64–83, 78. Paula Backscheider similarly claims that the purpose of travel in Defoe's novels is to prioritize the "quest for personal as opposed to social and family identity" (Paula R. Backscheider, "Defoe's Prodigal Sons," *Studies in the Literary Imagination* 15, no. 2 [1982]: 13–18, 13).

6. Kuhlisch, 344.

7. The observation that Moll is motivated by money, not love, is common in Defoe scholarship. For example, Jacques Sohier argues that Moll is a Machiavellian woman, a "materialist" who "gives precedence to security, status, and wealth over affection," one of the primary reasons, according to Sohier, that she refuses to confide even in her "close kin and loved ones" (Jacques Sohier, "Moll Flanders and the Rise of the Complete Gentlewoman-Tradeswoman," *The Eighteenth-Century Novel* 2 [2002]: 1–21, 16, 18). Ann Kibbie even argues that both *Moll Flanders* and *Roxana* focus so much on money they may be legitimately described as "companion pieces: a comedy and a tragedy of capital" (Ann Louise Kibbie, "Monstrous Generation: The Birth of Capital in Defoe's *Moll Flanders* and *Roxana*," *PMLA* 110, no. 5 [1995]: 1023–1034, 1024).

8. Daniel Defoe, *The Fortunes and Misfortunes of the Famous Moll Flanders*, in *The Novels of Daniel Defoe*, ed. Liz Bellamy (London: Pickering & Chatto, 2008–2009), 6:23–275, 86, 116. Hereafter cited in the text.

9. This is also true of the male and female protagonists of Defoe's other novels, none of whom crave the stability or hearth and home. Arguments explaining the fissure between the ideals Defoe advocates in his didactic texts and then violates gleefully in his fictional works, including *Moll Flanders*, focus largely on the difference between what is right in theory and what is realistic to do in particular circumstances. Shirlene Mason argues that in "his didactic works Defoe concentrates on the sin and its dire consequences. In his fiction he puts the sin in context of an evil situation in which sin is unavoidable if the person involved is to survive" (Shirlene Mason, *Daniel Defoe and the Status of Women* [Montreal: Eden Press, 1978], 97). Similarly, Srividhya Swaminathan argues that *Moll Flanders* answers the question of "[w]hat happens in a world when men

are largely absent, unable to give guidance, and act against the ideals of conduct manuals" (Srividhya Swarminathan, "Defoe's Alternative Conduct Manual: Survival Strategies and Female Networks in *Moll Flanders*," *Eighteenth-Century Fiction* 15, no. 2 [2003]:185–206, 204–5). Juliet McMaster makes a similar claim, noting "*Moll Flanders* deals with real situations women encounter in a world in which the "inglorious displacement of love by money" is the "operative standard" (Juliet McMaster, "The Equation of Love and Money in *Moll Flanders*," *Studies in the Novel* 2 [1970]: 131–144,132). Other scholars go further, claiming that in *Moll Flanders* Defoe in some sense debunks his own theories, demonstrating, as Austin Flanders writes in reference to the novel's incest incident, the "irrelevance of conventional codes of moral judgment for his rootless characters" (Austin W. Flanders, *Structures of Experience: History, Society, and Personal Life in the Eighteenth-Century Novel* [Columbia: University of South Carolina Press, 1984], 132). See also Richetti, 24.

10. Samuel Johnson, *An Universal Etymological Dictionary of the English Language* (London: W. Strahan for J. and P. Knapton, 1755), 2 vol.,1: *s.v.*), 356.

11. The father's plan for religious reform of his household and the response of each of its members is the subject of *The Family Instructor*. Only after a conversation with his youngest son, the first dialogue in the text, does he institute these changes. The edition consulted here is *The Family Instructor, in Three Parts, with a Recommendatory Letter by the Reverend Mr. S. Wright* (London: E. Matthews, 1715).

12. While Moll's first husband leaves her £1,200 when he dies, she describes her financial situation in negative terms—"not great"—explaining that he "had not receiv'd much from" his parents and "in the little time he liv'd" he "acquir'd no great Matters" (65).

13. Melissa Mowry, "Women, Work, Rearguard Politics, and Defoe's *Moll Flanders*," *The Eighteenth Century* 49, no. 2 (2008): 97–109, 105.

14. Gladfelder, 77.

15. David Blewett, "Changing Attitudes Towards Marriage in the Time of Defoe: The Case of *Moll Flanders*," *Huntington Library Quarterly* 44, no. 2 (1981): 77–88, 86.

16. Daniel Defoe, *Religious Courtship Abridg'd: Being Historical Discourses on the Necessity of Marrying Religious Husbands and Wives Only* (London, 1734), iv.

17. Daniel Defoe, *Conjugal Lewdness: or, Matrimonial Whoredom* (London, 1727), 119.

18. Blewett, 87.

19. Mona Scheuermann, "An Income of One's Own: Women and Money in *Moll Flanders* and *Roxana*," *The Durham University Journal* 80, no. 2 (1988): 225–239, 225.

20. Heavily revised and redacted editions of *Roxana* and *Moll Flanders* published in the 1770s provide additional evidence that readers, at least during the late eighteenth century, did not accept as culturally normative a mother's indifference to her children. In one such version of *Roxana*, Roxana's "intrigues

always include some arrangement for the children" and she assesses suitors based on whether they will be "devoted father[s]." Changes to *Moll Flanders* "are mostly by way of subtraction," leaving intact the protagonist's "promiscuity, and manipulative tendencies" but "systematically de-emphasiz[ing]" them "throughout the text," and omitting the criminal section entirely (Marshall, 212). Mark Vareschi specifically ties these revisions to Defoe's other works, particularly his didactic texts, speculating that the changes "may have been intended to . . . make the novels ideologically match the more widely known Defoe works like *Robinson Crusoe* and *The Family Instructor*" (Mark Vareschi, "Attribution and Reception: The Case of Defoe and the Circulating Library," *Eighteenth-Century Life* 36.2 [2012]: 36–59, 39–40).

21. Spielman concludes based on his calculations about the present day value of Moll's wealth at various points in the novel that "at no point in the course of [her] relationship does Moll experience anything like poverty" (David Wallace Spielman, "The Value of Money in *Robinson Crusoe, Moll Flanders,* and *Roxana*," *Modern Langugage Review* 107 [2012]: 65–84, 79). If correct, his figures tend to show that Moll is, at the very least, usually not so bad off as she claims when she uses poverty as an excuse to dispose of her children.

22. Michael Shinagel, "The Maternal Theme in *Moll Flanders*: Craft and Character," *The Cornell Library Journal* 7 (1969): 3–23, 8; Klaus Peter Jochum, "Defoe's Children," in *Fashioning Childhood in the Eighteenth Century: Age and Identity*, ed. Anja Muller (Burlington: Ashgate, 2006), 157–67, 161.

23. Marilyn Francus, "'A-Killing Their Children With Safety': Maternal Identity and Transgression in Swift and Defoe," in *Lewd and Notorious: Female Transgression in the Eighteenth Century*, ed. Katharine Kittredge (Ann Arbor: University of Michigan Press, 2003), 258–282, 262.

24. Lois A. Chaber, "Matriarchal Mirror: Women and Capital in *Moll Flanders*," *PMLA* 97, no. 2 (1982): 212–226, 219.

25. Chaber, 219.

26. Katerina Kitsi-Mitakou, "Whoring, Incest, Duplicity, or the 'Self-Polluting' Erotics of Daniel Defoe's *Moll Flanders*," in *Genealogies of Identity: Interdisciplinary Readings on Sex and Sexuality*, eds. Margaret Sonser Breen and Fiona Peters (New York: Rodopi, 2005), 79–94, 87.

27. Marilyn Francus, 269. Robert Erickson also describes Moll's governess as her "spiritual mother" (Robert Erickson, *Mother Midnight: Birth, Sex, and Fate in Eighteenth-Century Fiction* [New York: AMS Press, 1986], 51).

28. I do not think Moll is being ironic here, despite the number of children she discards. Rather, to her way of thinking and feeling, Humphry *really* is her only child because he is the only one who becomes profitable.

Imaginative Pleasures: *Fantomina*, Ideology, and Aesthetics

PATRICIA COMITINI

> The Pleasures of the Imagination, taken in their full Extent, are not so gross as those of Sense, nor so refined as those of the Understanding. The last are, indeed, more preferable, because they are founded on some new Knowledge or Improvement in the Mind of Man; yet it must be confest, that those of the Imagination are as great and as transporting as the other. . . .
>
> Joseph Addison, *Spectator* 411[1]

The British version of aesthetics is a peculiarly eighteenth-century phenomenon, with the pivotal role of the imagination, and the pleasures it provides, internalized as a natural and automatic part of the mind's primary understanding. As in Addison's famous rendering, the imagination mediates between sense impressions and mental cognition, creating a spontaneous reaction, what might be called an imaginary relation between "sense" and "understanding" that is experienced and felt, but never quite rationally construed.[2] On this view, the aesthetic becomes a means of ideological production, a way of constructing individual perception through representative forms like poetry and, somewhat more dangerously, fiction. Just how the aesthetic realm enables the imaginative experience of reading, shaping the way individual readers are to understand their cultural milieu, is the concern of this essay.

Eliza Haywood's *Fantomina* experiments with Addison's emerging notions of aesthetics and the pleasures of the imagination as a self-consciously imagined form of fiction. Its central plot is concerned with the way fictions motivate and exercise imaginative responses in the mind, playing with the sensory manifestations that produce the passions – what Addison points to as a "new Principle of Pleasure" resulting from an

"Operation of the Mind" (*Spectator* 418, 3: 566–67). Haywood's novella exposes the operation of an emergent kind of aesthetic pleasure, enabling the sensory domain to transcend the pleasures of the body in order to improve or ameliorate the imagination. A cultural novelty attracting a wide period readership, and a fiction that continues to prove attractive to critical attention today, *Fantomina* expresses a new relationship between the body and mind. It shows us fictive narrative attempting to do something different: to producc an aesthetic reading practice that engages readers in an imaginary experience privileged above rational judgment. In an expanding market of readers and publishers, Haywood crafts writing that adapts features of previous amatory and romance writing in order to create an imaginary relation of individuals to the transformative class and gender relations of the time. In *Fantomina*, ideology produces a form of consciousness that is enabled by the aesthetic. Arguably, the amatory form of the novella, as well as the reading practice it engenders, together produce a particular kind of imaginative thinking, or consciousness, that is separate from rational cognition, judgment, or knowledge. Through its serial form, sexual desire and passion are attached to the protagonist's particular imagination, and the reader is thus encouraged to use his or her imagination to take pleasure in the narrative and to desire more such fictions that (re)structure feeling and perception. *Fantomina* imagines fictions of desire that centrally engage and (re)produce the aesthetic by linking the body to the imagination, producing a desire inspired by narrative fiction, and enabling individual desire to be reproduced through literary forms. William Warner has claimed that Haywood's fiction generalizes the reader, but if we notice how fiction begins to work as an aesthetic practice of ideology, we may see how fiction generalizes not the reader, but rather the desire for reading.[3] That is, fiction works to engender ideology in its pleasurable responses,[4] and *Fantomina* in particular reveals how feeling (both sensory and emotive) precedes understanding, making the imagination just as "great and as transporting" as the understanding, as Addison suggests (*Spectator* 411, 3: 538).

My argument draws on previous interpretations, but offers another way to account for how desire, particularly feminine desire, operates in Haywood's fiction,[5] mapping changes in the development of fiction when the novel remains, at least, a suspect genre.[6] My analysis focuses on how *Fantomina* engages and stimulates passionate response from readers in order to reposition the body to the mind in an experience of imaginative pleasure—the same goal of aesthetic discourse. Repositionng imaginary pleasures as the associative hub of the body and mind duality in the early eighteenth century has been the context for some recent analyses of Haywood's early work. Kathleen Lubey, for example, has argued for an "amatory aesthetic," in which "Haywood conceives of her readers' imagination as a mediating force that, when employed purposefully, sustains the pleasures of the body and mind but forestalls a decline into unthinking sensual gratification."[7] Lubey's argument focuses on how readers can remain aware of Haywood's instructive warnings to resist and monitor their sensual desires. Likewise, Joseph Drury reads Haywood's early fiction as a "mechanical" fiction that makes readers conscious of the sensuous experience of reading while creating a different form for fiction's moral directive through the reader's "deliberating consciousness."[8] Rebecca Tierney-Hynes emphasizes that Haywood's fiction theorizes about the "role of the passions in human life and social engagement" and claims that Haywood argues for the "significance of passionate reading as a mode of moral and social arbitration, even as a model for cultural reproduction."[9] The passions are equated in Tierney-Hynes' argument with knowledge—"to know thyself" is effectively to know the passions, and fiction serves as an "epistemological quest" for an "empirical self."[10] Implicated in these assessments of Haywood's fiction is the assumption of a more or less pedagogical function for her fiction, focusing on how readers can manage the relationship between individual desire (stimulated in the body) and knowledge about them (stimulated in the mind).

What is at stake in these three readings is the idea of thinking that enables consciousness, and this consciousness is aligned with moral deliberation, cognition or judgment—all operations of the rational mind. In *Fantomina*, however, rational continuity consciousness is shown to be distinct from the operation of the imagination and the kinds of readerly pleasures it produces. If reading is to be a way to engender "moral" taste, then the imagination must energize the reader into feeling *first* before rational judgment can be engaged. Though Haywood's *Fantomina* in particular and aesthetic discourses in general conceive an absolute continuity between feeling and thought, body and mind, sense and cognition, the way this is achieved is through how one *imagines* the self. *Fantomina* emphasizes the fluidity of imaginative possibility that emerges through an aesthetic notion of taste, as well as the consistent amelioration of the imagination through a reading practice which produces and reproduces the imaginary effects of feeling and consciousness. If we consider imaginative pleasure as the starting point of an ameliorative reading practice that could lead to moral or aesthetic judgment, but also might not, then the novella produces a reading practice in which ideology becomes aesthetic. Generally speaking, ideology gives individuals a way to experience his/her relationship to the larger society;

it enables a subject to feel, to perceive, herself as an individual, and while this may be a form of knowledge, it is distinct from the realm of inquiry, truth and judgment.[11] As Terry Eagleton suggests, "if ideology is to work efficiently, it must be pleasurable, intuitive, self-ratifying: in a word aesthetic."[12] Haywood's experiment with aesthetic pleasure engenders this particular kind of reading practice—that the sensory pleasures enabled through reading reveals a spontaneous experience of desire, of passion, that is felt, perceived, but not quite consciously known. The subliminal imaginary rendering of fiction takes on the function of a more subjective, rather than objective, truth. This truth that *feels* spontaneous is the function of ideology, and this is seen as distinct from the realm of knowledge (inquiry) and from reason (judgment) in Haywood's narrative.

How does the novella do this? The answer lies in how imaginative pleasure is produced for both the protagonist in *Fantomina* and the reader. *Fantomina* distances the older pleasures of the rake—that is, transient and sensory pleasures—and produces new pleasures—that is, more enduring and transcendent pleasures linked to narratives of desire.[13] It experiments with those pleasures that are rooted in bodily sensation such as sexual desire, but it also presents a way to merge sensation and the abstract, such as the desire for love, transforming libidinal experience but not to a level of pure abstraction. It is here that the Lady's imagination becomes a mediating factor between body and mind.[14] Her imagination becomes a cause of "passion" that destabilizes reasonable cognition.[15]

Nothing is more obvious in the novella than that Fantomina (as well as the other personas) is a figment of the imagination—the Lady's, Beauplaisir's and the reader's. Haywood plays with the notion of imagination throughout the novel, thematizing it in the plot of disguises. Fantomina, and the other disguises, metonymically function to create a bridge in the novel between bodily and readerly pleasures, between the sensory experiences of sexual passion and the virtuous concepts of love and fidelity. The form of *Fantomina* does not give a true representation of woman's passionate desires, nor the motivations for her transgressive actions; in other words, the imaginative pleasure taken in reading *Fantomina* is not a matter of simple titillation (sensory perception), or about getting to the truth of feminine desire (the cause of an idea), or about judging a moral dilemma (the production of an ideal). Rather, the pleasure comes from *imagining* the aesthetic possibilities of textuality, and the desires that narrative is capable of creating, distancing, and reproducing. In doing this, the novella creates an ideology of ever-reproductive desire as the ultimate truth of subjectivity (masculine or feminine); the novella's source of pleasure is the Lady's endless desire for both Beauplaisir and for the stories she tells to him. Narrative helps readers, whether men or women, to imagine this desire as a possibility of texts and of individuals.

Fantomina's narrative connects textual pleasure to subjective desire through an aesthetic reading practice. The narrative engages bodily sensation through the depiction of sexual liaisons in order to have language embody desire, stimulate a sensory response in the absence of real physical sensation, and provoke the passions. This was a central question of the aesthetic, as a body of knowledge: to account for how language can stimulate a sensory response in the body which shapes both behavior and emotion. The desire for an object, be it pleasurable or painful should be physically inspired, but it could also be mental, a figment of one's imagination born from reading.[16] For Haywood, amatory fiction experiments with embodying the imagination in fictions of desire. The suggestions of seduction, rape, and sexual encounters—stock moments in amatory fictions—make it possible for fiction to have this stimulating effect in one's body and mind. *Fantomina* evokes desire and passion as a response to narrative. Consequently, it illustrates how sexual desire is less about looking at a particular woman's body (a physical prompt to sexual desire or love), and more about the fictions that make the feminine body attractive (as an imaginative perception of something real). The successive seductions of Beauplaisir by the Lady are contextualized by fictions, produced by the protagonist's imaginative mind, that perpetually restart Beauplaisir's desire for the same woman. Each disguise contains the fictional elements of storytelling: her three plots of Fantomina, Celia, and the Widow Bloomer are illustrative of various kinds of amatory stories across a class and social spectrum.

For example, as Widow Bloomer the Lady narrates for Beauplaisir a sorrowful tale about the lost love of her husband ("all that ought to be valuable to womankind"), her intense grief ("the most unhappy of my sex in out-living him"), her loss of her little income by her husband's greedy brother ("all will be carried off to Holland"), and her physical injury from a horseback fall in attempting to get to London to save herself: "[I] must be inevitably ruin'd in the Loss of all I have on Earth, without you have good Nature enough to admit me to take Part of your "Chariot".[17] Through the hyperbolic pathos of her story, Beauplaisir is inspired to imagine himself as the hero to her vulnerable heroine. The story, punctuated by "sighs and groans," invites Beauplaisir's sympathy which gives way to seduction (55). The Lady's stategem of telling Beauplaisir a story that connotes *The Ephesian Matron*, a story he remembers, enables him to take on the role of the seducer: "But bethinking himself of the celebrated Story of the *Ephesian* Matron, it came into his Head to make a trial, she who seem'd equally susceptible of *Sorrow*, might not be too of *Love*" (56). He attempts to engage her in a conversation about that "Joy-giving Passion" of love, reconnecting love to her bodily desires, her "Seeds of Fire, not yet extinguish'd" with his "kindling breath . . . to light into Blaze" (56). The Widow can become his conquest, just as the story of *The Ephesian Matron* predicts. Beauplaisir only becomes desirous of the Widow through the Lady's storytelling; it sets the seduction in motion. Rather than the surface of a disguise or a physical attraction to a body, her "Art of feigning" is created from a fiction that provokes his desire for pleasure—and his promises of love (57).

This kind of storytelling is missing from the Lady's last persona, Incognita. The letter Beauplaisir receives expresses her love toward his "Wit" and "Person" (63), but his passion is not aroused by a story. While he can see and enjoy her physical body, he cannot imagine who she is, and "he could not content himself with that which she was willing to reveal" (66). While bodily pleasure has been satisfied, his desire for her story and the pleasure it would give—the fictional context—is not. Here, the protagonist's persona is defined by her body alone, and Beauplaisir is left wanting her story. She provides a mystery, an intrigue, but that mystery proves too disturbing when her story is not revealed: "she would rather part with him forever, than consent to gratify an Inquisitiveness, which, in her Opinion, had no Business with his Love" (66). Yet, a story about her identity does have to do with motivating his love. To this end, Beauplaisir "went out of the House determin'd never to re-enter it, till she should pay the price of his Company with the Discovery of her Face and Circumstances" (67). The encounter seems dissatisfying for the Lady as well, as she must constantly conceal her identity from Beauplaisir's possession: wearing a mask, retreating to another room, lying together in utter darkness and refusing all entreaties to reveal her identity. Her misjudgment of her lover's desire for fiction leads her to "comfort" herself with the "Design of forming some other Strategem" (67).

In the stories of Fantomina, Celia and the Widow Bloomer, the novella has contextualized sexual desire in terms of imaginative narratives that befit each woman's social class, as in the example of the bourgeois Widow Bloomer's story, but does not define desire wholly in those terms, as in Incognita's. Incognita represents a universalized desire of women, but without the superimposition of a particular fiction; that is, sexual desire is generalized to transcend class in each story as a universalized bodily experience for both men and women, but how that desire is expressed becomes attached to a gendered and classed-based narrative about desire. These fictions enable Beauplasir, and the reader, to perceive and feel pleasures more intensely when given the particularities of a social position. Moreover, Beauplaisir's roving, rakish desire is taken almost as a physical imperative that has no particular object, but is then focused through the fiction the Lady presents to him, grounding his desire and heightening his pleasure through each story the Lady tells. Though not sustained for any length of time, the Lady fosters his sexual desire and his passion by the fictions she constructs, as in the Widow Bloomer's story. Without these fictions, Beauplaisir's conquests would not be as fulfilling as they seem to be for him; the Lady's conquest of Beauplaisir would also not be as fulfilling for her, or even believable: "but these Arts of passing on him as a new Mistress whenever the Ardor . . . begins to diminish, for the former one, I have him always raving, wild, impatient, longing, dying" (65). Desire for both men and women, as portrayed in *Fantomina*, necessitates a continual reproduction of new particular fictions to stimulate and structure that universalized sexual desire.

By reproducing different versions of narrative desire in her personas with the same physical object, Haywood is able to make distinctions between kinds of desire that are available for the reader's pleasurable consumption: the first is a transitory kind that is represented by the continual arousal, conquest, and gratifications of Beauplaisir, the typical rake. He is a stock character whose desires and pleasures are already known to the reader. He has no motivations beyond sexual conquests, and his manipulations of women are obvious and expected. His elegantly manipulating letters and his machinations as a matter of courtship and conquest of Widow Bloomer, "Never was a woman formed to charm like you . . . Since Yesterday we parted, I have seem'd a Body without a Soul" (58), exist expectedly alongside his infidelity to and deceit of Fantomina: "If you were half so sensible as you ought of your Power of charming, you would be assur'd, that to be unfaithful or unkind to you would be among the Things that are in their very Natures Impossibilities" (59). His letters voice lover's clichés, but his motives and desires lay at the surface of the narrative, so easily read by both the protagonist and the reader through the omniscient narrator's voice "'Traytor!' (cried she)," in case there was any doubt (59). His words are pure fiction—lies—a means to a lustful end. Beauplaisir lacks the imaginative ability to create a believable story, and so is easily exposed as a rake and his desires are easily manipulated by the Lady. Haywood uses the rake to expose the kind of transitory desires that emphasize only physical sensation. The reader is to understand that Beauplaisir is metaphorically blinded by this bodily desires, so blinded he does not see the duplicitous nature of his Lad(ies). By the end of the narrative, he is literally in the dark as Incognita seduces him. Beauplaisir, as a rake, is made into a parody of desire, rather than its instigator.

The rake's bodily pleasures are contrasted with the pleasures imagined by the Lady, pleasures that simultaneously transcend sensory gratification and occlude rationality, but enable an intuitive or naturalized feeling of sensuality and passion. This sensuality is what makes the Lady appealing: her desire is not impelled by her body, her overt sexuality alone, but is motivated by her passion expressed by each individualized story she conjures. In this way, the Lady represents emotional depth. To achieve this effect, the narrative alternates between the language of sexuality in describing her encounters with Beauplaisir and her internal thoughts of her perception of love. In doing so, Haywood can experiment with how the Lady can imagine herself as attractive to her object of desire, and this imagination is what deepens and continually reignites her desire, embodying the fictions that the novella reveals to its readers but keeps secret from Beauplaisir. Helen Thompson has made the point that the Lady "sustain[s] her fidelity to a rake by becoming in his mind a succession of different objects."[18] She does this by portraying herself as a *fiction* that can subsist in his mind, as a character in a narrative she imagines and constructs to enable his pleasure. The pleasure that the Lady takes in constructing her fictions is also the formal pleasure the reader takes in reading the novella.

Beauplaisir is desirable to the Lady not simply because he is the object of her love, but more importantly because he *is* the rake—this causes her desire. From the outset of the novella, the Lady is put in the position of imagining what it would be like to be desired by the men who swarm around the prostitutes at the theatre; Beauplaisir is one of these men. "Curiosity in her to know in what manner these Creatures were address'd" is the impetus to her creation of the role of Fantomina, her first plot (in the logic of the novella) to produce in Beauplaisir a physical attraction to her. She then enjoys "conversing with him in this free and unrestain'd manner" (43) which she could not have done without creating the fiction of herself as prostitute, and which he would not have done without believing her to be a prostitute. The fiction here, very literally, structures the pleasure each can take in one another. Thus, the Lady's imagination enables her enjoyment here and in other places in the narrative. Her fiction motivates her desire for him, as the narrative would have it; consequently, her desire motivates her continued fictions in an effort to continue to make herself attractive to him, becoming the template for plotting her subsequent seductions of Beauplaisir. Instead of focusing on the pleasures and dangers of the rake, the narrative provides a space for readers to experience a more sustained pleasure depicted through the imaginative fictions that embody the Lady, and create and renew desire for the next strategem. Jonathan Brody Kramnick reads the Lady's "narrated consciousness" in her last persona, Incognita, as a thinking "moment of deep internalization," which happens when she "sees herself as an object of another's person's desire" concluding that "to desire is to be serially the object of someone else's desire."[19] In addition, this culminating moment in the text would be impossible without the Lady's imaginative capability to design each strategem, or fiction, with which to enjoy Beauplaisir. While thinking is represented by her internal speech, her thinking is not wholly rational but motivated by her passion, as her strategems are willed into being by her imagination: "O that all neglected Wives, and fond abandoned Nymphs would take this Method!—Men would be caught in their own Snare, and have no Cause to scorn our easy, weeping wailing Sex!"(243). The ostensible contradiction between being an object of desire and subject of her own consciousness is mediated by her own imagination: the contradiction holds this object-subject relation in tension, enabling a shifting between sensory experience and the consciousness of passionate response. If, as Kramnick states, "she sees herself from outside of herself" or only "perceives herself" from within the "positions she *imagines* from the perspectives of Beauplaisir," then her imaginative capacity can challenge and shift social relations, albeit unevenly, because it exposes her position as an already constructed fiction that is distinct from the novella's construction of her "true" self.[20] The true self here, is not a social position, but an ideological one, represented as the Lady's bodily desire and her love. This imaginary relation—the fictive relationship ideology produces between the body and mind—is what coheres or abrogates social relations through existing practices, like seduction or courtship, which these fictions then express and reproduce.

Thus, being an object of desire and author of subjective agency is not necessarily a contradiction but are textual possibilities that can exist simultaneously. *Fantomina*'s range of fictions constructs an imaginary idea of women as both consumable objects *and* desiring subjects along a social spectrum. Her fictions enable the consumption of bodily pleasures, those associated only with sexuality, to be reconstituted by aesthetic pleasures that merge a sexualized body with the imaginative mind. For example, while the content of the plot seems to propel the assumption of women as interchangeable objects of desire for Beauplaisir, the satiric focus *on the plotting* of these disguises unifies the novella's disparate parts of fictional personas the Lady inhabits in order to sustain her desire. The suggestion is that the Lady is as gratified by her imaginary fictions as she is by Beauplaisir; she enjoys endlessly reproducing his desire for her. She is not simply "charmed" by him, but rather continually reconstitutes herself as an object of his desire so that she can be charmed by him again and again (44). After all, his pleasure can only be found where his body is; her imaginative mind enables her to physically inhabit and transverse the social spectrum safely and effectively without changing her object of desire. His pleasures are transitory; hers are sustainable and capable of being endlessly reproduced by being given a new fictional form, and she can be endlessly gratified because of it. Sustainable imaginative pleasure, posited as a universal desire, is a necessary requirement of fiction as it becomes an ideological form.

Note that the *re*production of the Lady in a new persona does not change what really matters—her sexual desire becomes merged with passion: she loves him because she can make herself his object of desire, endlessly. Her pleasure comes from being desired by Beauplaisir; her love comes from having him submit to this attraction. Both are structured by the fictions she creates. By associating sexual desire (of the body) with love (a concept in the mind) through the aesthetics of the narrative, Haywood transforms the Lady's characters from objects of sexual attraction into *a* subject who is capable of continually imagining, reimagining, and reproducing desire for herself, and one who is also continually capable of making herself desirable to others. In other words, the imaginary transcends the transitory social particulars. However, through the amatory plot devices, the hyperbolic prose, the stories that surround the personas and the satiric point of view, readers see Beauplaisir's limitations as a character type. While Haywood denaturalizes the cultural notion of women's objectification by means of her protagonist's ability to refashion herself as desirable in an endless array of disguises (that is, until her pregnancy stops her and the narrative ends), the rakish Beauplaisir does not, and does not need, this imaginative ability since his pleasures are wholly sensory and depicted as transitory rather than self-sustaining.[21]

Therefore, the stories that the Lady creates for Beauplaisir, and that the novella refracts for its readers, enable the aesthetic possibilities of textuality to merge sensation and imagination, and sustain a desire for more narratives about that relationship— primarily through the passionate feeling of love that is linked to sensory impressions made by language. This feeling of love, with both sensory and emotive connotations, is the aesthetic effect produced from narrative; feeling spontaneously enables agency.[22] The Lady's passionate feelings motivate her imagination as well as cause her to act on those passions. She does not form her schemes from principled reason or contemplative rationality or a moral cause; her consciousness and her agency are evoked by her passionate feeling. The narrative exploits this particular kind of feeling as the spontaneous truth of feminine consciousness that can motivate action and create agency for the Lady. The Lady privileges her feeling above knowing, resulting in the continual exercise of her imagination in conceiving her disguises and by producing stories. However, the novella does make a distinction between the truth of passions and other kinds of truth. After all, knowing Beauplaisir is a rake whose interest in women is transitory does not stop the Lady from pursuing him over and over again. The conundrum of the novella is that knowledge does not always lead to rational action, and it does not always lead to the right apprehension of a more socially or morally practiced truth—one that exists beyond the confines of the Lady's, and Haywood's, fictional world. What is at stake for the Lady more than knowledge or truth is that Beauplaisir remains the impetus to her imagination, to creating a new fiction that would renew his, and the reader's, desire for the next new fiction, the next "scheme" (51). That Beauplaisir is a rake makes for good storytelling especially when positioned against her constant devotion to him.

Haywood attempts to transcend the plot that is so linked to sensory desire and pleasure by referring to abstract ideas like virtue, constancy and love—romance ideals that have been unjustly cast aside by Beauplaisir's rakish actions. However, virtue, constancy and love remain abstractions throughout the text because they are clearly not the motivations for the Lady's conscious actions, or for the constructions of her fictions:

> She loved Beauplaisir, it was only he whose Solicitations could give her Pleasure; . . . Her Design was once more to engage him, to hear him sigh, to see him languish, to feel the strenuous Pressure of his eager Arms, to be compelled with equal Ardour, was what she wanted, and what she had form'd a Strategem to obtain, in which she promis'd herself Success. (51)

The motivational focus here is on the protagonist's desire, both physical and emotional, spoken from the privileged omniscient narrator's point of view. "She" is literally the subject here, and Beauplaisir, the object of her desire. Despite what the Lady claims, love is not an ideal in the mind, but rather is felt as a sensory experience, a literal feeling: her love is conceived as the "Pleasure" "to hear him," "to see him," "to feel the strenuous Pressure of his eager Arms." However, her love can only be fulfilled by embodying a fiction that makes her sensory desire—"what she want[s]"—possible. Here, as elsewhere in the text, readers are invited to participate in a spectacle of imaginative desire that motivates responsive action—"form'd a strategem"—rather than rationally thinking about ideas and values. In other words, the thinking represented by the plot–the ability to form a persona, to strategize, to manipulate a situation—is not always, and usually not, aligned with reason and judgment. With every persona that passes, a deeper commitment to the fulfillment of the protagonist's desire is made, damning the social consequences and deepening passion, motivating action. What is yielded, at the end of her story, is a Lady who is defined not just by her body, though that reality is implied by the pregnancy that undercuts her imagined perception of herself. The Lady is also defined by imaginative pleasures her own fictions create: a new way of experiencing the relationship between sensuous desire and love through an imaginative, seemingly-intuitive response to passion. Her fictions, through the writing of the novella, enable the reader's participation in a dialectical aesthetic experience, because desire and passion can be felt as a generalized, and naturalized, universal human construct borne from fiction.

As such, the relationship between sense and imagination, physical desire and sensory passion, produces and potentially reproduces the aesthetic ideology represented in the novella as the love that the Lady has for Beauplaisir. *Fantomina* imagines love as not chaste virtue that women must raise themselves to attain (an ideal conjured in the mind) or as devolving into sensuous sin (stimulation of the body), but rather reinvests love as the aesthetic experience in her narrative.[23] Love might be a consuming passion, but it takes ideological form in fiction, founded in the imagination, motivating the Lady's action, and thus the action of the plot. The reader is witness to her ever-deepening interiority because it expresses this passion: the imagination fosters a sustainable pleasure of its own conceived as love, seemingly divorced from social structures, concept or knowledge. The desire for love expressed by the form of the novella is a desire for imaginative experiences that fictions promise. The reader, not the protagonist, becomes aware of his/her position as a reader, as a witness to fictional possibility, and thus the reader's mind is engaged in contemplative response to the novella that signals for him/her a continuity between body and mind, between feeling and knowing. If there is moral deliberation, it happens in the minds of readers. How is this distinction achieved, and what is its cost?

Haywood's portrait of the Lady, her passions and actions, seems disengaged from any eighteenth-century social structure. The frame of the story, the Lady's upper-class position in society, is left out of the bulk of the narrative, and only exists to bring the reader back to the social circumstances of the protagonist that the text cannot fold into her "imaginary" world. Even the protagonist's thoughts are mediated through the omniscient narrator as if this imaginative space is detached from the reality of the Lady's life, and the lives of its readers.[24] This narrative maneuver suggests (creates a fiction, one might say) that the primary cause for meaning is the pursuit of sexual pleasure and passion for both the Lady and Beauplaisir, and which seems, though it is obviously not, detached from custom, Society or class. Social relations in this text become a transitory fictional context for the always renewable passion of the Lady and Beauplaisir, as we have seen. This happens not just in the successive seductive schemes that constitute the plot of the novel, but in the distancing aesthetic effect the novella produces to achieve a disinterested voice that is part of the narrative point of view and part of the amoral tone of the novel. While the plot of disguises enables *Fantomina* to explore and expose the rakish pleasures of Beauplaisir's sexuality and constructs an imaginary space across class lines to express the prohibited desires of the Lady, the novella also enables readers to engage in the more aesthetic, rather than just sensory, pleasures they might feel. *Fantomina* reshapes desire as an experience for the reader's consumption that is both detached from immediate sense perception and reasonable judgment. The possibility is that writing can operate as a way to foster new perceptions and experiences that are more dependent on emotion and pleasure, and less dependent on knowledge or reason. For Haywood, this possibility is a powerful one for her fiction, as we have seen, for fiction motivates the Lady and Beauplaisir's desire and love. However, the aesthetic form she experiments with in *Fantomina* also creates the possibility of a disinterested spectator, or reader, who witnesses these strategems, takes pleasure in them, but might not wholly identify with the protagonist's morality or actions. The distance between the reader's aesthetic experience of love and the love plot within the novella enables the novella to function as an emerging ideological form.

One way to get at this distancing effect is to look at how the fictions of the characters operate in the novella. While it may be true that the Lady is performing for her lover in these disguises, the novella depicts these characters as imitations of various different women of various socio-economic distinction, distancing them for the reader's consumption because they are separable from the Lady.[25] As a narrative, the reader's aesthetic relationship to the novella is built on witnessing the Lady's fictions, and sympathizing with them, if only momentarily. While the narrative creates an imaginative spectrum of possible social positions with which to foster new fictions of desire, the reader is not put in very dangerous proximity to these pleasures because Haywood does not force an identification of any character with the reader—the omniscient narrator is always there to direct the reader's attention to the fiction being presented; the personas are clearly stories made up with an expressed intent to attract Beauplaisir. The act of reading enables the sensory experience of titillation through imitation, but at a safe distance from the moral understanding of the Lady's radically transgressive behavior. The stories exist to exercise the reader's imagination, rather than to identify with the protagonist. When we learn in the frame that women will pay the price for their desire at the end of the novella, our sympathy for the Lady is not diminished but revealed as natural and distinct from judgment; readers have identified with an aesthetic experience—the fictions of this particular woman, and universal desire and love of all women—and not with a particular character as a model of fallen virtue. Passion may be felt by the reader, but the imaginative product of the narration is sympathy for the Lady cultivated by a rational distance from the protagonist.[26]

This sympathy for the Lady without an identification with her leads to the ambiguous ending of the novella that is the source of much commentary. The reason for this ambiguity lies not in the logical outcome of the development of the narrative, or in a feminized passion-based version of morality.[27] Passion rules, but morality and its consequences seem strangely beside the point, as do questions of agency and culpability. But perhaps the point throughout the novella has been to experiment with feeling: to stimulate bodily response in order to create a wholly aesthetic space to imagine fictional designs; to create fictions not bound by precept or concept, reality or social strictures, but by affective pleasure that both the protagonist and the reader desire without question or reasonable contemplation. *Fantomina* demonstrates the imaginative possibilities of fiction early on: as a space that ostensibly subordinates morality, politics, class and gender, to affective pleasure, in order to create the safe distance needed to consume that pleasure and produce desire for narratives.

That safe distance is produced by the reader's energetic engagement with aesthetics in which ideology is made to be felt; in other words, ideology *becomes* aesthetic. As an early aesthetic experiment in the imagination's mediating function between sense and rationality, readers engage *Fantomina* on its own amoral terms: belief suspended, moral judgment deferred, rational contemplation negated. *Fantomina*'s aesthetic achievement demonstrates that intense passion can be produced through narrative, and that aesthetic pleasures and pains can be consumed because of its fictional forms; pleasure and passion can be detached from a political or moral economy to concentrate ostensibly on individual feeling that is imaginatively constructed in the mind first, that then may be naturalized as ameliorating.

By mid-century, the natural sympathy of the passions is literature's greatest asset and its greatest liability. The result was an attempt to find a standard of taste by which to stabilize the reception of aesthetic objects which had proliferated. Edmund Burke, in one attempt, theorizes that the aesthetic forces of the sublime and beautiful are not produced in a reasoning mind, but rather "hurries us on by an irresistible force" because language affects us "sympathetically" rather than by "imitation."[28] Burke states that while the imagination can only rearrange what exists in reality, its power lies in how "the passions are represented, because by the force of natural sympathy they are felt in all men without any recourse to reasoning".[29] In other words, we can't "judge" a passion, like love, but we can all feel it. Aesthetic judgment only comes afterward by a facility with the standards of taste, and occurs only after the senses have been refined through the improvement of the imagination. But Haywood's fiction, its concerns with sensory feeling and imaginative pleasures, enables us to examine this emergent experience of the imagination, and how fiction becomes its vehicle to represent individual passion and desire, before a well-spring of caution about fiction is articulated. It also might point to why fiction persisted and its popularity grew despite these cautions.

Fantomina serves as an early experiment that merges feeling and language, body and mind, and aesthetics and ideology. It gave popular fiction a cultural and social function before the dangers of the imagination could be fully articulated or regulated by standards of taste. Overshadowed as Haywood's works were by the various fears that a print culture dependent on the "discourses of body"—that is, aesthetics—might bring, we might remember that the mediating effect of imagination to produce pleasures, not just regulate them, is the ultimate aesthetic achievement of the ideological form of *Fantomina*.[30]

NOTES

1. Joseph Addison, *No. 411, Saturday, June 21, 1712*, in *The Spectator*, ed. Donald F. Bond, 5 vols. (Oxford: Clarendon Press, 1965), 3:537–38. All references are to this edition.

2. For the idea of the imagination as mediating between sense and understanding in Addison, see Michael McKeon, "Mediation as Primal Word: The Arts, the Sciences, and the Origins of the Aesthetic," in *This Is Enlightenment*, ed. Clifford Siskin and William Warner (Chicago: University of Chicago Press, 2010), 391.

3. William Warner, *Licensing Entertainment: The Elevation of Novel Reading in Britain,* 1684–1750 (Berkeley: University of California Press, 1998), 111–16.

4. The term "ideology" needs clarification: we should remember Louis Althusser's definition of ideology as "a 'representation' of the imaginary relation of individuals to their real conditions of existence," but ideology is just as importantly the set of real material practices that enables us to engage the world. Though often misunderstood, ideology must exist in a practice, not as an idea or a representation of an idea. See "Ideology and Ideological State Apparatuses" in *Lenin and Philosophy* (NY: Monthly Review Press, 1971), 162–166. For a recent explanation of Althusser's notion of ideology, and a reinterpretation of the ISA essay, see Pierre Macherey, "Figures of Interpretation in Althusser and Fanon" *Radical Philosophy* 173 (May/June 2012): 9–20.

5. For a few representative examples of a broad body of scholarship, see Catherine Craft, *Masquerade and Gender: Disguise and Female Identity in Eighteenth-Century Fiction* (University Park: Penn State Press, 1993); Margaret Case Croskery, "Masquing Desire: The Politics of Passion in Eliza Haywood's *Fantomina*" in *The Passionate Fictions of Eliza Haywood: Essays on her Life and Work*, ed. Kirsten T. Saxton and Rebecca P. Bocchicchio (Lexington: University Press of Kentucky, 2001), 69–94; Joseph Drury, "Haywood's Thinking Machines," *Eighteenth-Century Fiction* 21.2 (Winter 2008–9): 201–228; Kirsten M. Girten, "Unsexed Souls: Natural Philosophy as Transformation in Eliza Haywood's *Female Spectator,*" *Eighteenth-Century Studies* 43.1 (Fall 2009): 55–75; Kathleen Lubey, "Eliza Haywood's Amatory Aesthetic," *Eighteenth-Century Studies* 39.3 (Spring 2006): 309–323; Juliette Merritt, *Beyond Spectacle: Eliza Haywood's Female Spectators* (Toronto: University of Toronto Press, 2004); Rebecca Tierny-Hynes, "Fictional Mechanics: Haywood, Reading, and the Passions," *The Eighteenth-Century* 51.1 (Spring/Summer 2010): 153–172; Helen Thompson, "Plotting Materialism: W. Charleton's *The Ephesian Matron*, E. Haywood's *Fantomina*, and Feminine Consistency," *Eighteenth-Century Studies* 35.2 (2002): 195–214.

6. For representative examples, see Ros Ballaster, *Seductive Forms: Women's Amatory Fiction From 1684 to 1740*, (Oxford: Clarendon Press, 1992) and "A Gender of Opposition: Eliza Haywood's Scandal Fiction" in *The Passionate Fictions of Eliza Haywood*, 143–167, in which she revises some of "political" effectiveness of Haywood's fiction; John Richetti, *Popular Fiction Before Richardson: Narrative Patterns, 1700–1739* (New York: Oxford University Press, 1992); William Warner, *Licensing Entertainment*; Paula Backscheider, "The Story of Eliza Haywood's Novels: Caveats and Questions" in *The Passionate Fictions of Eliza Haywood*, 19–47; and Melissa Mowry, "Eliza Haywood's Defense of the London's Body Politic," *Studies in English Literature*, 43.3 (Summer 2003): 645–665.

7. Lubey, "Amatory Aesthetic," 310.

8. Drury, "Thinking Machines," 204.

9. Tierney-Hynes, "Fictional Mechanics,"154.

10. Tierney-Hynes, "Fictional Mechanics,"155.

11. I am paraphrasing Althusser's explanation of the relationship of ideology

to art, "A Letter on Art in Reply to Andre Daspre" in *Lenin and Philosophy*, 222. It should be noted here that I do not agree with Althusser's concept of art, which relies too much on assigning a formalist notion of literary value. In my view, all writing produces ideology in relation to specific historical and cultural constructs, distanciating, producing and reproducing the relations of production that interpellate subjectivity. The function of Literature as an aesthetic form makes relationships of value possible. For this point, see Terry Eagleton, *The Ideology of the Aesthetic* (NY: Basil Blackwell, 1990), 3.

12. Eagleton, *Ideology*, 41.

13. In a different way, Paula Backscheider has made this claim as well: "[Haywood] was the most active experimenter with fictional forms and introduced themes, plots, characters, settings, and topics into English fiction," 22. My argument could be viewed as an extension of Backscheider's to focus on aesthetics, not just discursive forms. My focus is on how Haywood experiments with form to reconceive the imaginative, pleasurable and ideological work that novels do to engender a specific reading practice that will be useful to bourgeois social relations.

14. As mentioned above, Lubey suggests this as well, 309–10. However, while Lubey's interpretation of Haywood's fiction stems from a didactic design which teaches readers to remain "mentally attentive to the instructive warning contained" in her novels and therefore manages "aesthetic pleasure," I am not sure Haywood's pedagogic ends are clear. The aesthetic as a category, at least for the 1720s, is quite unstable. As Michael McKeon has recently shown, the origins of British aesthetics is a response to the problem that the faculty of the imagination poses to reason and sensibility: its early origination is as a science of sense and reason, in order to explain how the body and mind together construct mental representations of ideas. See McKeon, "Mediation as Primal Word," 385–412. While Haywood's intention may be to instruct, her fiction also teaches readers to be stimulated by fiction before managing their aesthetic pleasures can happen, which suggests contradictory purposes for her novels. Moreover, the implication of instruction is to accept the societal notions of morality and immortality, which would make regulating women's body, pleasure and emotion necessary. The idea of aesthetics, and the role of the imagination, needs to be constructed and produced in fiction before it can be contained. Haywood's early fiction can show us how this process occurred.

15. This is what psychologist Kurt Danziger traces as the "Great Transformation" of subjectivity. See Danziger, *Naming the Mind: How Psychology Found Its Language* (London: Sage, 1997), 36 49. The focus of the chapter is the conceptual movement from passion to emotion as the defining characteristic of one's subjectivity; in other words, we perceive ourselves through subjective feeling. Likewise, Geoffrey Sill in *The Cure of the Passions and the Origins of the English Novel* (New York: Cambridge University Press, 2001), locates the problem of the passions as a motive force for the emergence of the novel in the eighteenth century; the novel attempts to account for, understand and transform the passions into vehicles for truth and virtue.

16. Both Addison, earlier in the century, and Burke, later in the century,

suggest that representational forms—images in language—enable a powerful relationship between body and mind, sense and concept. For Addison, through reading language, the object described is made not just pleasurable but desirable, and its reality is more natural than its being in nature: the poet "get[s] the better of nature" (*Spectator* 416, 3:560). How language creates an aesthetic response is the subject of Part V of the *A Philosophical Enquiry into the Origins of our Ideas of the Sublime and Beautiful*, ed. J.T. Boulton (New York: Columbia University Press, 1958) where Burke claims that "words have as considerable a share in exciting ideas of beauty and of the sublime as any [other kinds of visual art], and sometimes a much greater than any of them," 163. For Burke, it is not the image of the thing in one's mind that conjures a passionate response nor is it an idea of the thing in reality; rather it is an aggregate response of sympathy to the union of words that cause an association of ideas: "to display the effect of things on the mind" but not imitative of things themselves (*Enquiry*, 172).

17. Eliza Haywood, *Fantomina and Other Works*, Alexander Pettit, Margaret Case Croskery, and Anna C. Patchias, eds. (Peterborough, Ontario: Broadview, 2004). References are to this edition.

18. Helen Thompson, "'In Idea, a thousand nameless Joys': Secondary Qualities in Arnauld, Locke and Haywood's *Lasselia,*" *The Eighteenth Century* 48.3 (Fall 2007): 239.

19. Jonathan Brody Kramnick, "Locke, Haywood, and Consent," *ELH* 72 (2005): 466.

20. Kramnick, "Locke," 467 (emphasis mine).

21. Admittedly, woman as "agent" is a vexed issue given the patriarchal social strictures of the eighteenth century as Helen Thompson has already pointed out. See Thompson, "Plotting Materialism,"196.

22. As David Hume will argue later in the century in *An Enquiry Concerning the Principles of Morals*, (Oxford: Oxford University Press, 1975): "the ultimate ends of human actions can never…be accounted for by reason, but recommend themselves entirely to the sentiments and affections of mankind, without any dependence on the intellectual faculties" (293). Passion thus "becomes a motive to action, and is the first spring or impulse to desire and volition" (294).

23. In Haywood's "Reflections on the Various Effects of Love" (1726), she is quite explicit in arguing that "love" is usually perceived as either "insensible" or "brutal" and thus the current narratives that depict these types of love are problematic because they are too idealized and unrealistic, inviting people to "imagine it of much greater force than in Reality it can boast," *Fantomina and Other Works*, 107–8. Haywood's new conception of love posited in "Reflections" solves this problem: "Let us take away a little of that almighty Power which we ascribe to Love, and allow something more to Nature and those inclination born with us, and we shall immediately reconcile the seeming impossibility" of individuals ever truly understanding love (113–14).

24. As Marta Kvande has pointed out, outside narrators are an important narrative strategy for Haywood's political novels. See Kvande, "The Outside Narrator in Eliza Haywood's Political Novels," *SEL* 43.3 (2003): 625–643.

25. See Emily Hodgson Anderson, "Performing the Passions in Eliza Haywood's *Fantomina* and *Miss Betsy Thoughtless,*" *The Eighteenth Century* 46.1 (Spring 2005): 1–16.

26. Burke claims that imitation is a natural passion that produces pleasure and moves the reader to have sympathy toward the object of imitation. See Burke, *A Philosphical Enquiry*, 49.

27. As Margaret Case Croskery suggests that "emotions will best be ruled—not by reason—but by other emotions" and this will lead to one's moral education. See Croskery, "Novel Romanticism in 1751: Eliza Haywood's *Betsy Thoughtless,*" in *Enlightening Romanticism, Romancing the Enlightenment: British Novels From 1750–1832*, ed. Miriam L. Wallace (Aldershot: Ashgate, 2009), 29.

28. Burke, *A Philosophical Enquiry*, 57, 172.

29. Burke, *A Philosophical Enquiry*, 22.

30. Eagleton, *Ideology*, 13. "Discourse of the body" is Eagleton's descriptive term for the many aesthetic treatises in the mid-eighteenth century in Europe.

Rousseau and the Revolutionary Repertoire

REBECCA DOWD GEOFFROY-SCHWINDEN

Jean-Jacques Rousseau's *Lettre à d'Alembert* provides a detailed account of a spontaneous festival fueled by wine and music that he supposedly witnessed as a child in Geneva during the 1720s. Let me begin by quoting from it at length, because I shall be circling back to the scene as a certain touchstone of historical continuity:

> Le Régiment de St. Gervais avoit fait l'éxercice, et selon la coutume, on avoit soupé par compagnies. La pluspart de ceux qui les composoient se rassemblérent après le Soupé dans la place de St-Gervais, et se mirent à danser tous ensemble, officiers et soldats, autour de la fontaine, sur le bassin de laquelle étoient montés les Tambours, les Fifres, et ceux qui portoient les flambeaux. Une danse de gens égayés par un long repas, sembleroit n'offrir rien de fort intéressant à voir. Cependant, l'accord de cinq ou six cens hommes en uniforme, se tenant tous par la main, et formant une longue bande qui serpentoit en cadence et sans confusion avec mille tours et retours, mille espéces d'évolutions figurées, le choix des airs qui les animoient, le bruit des Tambours, l'éclat des flambeaux, un certain appareil militaire au sein du plaisir; tout cela formoit une sensation très vive, qu'on ne pouvoit supporter de sang-froid.

> Il étoit tard; les femmes étoient couchées, toutes se relevérent; bientôt les fenêtres furent pleines de Spectatrices qui donnoient un nouveau zéle aux acteurs. Elles ne purent tenir longtems à leurs fenêtres; elles descendirent; les maitresses venoient voir leurs maris, les servantes apportoient du vin; les enfans même eveillés par le bruit, accoururent demi-vétus entre les Péres et les Méres. La danse fut suspendüe . . . Il résulta de tout cela un attendrissement général que je ne saurois peindre, mais que dans l'allegresse universelle, on éprouve assés naturellement au milieu de tout ce qui nous est cher.[1]

During the French Revolution, Rousseau's ideas about the role of music in a democratic community found expression in a variety of popular contexts— in public singing at festivals, in *chansonniers* that set new song lyrics to well-known melodies for the musically illiterate, and in the mobilization of music toward politically unifying goals. Many of these ideas are set forth in Rousseau's *Essai sur l'origine des langues où il est parlé de la mélodie et de l'imitation musicale*, a work Rousseau grappled with and rewrote from the 1750s until 1761. Published posthumously in 1781, the work remained largely unexplored until the twentieth century. In the essay Rousseau posits a theory of cultural evolution in which music devolved from a tool integral to the creation of community at some unspecified moment in pre-history to a symptom of the moral decay of contemporary French society, a decay resulting from the combined degeneration of music and language caused by historical progress. Rousseau's prescriptions for the place of music in politics, as found in this essay as well as his *Lettre à d'Alembert*, became articulated in revolutionary society even though citizens neither circulated nor discussed the texts, and developments in Parisian popular musical practices from 1749 to 1794 may be seen to shed new light on the living sources for Rousseau's writing about music.

It has long been acknowledged that Rousseau philosophized from a deeply subjective position, and so his life experiences provide an entryway into his works. Contextualizing Rousseau's philosophy within mid-eighteenth-century Parisian musical practice illuminates the relationship between musical performance during the Revolution and his political thought. Indeed, what I want to argue is that Rousseau's political writing actually grew from his lived experience of music as a writer[2] in mid-eighteenth-century Paris rather than from a utopian community he imagined against the backdrop of an earlier philosophy of cultural acquisition.[3] When we examine the role that political opinion plays in French popular song across the century, it becomes evident that Rousseau did not create an entirely new concept of musico-political performance later perpetuated during the French Revolution, but rather that he participated in an ongoing process of appropriation and expression that reached a pinnacle with the politics of music in revolutionary culture. Where it has been suggested that Rousseau's *Lettre à d'Alembert* is only tenuously connected to revolutionary festivals,[4] my thesis is that the interaction between intellectual and popular musical cultures during the eighteenth century serves to explain certain trans-historical similarities between written artifacts and performance practices, and in fact that the Genevan festival described in my opening paragraph could easily be mistaken for the account of a *fête révolutionnaire* held some thirty-six years after Rousseau composed the letter.

At the time Rousseau began distilling his perspectives on music the Affair of the Fourteen became a much-discussed public matter. Robert Darnton has recently shown that throughout the spring and summer of 1749 French subjects across Paris were being arrested for the dissemination of spoken, written, or sung poetry that criticized the king and his mistress.[5] During the first half of the eighteenth century, following Louis XIV's death, the ideological tone of musical performances in Paris began to enjoy a series of changes. These transformations occurred at first only in fair theatres and the nascent genre of *opéra-comique*, and gradually evolved from innocent *divertissement* to outlets for social and political dissent.[6] Though official theatres still frowned upon such critiques, music in popular milieus became a forum for voicing dissent against the royal regime and noble privileges. Scholars have long debated whether it is anachronistic to speak of public opinion before the Revolution: Darnton himself insists that "in eighteenth-century Paris, a public peculiar to the Old Regime took form and began to impose its opinions on events" (139); Arlette Farge avers that "while there was no public opinion, in the modern sense, in the eighteenth century, there were popular opinions, whose form, content, and function developed within a monarchic system whose attitude gave them life even as it rejected them;"[7] and Michael Sonenscher has pointed out that Rousseau seems to be the first writer of note to use the term "public opinion" (161). Rousseau labeled the popular opinions that circulated throughout Paris as public—and so it seems safe to use the term here.

First, I will begin by reading Rousseau's *Essai sur l'origine des langues* through the lens of the Affair of the Fourteen. Next, two musical artifacts from 1794 dedicated to Rousseau will be set in relation to the Affair of the Fourteen: a text from a revolutionary chansonnier; and a performance described in a published account of a revolutionary festival. The similarities between the Affair of the Fourteen of 1749 and these revolutionary musical experiences of 1794 will illustrate that Rousseau's prescriptions found in the *Essai sur l'origine des langues*, though never read by those who enacted them, reflect living Parisian musical practices. These case studies will illuminate the continuity between Rousseau's work and the enactment of these unread texts in revolutionary Paris, disentangling the interwoven discourses about philosophies and performances of music from the French Enlightenment through the French Revolution. Our exploration of Rousseau's *Essai sur l'origine des langues* within the context of Parisian musical practices of 1749 serves three purposes: to propose a reading of Rousseau's essay that connects French Enlightenment texts to lived experiences of eighteenth-century music; to situate Rousseau as an individual agent within his historical and cultural environment, rather than as a philosopher who thought and wrote in isolation; and to elucidate the process by which Enlightenment texts about music became enacted in the everyday political culture of the French Revolution despite general ignorance of these texts on the part of performers.

Performance studies provide a productive theoretical framework through which to examine this phenomenon. Diana Taylor defines the archive as cultural memory that exists as material documents and the repertoire as enacting "embodied memory."[8] The repertoire includes musical performances in which as she says "people participate in the production and reproduction of knowledge by . . . being part of the transmission" (20). If public performance generates, records, and transmits knowledge, as Taylor goes on to describe its functioning, then this 1749 singing affair and Rousseau's re-writing of it might provide a glimpse into the process by which Parisian song practices became transmitted, as well as transformed, trans-historically. A recent publication on current methodologies in performance and music studies pinpoints the benefits of such an approach: "In shifting the focus of musical analysis from composition and text to performance, [this] approach highlights the interactional, political, emotional, and emergent in music."[9] While we can never experience the live quality of eighteenth-century Parisian musical performances, we can engage with textual artifacts that allow glimpses into popular performance practices. In this case, the musical enactment of beliefs and identity proves to be a repeating political and performative scenario that continues in Paris over the course of the eighteenth century, a scenario that in turn became legitimized by the changes achieved through the French Revolution.

The Affair of the Fourteen and Rousseau's Essay

The Affair of the Fourteen consisted of the capture, interrogation, and in some cases, imprisonment of fourteen Parisian students, clergymen, clerks, and professors accused of composing or disseminating slanderous songs about the king's mistress, Madame de Pompadour. Darnton asserts that "the links among the Fourteen formed only a small segment of [a] larger entity—a huge communication system that extended everywhere, from the palace of Versailles to the furnished rooms of the Parisian poor" (55). This network of communication crisscrossed social categories and their dwelling spaces, and the swift broadcasting of the songs throughout Paris proves that the influence of social networks on public opinions did not begin with twenty-first century media. Song and poetry acted as the primary medium for this social network. Darnton confirms that at least two of the songs passed among the Fourteen "could be heard everywhere in Paris at the time" (174–75).

In his eagerness to debate all things musical and political, Rousseau necessarily thought, conversed, and wrote from within this Parisian web. Though little extant works remain from this period of Rousseau's life, writings from both Denis Diderot and Rousseau reveal that the two were quite close during 1749, when Diderot, Rousseau, and the abbé de Condillac would meet for weekly dinners at the Panier Fleuri in Paris.[10] Both the relationship with Diderot and material traces of the social network of intellectuals in Paris during the late 1740s and early 1750s clearly link Rousseau to several gentlemen involved in the Affair of the Fourteen. Darnton eloquently recounts the following relationships in *Poetry and the Police*. In July 1749, Pierre Sigorgne, professor of philosophy and disseminator of the scandalous songs, awaited his fate in the Bastille, while Denis Diderot sat imprisoned in the Château de Vincennes because his recent writing, the *Lettre sur les aveugles à l'usage de ceux qui voient*, offended both the government and the clergy. Sigorgne and Diderot had mutual intellectual apostles, André Morellet and Anne Robert Jacques Turgot. In fact, a written transcription of Sigorgne's dictation of one of the Affair poems was transmitted among the accused within a copy of Diderot's *Lettre sur les aveugles*. Sigorgne's students, Morellet and Turgot, and Rousseau, all contributed to Diderot's *Encyclopédie*, the publication of which was delayed because the editor Diderot spent part of the summer in prison (25). Finally, Nicolas René Berryer, lieutenant-général of the police, and his secretary Duval both worked on the Diderot case and the Affair of the Fourteen case that summer. Rousseau's *Enclycopédie* associates, at least through the eyes of the police, belonged to the same mischievous group of intellectuals involved in the Affair.

There can be no doubt that Rousseau at least knew of these songs and the Affair, and he likely had more intimate knowledge of the investigation through the circle of *encyclopédistes* with whom he was closely involved in 1749. Rousseau certainly would have been aware of the stir that poetry and music were creating: encouraging popular opinions in the streets of Paris and creating paranoia within the bureaucratic offices that cocooned the monarchy. Though the document has never been found, Rousseau claimed to have written a letter to Mme de Pompadour in the end of July or beginning of August 1749 supposedly begging for Diderot's freedom from prison and insisting that if the request were not granted then he should like to be imprisoned with his friend. The fabled letter is noted in Rousseau's correspondence and the editor states that it was a "lettre trop peu raisonable pour être efficace."[11] Years later, in 1783, Thérèse Levaseur referenced this letter in a discussion with l'abbé Gabriel Brizard (120). If the letter is yet to be substantiated, it is nonetheless important to note that Rousseau at least acted as if he had contacted Mme de Pompadour regarding Diderot. This fact in itself provides an important piece of historical evidence: Rousseau believed Mme de Pompadour was the power behind Diderot's arrest. According to Darnton, she was surely the power behind the arrests in the Affair of the Fourteen.

This year also proved to be a turning point in Rousseau's philosophy. In his *Confessions* and *Lettre à M. Malesherbes*, Rousseau claims that during the summer of 1749, while walking to visit his friend Diderot in prison, he experienced what has been called the illumination of Vincennes. Rousseau recalls reading an announcement by the Academy of Dijon published in the *Mercure de France* offering a prize to the best essay regarding the topic, "Whether the restoration of the sciences and arts has contributed to purify morals." The subject triggered Rousseau's so-called illumination and he recounts a sweaty, hallucinatory experience of composing a hasty, negative response. He concluded that man, naturally good, had been tainted by the immorality of modern civilization, and more specifically by modern institutions.[12] Though scholars now date the illumination to the autumn rather than the summer of 1749, Rousseau's own connection of this revelation to the same summer as Diderot's imprisonment and the Affair of the Fourteen remains crucial.

Rousseau's conceptions of music and politics, as put forth in his *Essai sur l'origine des langues*, can be re-read when placed within the context of this vast social network of song on the one hand and a critical moment in his philosophy of the arts on the other. Rousseau wrote his first musical entries for Diderot's *Encyclopédie* from 1749 until 1751. Furthermore, scholars have linked Rousseau's response to the Academy of Dijon, better known as his *Discours sur les sciences et les arts* (1750), to the *Essai sur l'origine des langues*, originally a fragment discarded from his *Discours sur l'origine de l'inégalité* in 1754.[13] Rousseau continued to work on the *Essai sur l'origine des langues* until 1761, however he established the foundation of his views on music, language, government and historical progress, through these earlier writings, which commenced with the illumination of Vincennes. Robert Wokler has pointed out the significance of Rousseau's *Premier Discours* that resulted from the illumination of Vincennes, specifically because it seems to have paved the writer's way toward key themes found in both the *Discours sur l'origine de l'inégalité* and the *Essai sur l'origine des langues*, in particular the equation between hyper-civilization and moral degradation (392). The essay's connection to the *Discours sur les sciences et les arts* is especially salient in regards to Rousseau's discussion of music, which Rousseau identifies as degenerate as a result of increasingly convoluted compositional and performance techniques, both the result of historical progress, or civilization.

The Affair of the Fourteen, in combination with the illumination of Vincennes, sheds critical light on the following three features Rousseau prescribes in his musico-political philosophy: a codependent relationship between music and speech; an uncomplicated melody and accompaniment; and a prominent role played by music within its native governmental system. In his *Essai sur l'origine des langues*, Rousseau describes a close connection between speech and music in the language of the first societies. He explains, "les infléxions mélodieuses des accens firent naitre la poesie et la musique avec la langue, ou plustôt tout cela n'étoit que la langue."[14] These first societies began to articulate utterances that combined speech and song and, in Rousseau's opinion, produced an effective speech that directly expressed and evoked emotions. Such speech would be conveyed in images, sentiments, and figures of speech, and it would be sung rather than spoken. Ideal communication would neglect grammar in favor of beautiful sounds.

Rousseau describes a musical communication that would "persuade without convincing" (383). This phrase, although one of Rousseau's enigmatic descriptions of his utopian musical culture, can be understood within the context of eighteenth-century Parisian singing practices. Persuasion implies a direct moral response evoked from the listener as opposed to the logic required to convince. If eighteenth-century Parisians hoped to convince one another of political opinions, speeches and essays would have proved much more effective than songs and poems. Unfortunately, such public expressions would have quickly attracted government attention, yet clandestine songs and poems provided a more veiled critique. The singers along the 1749 communication network did not hope to overtly convince one another of new ideas; rather, they shared musical performances as a means of commentary that could sway beliefs. Ideas stem from the hyper-civilization of the mind that Rousseau condemns. Beliefs result from the natural emotions that humans, according to Rousseau, innately possess. The 1749 performances aimed to subtly persuade rather than forcefully convince, a true communication involving an open exchange of natural beliefs rather than the imposition of convoluted ideas. Though the concept of persuading without convincing may seem perplexing within the context of Rousseau's essay, it becomes clear within the context of his musical experiences in Paris.

In the Affair of the Fourteen, much in accordance with Rousseau's supposed prescriptions, a combination of poetry and music expressed emotions about social and governmental events and sought to evoke similar emotions from the listener. The songs that circulated in the Affair of the Fourteen were as much poetry as they were music; like "les prémiers discours," they were "retours périodiques et mesurés du rhythme . . . les infléxions mélodieuses des accens" (383). Poetry inherently requires "de la cadence aux périodes et de la rondeur aux phrases." The poetry used in the Affair songs varies in sophistication—from basic romance structure to sophisticated alexandrine verse. Nonetheless, in all cases, images, feelings, and figures of speech play a crucial role in the communicative effectiveness of the songs. Although overt criticisms and characterizations were not unheard of in these ditties, subtlety and turns of phrase are clearly preferable.

Take for example "the attack on Mme de Pompadour" sung to the exceedingly popular tune of "Quand le péril est agréable," shown in Example 1:

> Par vos façons nobles et franches,
> Iris, vous enchantez nos coeurs;
> Sur nos pas vous semez des fleurs.
> Mais ce sont des fleurs blanches. (Darnton 176)

Darnton concludes that the "white flowers" that Mme de Pompadour strews about in the last line of this stanza are actually a venereal skin infection resembling white blossoms (182). This text comments on current events eloquently, and whenever possible without succumbing to obvious slander. Artful play with language, combined with well-known music, creates an easily comprehensible and transmittable work, and though the goal of these

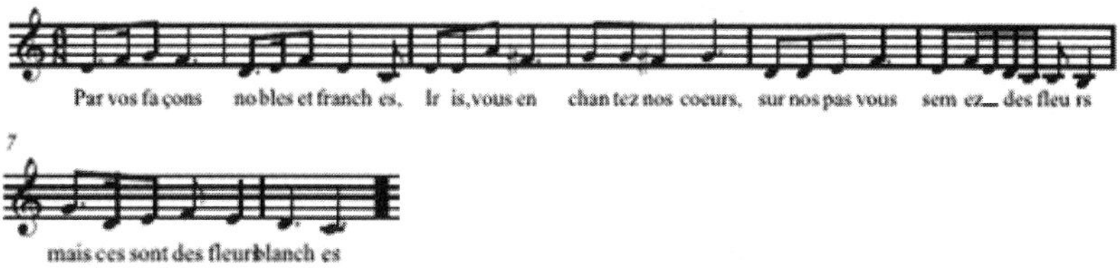

Example 1. "The attack on Mme. de Pompadour" sung to "Quand le péril est agréable," as transcribed from the recording on Darnton's electronic cabaret.[15]

songs tended toward social commentary, ultimately such songs worked to persuade listeners along the communication network to agree with the criticism they present.

The musical features of this example also conform aesthetically to Rousseau's conception of ideal music, particularly through the predominance of the unison, the sparsely or un-accompanied vocals, and the clear underlying moral purpose. Example 1 provides a transcription of the online recording that accompanies Darnton's *Poetry and the Police.* It is appropriate to transcribe the work as a performance rather than from its notation because most Parisians would have only experienced the melody through oral transmission, never seeing it notated in a text.[16] In the transcription, we can see dotted rhythms and sixteenth notes that likely would have been improvised by performers and perhaps not notated within the original sources. The harmony one can extrapolate from this simple melody is quite basic: from the tonic, to the supertonic, to the dominant and back again. The interest of the music is not in technical musical features like harmonic motion, but in the folk-like and wholly memorable melody, a melody that complements rather than dominates the text. Rousseau advocated just such a natural music, in which speech and singing become indistinguishable and in which melody takes primacy over harmony.[17] The Affair songs utilize basic musical techniques to evoke moral responses from listeners, with a goal of communication rather than artistic performance. Rousseau claims that music degenerates when the melody becomes disconnected from discourse and obtains a separate existence from words.[18] In the case of the Affair of the Fourteen songs, melodies are both conceptually and aesthetically interwoven with discourse, precisely the aesthetic Rousseau promotes. In this practice, pre-existing melodies that all Parisians would have known were attached to new words. These recycled melodies existed for the purpose of accompanying the sort of poetry which itself could not be complete without musical vocal inflection.[19]

When the French Revolution appeared to offer a radically new venue in which to perform political beliefs, Parisians still turned to centuries-old melodies to express themselves. Rousseau's own musical compositions also clearly drew upon the same tradition of popular song. Rousseau has come down to us in history as the composer who helped to bring folk-like music into the mainstream with his exceedingly popular *Le Devin du Village*. If we look at these traditions of music, poetry, and communication on a macro-historical scale, the link between Rousseau's writings on music and French revolutionary musical practices becomes comprehensible and even unsurprising.

In Rousseau's ideal society, music and language are not only intimately associated, but they also work to unify humans into a community. According to Rousseau, music "rapproche plus l'homme de l'homme et nous donne toujours quelque idée de nos semblables . . . sitôt que des signes vocaux frapent vôtre oreille, ils vous annoncent un être semblable à vous, ils sont, pour ainsi dire, les organes de l'ame, et s'ils vous peignent aussi la solitude ils vous disent que vous n'y étes pas seul."[20] In Rousseau's *Essay*, successful music is fundamentally social, and the modifier is not to be confused with civilized. These first societies were unified in purpose and in voice, and their natural communication was musical, rather than artistic. Rousseau bemoans modern politics in which "the subjects must be kept scattered" (428). Implicit in this critique is the belief that modern politics, that is, absolute monarchy, can only function if the subjects are prevented from unifying and thus remain voiceless (un-unified voices merely create noise according to Rousseau). Rousseau insists, it is not that the French do not listen to one another's voices and cries, but that their language is not disposed to being heard (429). He states simply: "Il y a des langues favorables à la liberté" (428), and he does not consider French one of them. Here we find a quintessential Rousseauean paradox: the French language is not particularly well suited to liberty, but it seems Rousseau conceived of his philosophy of music and politics against the backdrop of this Parisian singing scandal. The songs from the Affair of the Fourteen were a perfect combination of music and poetry, a combination that united people in a common will in search of a mutual moral purpose. Rousseau creates such paradoxes within his writing in order to establish the binaries that are so integral to his way of thinking.

Rousseau thrived on binaries between thought and lived experience, yet these binaries exist as two sides of the same coin. In his discussion of Rousseau's writing, Louis-Sébastien Mercier points out the writer's tendency toward paradox: "Jamais écrivain n'avoit montré qu'on pût toucher à la fois deux points aussi éloignés, aussi opposés que l'éloquence de l'amour passionné, et celle de l'obscure et profonde politique."[21] In Rousseau's utopian musical society, music and language come together as one in order to express the passions of the soul. Rousseau took his dystopian experience of music in mid-eighteenth-century Paris, where French citizens sang in discord to communicate their frustrations, and transformed it into his idealistic view of music's political role in a utopian society, in which citizens would sing in moral harmony.[22] In short, through his *Essai sur l'origine des langues*, Rousseau creates a written, utopian reflection of the Affair of the Fourteen, which to him likely represented a performed, dystopian reality.

If Rousseau's philosophy of music in politics does, in fact, stem from this pre-existing music practice, then we should be more inclined to connect his philosophy of music to music's fundamental role in the political culture of the French Revolution. Clearly, the Affair of the Fourteen did not foretell revolution in any way; yet, it did belie a nascent musical culture of performing opinion, idealized and re-written by Rousseau. The Affair of the Fourteen confirms that the social networks and performance techniques were already accessible in the Parisian repertoire in 1749 and therefore could be reincarnated through cultural and musical memory forty years later, in 1789.

Text: *Chansonnier de la République, pour l'an 3è* (1794)

One of the social networks already in place by 1749 belonged to a long tradition of popular tunes that circulated through Parisian society via chansonniers. As shown through the Affair of the Fourteen, these tunes could be reused and recycled to fit changing social and political situations. This tradition did not merely persist, but actually thrived during the French Revolution. The dedication page of the *Chansonnier de la République, pour l'an 3è* (1794) announces its homage to "friends of liberty"[23] and to four historical figures, all of them ancestors of the French Revolution who served or shaped *la patrie* "en temps différents": Junius Brutus, Mutius Scévola, Guillaume Tell, and Jean-Jacques Rousseau. In the brief elegy to Rousseau found in the introduction of the chansonnier, he is described as a genius persecuted for the truth he spoke, preacher of "la loi naturelle" (11) and carrier of "le flambeau de la raison" (11).

Rousseau proves the only dedicatee worthy of a song in his honor. "Couplets à J.J. Rousseau" (Example 2) is set to a romance melody from Rousseau's apocryphal, posthumously published collection of romances

(139)

COUPLETS

A J. J. ROUSSEAU.

AIR : *Je l'ai planté, je l'ai vu naître.*

Bienfaiteur de la tendre enfance,
Qui protégeas nos jeunes ans,
Rousseau, de la reconnaissance
Entends les timides accens.

Loin des sentiers de la nature
Nos pères étaient entraînés ;
Mais ta voix bienfaisante et pure
A ses loix les a ramenés.

Nous n'entrerons plus dans la vie
Sous l'escorte de la douleur :
Par toi notre enfance embellie
Sera l'aurore du bonheur.

Nos jours à des mains étrangères
Ne seront plus abandonnés ;
Nous pourrons, sous l'œil de nos mères,
Croître libres et fortunés.

Example 2. "Couplets à J.J. Rousseau," *Chansonniers de la République*, *an 3è* (1794) and airs, *Les consolations des misères de ma vie* (1781). Unlike the melodies within the *Chansonnier de la République* that had to be written for citizens to learn, Rousseau's melody proved sufficiently popular that it did not need to be notated within the chansonnier. French citizens should have already been familiar with the tune. This romance was clearly chosen for a variety of reasons: Rousseau composed the original work, the melody is traditional-sounding and uncomplicated, and a close relationship exists between the old and new lyrics.

The dedication of a chansonnier to Rousseau seems appropriate when considering his belief that music should be at the core of a democratic community. The chansonnier contributed to the maintenance of a common, uncomplicated musical vocabulary for festivals and patriotic gatherings, and enhanced feelings of unity and equality among citizens. Yet this text has a pre-history, even before Rousseau's prescriptions for an accessible and democratic popular music. Such chansonniers already existed during the sixteenth century (see footnote 16), and it was precisely these older songbooks that provided some of the popular tunes used to accompany poetry during both the Affair of the Fourteen and the French Revolution. This particular chansonnier materializes the interaction among Rousseau's experience of music in mid-eighteenth-century Paris, the oral history of his role as a founding father of the Revolution, and the unification of these two cultural artifacts into a symbol of the so-called new revolutionary political culture. Rousseau himself experienced, as exemplified through the Affair of the Fourteen, the Parisian practice of singing as a means of sharing political beliefs. Rousseau then became idealized as father of the new republic that sprang forth through the French Revolution. Revolutionary chansonniers and the veneration of Rousseau were portrayed as unique features of this new government. Despite these efforts to create something completely different, Parisians only had past texts and performances to draw upon for inspiration and they continued to express themselves through this trans-historical repertoire, in fact the very same repertoire that Rousseau experienced as he wrote his *Essai sur l'origine des langues* and the *Lettre à d'Alembert*.

Implicitly, this chansonnier attributes both the philosophical and musical birth of the French Revolution to Rousseau. Parisians understood that Rousseau's legacy melded music and citizenship into a symbiotic whole, each requiring the other. Although citizens knew of Rousseau through revolutionary rhetoric that circulated throughout Paris during the early stages of the Revolution, it remains very unlikely that those who performed from this chansonnier were aware of Rousseau's nuanced prescriptions for the ideal role of music in political culture. The *Essai sur l'origine des langues* did not circulate widely in France, or anywhere else for that matter, until the twentieth century. Nonetheless, as Rousseau would prescribe, this chansonnier provided an opportunity for those who were not musically literate to perform and participate at patriotic gatherings meant to strengthen sentiments of *patrie*. Through the example of the Affair of the Fourteen, we see that French citizens already practiced oral transmission of public opinions through song. Rousseau, who rewrote mid-century performances in a utopian nature, became reintegrated into these practices once his revolutionary legacy became solidified.

Performance: Une Fête Révolutionnaire en l'honneur de Jean-Jacques Rousseau

Although texts remain our only traces of revolutionary repertoire, they nonetheless provide testimony to what a revolutionary musical performance could have communicated and transmitted among spectators and participants. A text entitled *Fête champêtre célébrée à Montmorency en l'honneur de J.J. Rousseau* recounts a festival given in honor of Rousseau on the 25th of September 1794, when the village of Montmorency erected a monument in the writer's honor. The small village just outside of Paris prided itself as the location where Rousseau lived when he wrote numerous famous works, including *Du Contrat Social* (1762). Typical of other festivals during the French Revolution, the proceedings of this particular festival were documented in a pamphlet published for a variety of purposes: to make the new government aware of the town's revolutionary activities, to record specific details of the festival, contributing to the new history of the Republic, and to make festival customs available to other villages so that they might emulate Montmorency's exceptional citizenship. As was the custom during revolutionary festivals, town members, public officials, soldiers, and artists gathered to read speeches, perform music, and celebrate a republican icon, in this case, Rousseau.

Striking similarities surface between this revolutionary festival in honor of Rousseau and the citizen celebration of the regiment of Saint-Gervais, quoted above. Tracy B. Strong identifies five elements of the Saint-Gervais public demonstration of citizenship that, for Rousseau, made it an ideal performance modeling commonality: formless dance resulting from music, a celebration of citizenship, female participation, loss of self-consciousness in favor of public identity, and focus on the present moment.[24] The revolutionary celebration following the Montmorency festival in Rousseau's honor resonates with Rousseau's own description of the impressionable "bacchanalia of the political" (123) he witnessed as a child:

> Ces couplets [du Devin du Village] finis, la musique prit un caractere plus général; les airs consactés par le patriotisme, donnerent le signal de la joie & des danses. La nuit qui s'approchoit n'apporta point d'obstacles à ce plaisir, qui semble l'ame & le caractere des fêtes champêtres; des lampions posés dans les arbres, prolongerent la fête qui dura jusqu'à minuit.[26]

At this revolutionary festival, the music drives the citizens' desire to continue celebrating and performing their public identity, living in the present moment without concern for the nearing midnight hour. The music's patriotism sparks these feelings and moves the participants to dance. The reference to "fêtes champêtres" invokes naturalness like that of Rousseau's ideal political culture in which music and language work to perform commonality among citizens. The citizens' actions do not result from civilization, but from an inner, visceral connection with the community and the moment. All of these features mirror those found in Rousseau's description of the spontaneous Saint-Gervais festival.

Rousseau's own musical composition, an air from *Le Devin du Village*, layers upon this Rousseauean ideal of musical performance (Example 3). The timbre used is "Ici de la simple nature," from the vaudeville of Rousseau's one-act opera. By this point in the Revolution, vaudevilles had a long history as musical works that could be reused in a variety of situations and that demanded audience participation. We must wonder, then, whether Rousseau's music was employed in these festivals for its aesthetic appeal or for its meaning. From revolutionary chansonniers and festivals, it seems French taste in music had indeed decided in favor of the musical style Rousseau promoted throughout his life and works: simple melodies set to sparse harmonization, accessible to musicians and non-musicians alike, evoking affect and participation rather than awe. An added benefit was that Rousseau himself had written this music. Despite these correlations with Rousseau's musical preferences and compositions, in popular milieus such melodies had persisted since the seventeenth century, and it is unlikely that Rousseau imagined such music in isolation. Simply by crossing the Pont Neuf at any point during his time in Paris, he would have heard such tunes. Rousseau contributed to this musical repertoire with his *Le Devin du Village* and the apocryphal book of romances, which contributed to the popular folk-like genres and styles of the mainstream

O tendre ami de la nature,
Jean-Jacques ici reçois nos vœux,
D'une morale douce & pure,
Vois en nous le ſuccès heureux;
La reconnoiſſance,
L'aimable innocence,
Tout t'aſſure un tribut d'encens,
Dans nos enfans (*bis.*)

Example 3. Couplets set to "Ici de la simple nature," from *Le Devin du Village*, for the *Fête champêtre célébrée à Montmorency en l'honneur de J.J. Rousseau* (1794)

Parisian musical scene.[27]

The changes in song culture that occurred from 1749 to 1794 can be understood through the Affair of the Fourteen, Rousseau's *Essai sur l'origine des langues* and this festival at Montmorency. Unfortunately, little evidence remains regarding the actual musical performances that must have been part of the Affair of the Fourteen. We do know two key facts: that this music was performed and that there was a tradition of street singing in eighteenth-century Paris. Citizens performed the Affair of the Fourteen songs enough for us to know, even centuries later, that the songs were widespread throughout the city (Darnton 174). As mentioned above, Rousseau complains that his contemporaries, that is, mid-century Parisian citizens, were "kept scattered"— mid-eighteenth-century performances of dissident songs were clandestine and conspicuously undocumented. With changes that occurred through the Revolution, at least for a moment, street singing became a legitimate form of political activism, rather than a form of dissent to be hidden.[27] After the Terror, the danger of unrest caused by singing became evident,[28] and as an end result, authorities demanded that songs be performed in a controlled environment such as sanctioned festivals. Consequently, sung performances by 1794 looked eerily similar to the ideal set forth by Rousseau: French citizens unified to sing common beliefs in supposedly spontaneous, natural festival settings. In reality these performances conflicted with the spontaneity prescribed by Rousseau because revolutionary festivals became increasingly scripted as fear of violent outbreaks increased. Ironically enough, performances during the 1749 Affair of the Fourteen proved more spontaneous, and more in line with Rousseau's prescriptions, than the carefully planned revolutionary festivals that followed the Terror.

These two examples of text and performance from the Revolution exhibit the interaction of mid-century Parisian musical practices, Rousseau's written philosophy of music in politics, and the legend of Rousseau that became incorporated into the new political culture during the French Revolution. The chansonnier from 1794 materializes Rousseau's demand for music as a tool for creating community among citizens. The songs within the chansonnier are transparent because they are set to music that every citizen already knew through prior collective experience. The Parisian tradition of singing subjects and Rousseau's promotion of music as politics interweaves. The festival in Rousseau's honor exemplifies the writer's belief that appropriately patriotic music could move citizens to perform community and public identity. As shown by Darnton, performances of opinion already circulated, in some form, during the Affair of the Fourteen. Most significantly, both examples use music composed by Rousseau. Both the chansonnier and the festival evince Rousseau's material influence on the music performed and circulated during the French Revolution and his conceptual influence on the imperative relationship between music and democracy. It is this second, theoretical influence that the Affair of the Fourteen elucidates. The possibility for this influence can only be explained through the interaction between popular and intellectual experiences and practices over the course of the eighteenth century.

Conclusion

Initially, Rousseau's musical influence on the French Revolution may appear both logical and unsurprising. As a leading figure of the Enlightenment long since credited in Mercier's memorable phrase as one of the "first authors of the revolution" (1), Rousseau's fingerprints are found on almost every aspect of the revolutionary enterprise, from the *Déclaration des droits de l'homme et du citoyen* to the first festival of the federation. Because he suggested that man could go back to a pre-civilized state where democracy and common will ruled, some considered the Revolution to be Rousseau's own brainchild. Yet the question persists as to how Rousseau's philosophy of music and politics became articulated in revolutionary society when citizens neither circulated nor discussed his *Essai sur l'origine des langues*. Enlightenment theories of music consistently intertwine with the political culture of the French Revolution, but rarely do we find the material evidence of how these lofty ideas trickled down to what Lynn Hunt has called the "politicized everyday."[29] The mid-century Affair of the Fourteen illuminates this phenomenon of exchange. If the Affair of the Fourteen influenced Rousseau's philosophy of music, then we find a writer who mirrors and manipulates a musical culture, then reflects his own interpretation of that musical culture back into his environment. Although citizens during the French Revolution did not read Rousseau's writings on music and democracy, this was in any case unnecessary, since Rousseau's writings were in fact derived from a mid-eighteenth-century Parisian musical practice that had existed during the pre-revolutionary period.

In 1749, Parisians added new verses to simple, traditional melodies to subtly persuade one another about a variety of political agendas. The critique put forth by these performances jibe with Rousseau's own criticisms of French society: a hyper-civilized government in which citizens remained physically alienated and voiceless. By the 1790s, particularly following the Terror, French citizens temporarily returned to a Rousseauean, pre-civilized state in which all citizens had a unified voice with which to express their love for *la patrie* and their commonality as its children. Since the musical culture of political expression, described by Rousseau in utopian terms, was already in place since at least the mid-eighteenth-century, the French public proved amply prepared to pick up the musical ideals of Rousseau when the opportunity presented itself during the French Revolution. This is not to say that the French Revolution was in the making by the late 1740s. Rather, the range of musical and political possibilities extant in 1749 Paris, first, made possible Rousseau's imagination of a more utopian use of music, and second, laid the foundation for the politically focused musical culture that so quickly developed during the 1790s. By connecting Rousseau's lived experience of music in 1740s Paris with his utopian writings on music within a political community, we find a bridge that connects intellectual music history to cultural music history. This relationship bears witness to the simultaneous persistence and transience of the archive and the repertoire in action, and more importantly, in interaction. A tradition that saw public opinion as part of popular musical performance was already available to Parisians by mid-century. Eventually enriched by new political beliefs and identities, it could easily be recycled and reintegrated into revolutionary political culture, without everyday citizens having ever read Rousseau's highly topical *Essai sur l'origine des langues*.

NOTES

1. Jean-Jacques Rousseau, *Lettre à d'Alembert*, ed. E. Gagnebin and M. Raymond, *Œeuvres complètes: Écrits sur la musique, la langue, et le théâtre* (Paris: Editions Gallimard, 1995), 5: 1–125 (123–124).

2. Rousseau described himself as a writer during this period, and continued to avoid the title "philosopher" throughout his lifetime. He was also viewed that way by others. Denis Diderot writes in 1742 of their first introduction: "Au cours de février, l'un de ses compagnons de bohême, Daniel Roguin, ancient officier de l'armée hollandaise, mais vaudois d'origine, lui présente, au Café de la Régence, un jeune joueur d'échecs *arrivé de Genève pour tenter sa fortune littéraire à Paris*; il se nomme Rousseau." Denis Diderot, *Correspondence* (1713–1757), ed. Georges Roth (Paris: Editions de Minuit, 1955), 1: 27, emphasis added.

3. Michael Sonenscher, in *Sans-Culottes: An Eighteenth-Century Emblem in the French Revolution* (Princeton and Oxford: Princeton University Press, 2008), 166, attributes Rousseau's philosophy of music and language in politics to a theological philosophy, the genealogy of which ends with Giambattista Vico (1668–1744), and cited further in the text.

4. Sonenscher writes, for example: "It is tempting to think that much of the content of the many public festivities put on, not only during the period of the French Revolution, but right up to the banqueting campaign that heralded the revolution of 1848, can be traced back to Rousseau's *Letter to d'Alembert*. In a weak sense, this must be true. But Rousseau's interest in the causal relationships linking political institutions like festivals or cercles, the content of public opinion, and the real power of legitimate government overlapped with a rather different and much older interest in the related subjects of singing, dancing, morality, and government" (164). However, later in the same chapter, Sonenscher claims that "it may be more historically accurate not only to position Rousseau's own historical conjectures against this older, and broader intellectual context, *but also to describe Rousseau's conjectures as the intellectual stimulus that brought them back to life*" (170, emphasis added).

5. Robert Darnton, *Poetry and the Police: Communication Networks in Eighteenth-Century Paris* (Cambridge, MA, and London: The Belknap Press of Harvard University Press, 2010), and cited further in the text.

6. See Georgia Cowart, "Carnival in Venice or Protest in Paris? Louis XIV and the Politics of Subversion at the Paris Opéra," *Journal of the American Musicological Society* 54, no. 2 (Summer 2001): 265–302.

7. Arlette Farge, *Subversive Words: Public Opinion in Eighteenth-Century France*, trans. Rosemary Morris (University Park, PA: The Pennsylvania State University Press, 1994), 4. As Farge later explains: "It would be tempting to think that public opinion was born at just this time [1760s–1770s], as it laid claim not to its objects or its content, but to its own existence. It would be rash to do so, however. For a long time, as we have tried to show in this book, individuals had been reflecting on events, fabricating morsels of personal opinion on the basis of precise facts. Now they were considering the monarchic system, brushing aside

a king who they thought was absent from himself, and especially breaking the fetters into which the monarchy had compelled them, in the belief that not only were they equipped to speak out, but that they had a legitimate right to do so, and must exercise that right openly. Secrecy was out of fashion [. . .] This attitude undoubtedly represents a major shift away from the position of those—probably still numerous at that time—who boasted of having a secret which they would tell only to the king. But most of the people had moved on, to a place where they had access to other forms of identity; where new situations, each more novel than the last, could be created" (191).

8. Diana Taylor, *The Archive and the Repertoire: Performing Cultural Memory in the Americas* (Durham, NC: Duke University Press, 2003), 19–20.

9. Stacy Holman Jones, "Singing it the Way She Hears It," *Cultural Studies<=>Critical Methodologies* 10, no. 4 (2010): 268.

10. Rousseau, *Les confessions*, *Œuvres Complètes: Les confessions et autres textes autobiographiques*, ed. Bernard Gagnebin et Marcel Raymond (Paris: Editions Gallimard, 1959), 1: 277–348 (347).

11. R. A. Leigh, *Correspondance complète de Jean Jacques Rousseau*, (Genève: Institute et Musée Voltaire, 1965), 2: 120, and cited further in the text.

12. Rousseau, *Les confessions* and *Lettre à M. Malsherbes, Œuvres Complètes: Les Confessions et autres textes autobiographiques*, ed. Bernard Gagnebin et Marcel Raymond (Paris: Editions Gallimard, 1959), 1: 277–348 and 1130–1147.

13. Robert Wokler, *Rousseau on Society, Politics, Music and Language: An Historical Interpretation of his Early Writings* (New York and London: Garland Publishing, Inc., 1987). Wokler has established that Rousseau worked out his conception of music's integral role to language and government, eloquently put forth in his *Essai sur l'origine des langues*, in this first work on the topic, *Le Premier Discours*.

14. Rousseau, *Essai sur l'origine des langues, où il est parlé de la mélodie et de l'imitation musicale*, ed. Jean Starobinski, *Œuvres complètes: Écrits sur la musique, la langue, et le théâtre* (Paris: Editions Gallimard, 1959), 5: 375–429 (410).

15. Hélène Delavault, "Par vos façons nobles et franches," *An Electronic Cabaret: Paris Street Songs, 1748–50*, a supplement to *Poetry and the Police: Communication Networks in Eighteenth-Century Paris* by Robert Darnton, accessed June 21, 2013, http://www.hup.harvard.edu/features/darpoe. Musical transcription my own.

16. The *chanson* "Réveillez-vous belle dormeuse" is even older than Darnton would suggest, since a printed version dates to nearly 200 years prior to the 1717 publication, in the 1535 *La fleur des noels*, reprinted in Pierre Louÿs, *Revue des livres anciens: documents d'histoire littéraire, de bibliographie et de bibliophile* (Paris: Fontemoing et Cie, 1913–1917). Indeed, earlier transcriptions may well exist, and the song continues to appear in chansonniers from the nineteenth and twentieth centuries. See, for example, Halbert d'Angers, *Chansonnier complet et universel, contenant des chansons pour naissances, baptêmes, mariages, nous, réunions de famille, fêtes et assemblées d'amis* (Paris: tous les marchands de nouveautés,

1846), and Camille Daux *Les chansons des pélerins de Saint-Jacques: paroles et musique* (Montauban: E. Forestié, 1899). In comparing the transcription of the tune from Darnton's *Poetry and the Police* recording with that found in the 1535 publication, it becomes clear that improvisation and oral transmission contributed to variations in the melody over time and geographic space. Nonetheless, the tune remained popular during the Revolution. In publication from 1794, we find the titles "Réveillez-vous, belle dormeuse" and "Réveillez-vous, belle endormie" used interchangeably for the same tune. The reason to highlight the deep historical roots of this tune is not a quest for origins, but rather for a distinct musical thread that can be traced through at least four centuries of French history. This melodic continuity across time emphasizes the common performance archive and repertoire upon which French citizens and Rousseau drew.

17. The most extensive exploration of the sources for Rousseau's concept of *unité de mélodie* and primacy of melody can be found in Jacqueline Waeber, "Jean-Jacques Rousseau's 'unité de mélodie'," *Journal of the American Musicological Society* 62, no. 1 (2009): 79–143.

18. Rousseau, *Essai sur l'origine des langues*, 425.

19. Although poetry clearly existed without musical melodies throughout French history, from at least the sixteenth century onward, popular poetry was often set to music as a mnemonic device to facilitate easy transmission. In this context, the two required one another, as in Rousseau's musico-political philosophy.

20. Rousseau, *Essai sur l'origine des langues*, 421.

21. Louis-Sébastien Mercier, *De J.-J. Rousseau considéré comme l'un des premiers auteurs de la Révolution* (Paris: Chez Buisson, 1791), 4.

22. See Julia Simon, "Singing Democracy: Music and Politics in Jean-Jacques Rousseau's Thought," *Journal of the History of Ideas* 64, no. 3 (July 2004): 433–454, for an explanation of Rousseau's concept of general will in terms of musical performance.

23. *Chansonnier de la République, pour l'an 3è. Dédié aux amis de la liberté, orné des portraits de Brutus Mutius Scévola, Guillaume Tell et Rousseau, enrichi d'himnes patriotiques chantés aux fêtes nationales avec les airs notés. l'an 3e* (Bordeaux et Paris: Barba Libraire et Louis Libraire, 1794), 11.

24. Tracy B. Strong, "Theatricality, Public Space, and Music in Rousseau," *SubStance* 25, no. 2, Issue 80 Special Issue Politics on Stage (1996): 122–124, cited parenthetically in the text.

25. Anonyme. *Fête champêtre célébrée à Montmorency en l'honneur de J.J. Rousseau: avec les discours qui ont été prononcés le jour de cette fête* (1794), 35–36.

26. See David Charlton, "Genre and Form in French Opera," *The Cambridge Companion to Eighteenth-Century Opera*, ed. Anthony R. DelDonna and Pierpaolo Polzonetti (Cambridge and New York: Cambridge University Press, 2009).

27. Laura Mason, *Singing the French Revolution* (Ithaca and London: Cornell University Press, 1996).

28. See Mason and Michael E. McClellan, "Counterrevolution in Concert: Music and Political Dissent in Revolutionary France," *The Musical Quarterly* 80,

no. 1 (Spring 1996): 31–57.

28. Lynn Hunt, *Politics, Culture, and Class in the French Revolution* (Berkeley, Los Angeles, London: University of California Press, 1984/2004), 56.

How Body Matters in Berkeley's *Siris*

JOANNE E. MYERS

In the mid-eighteenth century it can seem as if everyone in Britain and Ireland is either drinking, or at least talking about drinking, tar-water. Readers of the *Gentleman's Magazine* for June 1744 curious about competing recipes for the medicinal preparation of pine resin are told that "*Norway Tar* . . . is fittest."[1] Edmund Burke writes from Dublin in July of the same year to inform an Irish correspondent that "tar is the universal Medicine here, notwithstanding the opposition of its Enemy's the Physicians."[2] In 1748, *The Gentleman's Magazine* reports that one Martin Mackrel, a Southampton laborer, has by the regular consumption of tar-water been cured of "a large tumour . . . as big as an egg, under his jaw."[3] Henry Fielding would later recall how, having "dosed [himself] morning and evening," he observed "some visible effects . . . far beyond what [his] most sanguine hopes could with any modesty expect."[4] Tar-water could not save Fielding from dropsy but according to the man most responsible for its popular use, it did save "a gentleman with a withered arm, [who] had it restored by drinking tar-water" and "[a]nother who, by running his head against a post, had a concussion of the brain," a third who "had lost the use of his limbs by poison, [and] another [who] had been bitten by a mad ass,. . ."[5] The figure in question is George Berkeley: immaterialist philosopher, Bishop of Cloyne, failed projector of a college in the Bermudas, and friend to anyone tormented by a mad ass. In the 1740s, having removed to County Cork, Berkeley's first-hand witness of famine and disease drove him not only to direct charitable relief but to the prescription and promotion of tar-water, whose curative powers seem to have been known to Native American tribes, and about which Berkeley may have learned during his time in the Americas.[6] His last major work, *Siris: A Chain of Philosophical Reflexions and Inquiries concerning the Virtues of Tar-Water* (1744), expounds on tar-water's virtues as a potential panacea. In Horace Walpole's witty formulation, *Siris* "contains every subject from tar-water to the Trinity," and as its full title suggests, ranges from practical advice about preparing tar-water to metaphysical speculation informed by various Platonic, Stoic, and alchemical traditions.[7]

The idiosyncratic genre of *Siris* has often prevented critics from engaging squarely with Berkeley's real commitment to his panacea and the public interest that made the text a best-seller amongst Berkeley's works during his lifetime. Readers focused on Berkeley's position within the British empiricist tradition as well as those more interested in *Siris*'s lyrical rhetoric have had less to say about tar-water itself.[8] In part, understanding the intimacy between Berkeley's metaphysics and his charitable objectives may have been hampered by a tendency to shy away from engaging directly with his religious beliefs, which tend to be treated either as superfluous to his philosophy or as an essentially aesthetic element of his texts.[9] Accounts of the good Bishop, of course, have long acknowledged his efforts to fit modern epistemology to "the demands of Christian orthodoxy."[10] Some recent studies, moreover, have drawn attention to the importance of Berkeley's religious and practical projects.[11] Yet while such attempts draw valuable attention to the importance of Berkeley's faith, there remains in much of the criticism on Berkeley a tendency to locate that faith within a paradigm of "reasonableness" that, as David Sorkin has shown, was a powerful tool throughout the eighteenth century for harmonizing the claims of reason and religion.[12] *Siris*, however, with its rapid move from tar-water to a view of the aether as a divine instrument, its insistent trinitarianism, and its invocation of a Christianized world soul, elaborates its orthodoxy in abstruse, mystical directions whose potential *un*reasonableness is hard to ignore.[13] What is still needed is a way to understand how exactly Berkeley's arguments on behalf of tar-water contribute to his philosophical claims in *Siris*, and it may be useful to extend J.G.A. Pocock's call to recognize "a family of Enlightenments"—developing differently in varied national, disciplinary, and even confessional contexts—and consider the possible existence of a less "reasonable" Enlightenment.[14] Pocock himself has in fact identified a vein of enthusiasm, of the sort that alarmed *Siris*'s critics, as constituting an alternative to the mainstream Enlightenment, and recent critical attention to enthusiasm as the necessary other to modernity provides the foundation for considering how even figures long thought to be part of mainstream Enlightenment culture are only partly at ease there.[15] Though Berkeley hardly seems a wild-eyed dogmatist, this article suggests that in *Siris* he in fact courts enthusiasm in order to defend—over the objections of some contemporary readers—an epistemology from which faith is not excluded. Faith, he holds, forges the chain of *Siris*'s analogical arguments, enabling the perception of similitude amongst seemingly disparate particulars and generating use-based forms of understanding that make a panacea not altogether "morally impracticable," as one of Berkeley's anonymous contemporary critics claimed.[16]

Central to these arguments, unlikely as it may sound, is the body. If Berkeley's contemporary reputation for politeness makes his turn to enthusiasm surprising, his immaterialism may seem to make his turn to the body even more incongruous.[17] Yet, as Berkeley moves from the practical sections on tar-water to metaphysical speculation, the body is not simply transcended. It plays an important role in *Siris*'s argument against mechanical causality, one of Berkeley's lifelong bugbears, where it figures as a sign of God's power to work multiple and contradictory effects. As a sign, the body in *Siris* cannot be penetrated by the discriminating gaze; rather, it demands to be read faithfully. A faithful reading of the body teaches not so much *how* tar-water works as *that* it works: the knowledge acquired both derives from and serves practical, use-based ends. Berkeley promotes this vision of the body, and the practical knowledge it yields, in order to curb the authority of contemporary natural philosophers and physicians. *Siris* takes the mysterious action of tar-water in the body as a paradigm for God's action in the world, thereby reducing the efforts of natural philosphy to what Berkeley terms "*natural vaticination*" and contesting what Roy Porter has described as the gradual secularization of the body within a post-Cartesian framework.[18] The criticism that *Siris* garners suggest that skeptical readers saw what Berkeley was up to, and the author of *Anti-Siris* (1744) complains that "what is difficult and abstruce to secular Brains" in Berkeley's treatise "may be plain and easy to the spiritual" (27).

The status of the body as a sign in *Siris* also allows it to anchor the chain of analogies that structures the text. Analogy in *Siris* links the body to the fiery "Aether" that animates the universe and thence to the activity of superintending divine Mind. Berkeley's preference for analogical reasoning again puts him at odds with modern epistemology's tendency to privilege distinction over resemblance in the production of knowledge.[19] Furthermore, the emphasis on analogy in *Siris* represents a development in Berkeley's use of the trope. Here the things analogized—most notably finite mind and divine Mind—are joined in an ontologically real, participatory relationship that contrasts with the general eighteenth-century tendency, in which Berkeley sometimes shares, to reduce analogy to mere "similitude" or heuristic fiction.[20] This participatory relationship, in which the body remains crucial, also allows Berkeley to amend the problem of how human agency can be understood given the immaterialist assumption that all sense experience derives from divine rather than human action. *Siris* offers a curious, fleeting vision of human agency that derives from embodied experience and depends on an intuition of power and unity linking the individual to God. As in the argument for tar's curative powers, where practical know-how matters more than theoretical knowledge, the argument that embodiment links us to God depends on a use-based claim: in knowing how to use our bodies, *Siris* implies, we achieve a power that we understand only by analogy with divine power at work in the body of the cosmos. This power, which might for lack of a better word be called poetic, conveys what might then be termed a lyric agency to the embodied individual.

"We move our Legs our selves," Berkeley writes in his early notebooks; "'tis we that will their movement. Herein I differ from Malbranch."[21] Narrowly, the claim distinguishes Berkeley's immaterialism from his contemporary's occasionalism. The statement implies that immaterialism can accommodate a greater role for individual will, which for Berkeley always does more than simply make space for God's will to operate. More broadly, the claim opens a way to think about the role played by the body in a philosophy best remembered for seeming to dismiss the body altogether. This snippet from the notebooks suggests that, however counter-intuitive it might seem, body for Berkeley is ready-to-hand as a source of evidence. This essay will show that body matters for Berkeley because it teaches the properly faithful and analogical shape of epistemological inquiry and joins us as agents to divine Mind. Reading *Siris* not as a diversion from Berkeley's main philosophical program but an extension of it allows his distance from the analytic philosophical tradition in which he is often situated to become clear and contributes to the reassessment of religious belief's role in the Enlightenment period.[22]

"*Natural Vaticination*"

Burke's remark that tar-water found foes in the medical community suggests that *Siris* attracted criticism by igniting a disciplinary turf war. As Marjorie Nicolson and George S. Rousseau have documented, many of Berkeley's critics were indeed doctors affronted by his "Priestly *Vanity*" (*Anti-Siris* 30).[23] Yet the censure of Berkeley is more than a debate over professional boundaries. Thomas Reeve, a future President of the Royal College of Physicians, was chagrined by the fact that Berkeley was "meddling with a Subject, that does not belong to his sacred Function."[24] He goes on to note, though, that "there is an infinite Fund of *Enthusiasm* in the Composition of *human Nature*," adding that "in every Age of Physick this *Hydra of Enthusiasm* has reared a *new* Head." Reeve laments that "an understanding like [Berkeley's] should be a prey to This *Enthusiasm!*" (64–65). A remnant from the era of the Civil Wars, the accusation of enthusiasm had grown by mid-century into a flexible, capacious charge that targeted not so much sectarianism as any form of knowledge—mystical, hermetic, or broadly 'impolite'—that did not fit the dominant skeptical paradigm.[25] Like Reeve, some respondents to *Siris* levy the charge directly: James Jurin, a former Secretary of the Royal Society and Berkeley's antagonist since the *Analyst* controversy, marvels ironically at the "Enthusiasm" that Berkeley, in composing *Siris*, "hast . . . tack'd to the convincing Truths" of classical authors.[26] Other critics indirectly allege Berkeley's enthusiasm by allying him to groups that frequently merited the charge, from Catholics to Quakers and alchemists—all of whose claims to truth were taken to be unfortunately dogmatic. *Anti-Siris* accuses Berkeley's text of purveying a "*Jesuitical Spirit*" that amounts to "a Preparation for the Introduction of Popery" (38) and claims that *Siris* seeks to reestablish "*Tradition* . . . in direct Opposition to the Tenets of the Reform'd Church" (33). Reeve claims that the idea of a panacea is "as mad a Story as the maddest Chymist" might tell (9).[27]

Why does *Siris* elicit this charge of enthusiasm? Why, as *Anti-Siris* puts it, will secular readers struggle with its claims? The problem is not simply that Berkeley advocates an improbable panacea, but that he uses the possibility of a cure-all to build a case against mechanist physiology and the claims of mechanism more broadly. In so doing, he insists that science is limited in its ability to explain the world and that faith is requisite for understanding. Aiming to prune the pretensions of the moderns, Berkeley recasts natural-philosophical and medical analysis as forms of divination: "[H]e that foretells . . . the effects of medicines, or the results of chemical or mechanical experiments," Berkeley tells readers, "may be said to do it by *natural vaticination*" (§252, 120). A panacea appeals because, by defeating tidy alignments of causes and effects, it puts mechanism in its place and highlights this divinatory character of human understanding. Throughout *Siris*, Berkeley insists "that the virtue of tar-water extends to a surprising variety of cases, very distant and unlike" (§72, 55). A panacea "must seem chimerical," he admits, but, rather than let the admission scuttle his argument, he amplifies tar-water's mysterious efficacy by offering readers catalogues of disparate illnesses his remedy has relieved (§72, 55). It is Berkeley's willingness to credit the "chimerical" or, more precisely, his insistence that his readers have faith in the marvelous, that earns him the status of an enthusiast.

Though it has a polemic edge, the reframing of natural philosophy and physiology as forms of "*vaticination*" is not wholly scornful. It is Berkeley's lifelong belief that knowledge develops not when we penetrate and analyze the world's depths but when we attend to the signals that God sends through sense experience. "To explain the *phenomena*," Berkeley explains in *A Treatise concerning the Principles of Human Knowledge* (1710), "is all one as to shew, why upon such and such occasions we are affected with such and such ideas," offered to us by God.[28] This claim receives fresh treatment in *The Theory of Vision . . . Vindicated* (1733) and recurs in *Siris*, where Berkeley insists that "[t]he mechanical philosopher . . . inquires properly concerning the rules and modes of operation alone, and not concerning the cause; forasmuch as nothing mechanical is or really can be a cause" (§249, 119). Practiced with appropriate humility, natural philosophy is simply a faithful attempt to apprehend God's creation.[29] Not all medical theory in Berkeley's day falls outside such a model; as Porter, John Yolton, and others have shown, the post-Cartesian challenge to explain how mind and body interacted also generates theories that accommodate dynamic accounts of the body as the home of elastic and vital powers, some of which influence the nerve theory that gains ascendancy later in the century.[30] But Berkeley identifies as his target in *Siris* an influential vein of Newtonian physiology that elaborates on Newton's speculations about aether in the 1717 *Opticks* to propose a materialist view of the body and its workings.[31] Such theories, in Berkeley's eyes, crystallize the "proclivity of mankind to realise their notions" so rampant in modern times (§250, 119). In the poem "On Tar" prefixed to the second Dublin edition of *Siris*, his tone sharpens as he makes clear his belief that mechanists had overstepped their bounds: "Go learn'd Mechanic," he writes, "stare with stupid Eyes,/Attribute all to Figure, Weight, and Size;/ Nor look behind the moving Scene . . . To Real Agents, and true Causes blind."[32]

As an object of the sort of faithful inquiry that Berkeley imagines, the body is not an intricate mechanism but rather a signifying token. Body matters to the extent that it can be cured and thus stand as a sign of divine omnipotence unconstrained by mere mechanical laws. This vision of the body emerges gradually. At first glance, the natural-philosophical detail and accounts of tar-water's cures that fill the early sections of *Siris* seem not uncongenial fare for a mechanically-inclined reader. However, the text goes on repeatedly to blur the sort of fine-grained distinctions that Lester S. King has argued were increasingly favored in the eighteenth century as humoral theories of illness lost ground.[33] Distinctions between particular cases collapse: "Having tried [tar-water] in a great variety of cases," Berkeley writes, "I found it succeeded beyond my hopes: in a tedious and painful ulceration of the bowels; in a consumptive cough, and . . . an ulcer in the lungs; in a pleurisy and peripneumony. And when a person who for some years had been subject to erysipelatous fevers perceived the usual forerunning symptoms to come on, I advised her to drink tar-water, which prevented the erysipelas" (*Siris* §5, 33). Such catalogues risk absurdity, but they testify to Berkeley's belief that, from the vantage of faith, the particular body can stand for any body. Differences between and amongst diseases and patients fade if one focuses on the body's susceptibility to tar-water, and this focus allows Berkeley rapidly to analogize from case to case. If his critics find the links in his chain of cures fanciful—forged in a negative sense—for Berkeley they bear out and exemplify the faithful humility required for true understanding.

Berkeley's respondents are unsparing of what they see as his hopeless imprecision—his "methodical want of Method," as the author of *Siris in the Shades* puts it.[34] The substance of their criticisms reveals their confidence that an appropriately refined scientific technique will yield truth, while the tenor of their replies shows how outrageous they found Berkeley's refusal to grant the body's essential secularity and, by extension, the adequacy of essentially secular modes of epistemological inquiry. They find faults both petty and sweeping: several harp on Berkeley's dosing instructions, which are vague. "In very dangerous and acute cases," he advises, "much may be taken and often; as far as the stomach can bear" (§116, 71). The author writing under the derisory pen-name Risorius complains that Berkeley "has given us only some lax, and general, Rules for [tar-water's] Use herein."[35] Lack of sufficient detail is a common complaint. Reeve speaks for other pamphleteers when he criticizes Berkeley's "loose and general way of reporting" facts and his "careless exceptionable way of relating . . . Evidence" (13). Perhaps the most frequent charge is that Berkeley has failed adequately to distinguish between and amongst cases. "[Y]our Remedy . . . must be in great Perplexity for Want of knowing what Part it is to act," scoffs the author of *Siris in the Shades*.[36] "[H]ocus pocus, Tar-water, presto pass quick," mocks Risorius, who labels tar-water a veritable "Proteus"; "the Bishop," he writes, "has acquired the Art of changing it's Properties when, and as often as, he thinks proper" (22).

Reeve's comments highlight the confidence that he, like other critics of *Siris*, reposed in the skill and technique of the individual he calls the "Experimenter":

> Does not your Lordship well know that all Facts, from which such important Consequences follow, ought to be fairly and nicely examined? Are there not many accidental Circumstances in every Experiment, which unwary Observers or hasty Concluders frequently mistake for essential? And ought not such Circumstances to be carefully distinguished and separated from those that are essential by every Experimenter? (13)

Reeve's stance bears out what Yolton identifies as the increasingly common eighteenth-century view that "[m]an the machine may be eased into action by God, but thereafter physics, chemistry, anatomy, and optics will give us the account of human thought and action."[37] Reeve eagerly sets out to dismantle Berkeley's claim to "having had twenty-five fevers in my own family cured by this medicinal water, drunk copiously" (*Siris* §77, 56). Reeve's response illustrates his confidence that careful experimental design and enumeration of particulars would produce truth. "Does your Lordship by this ambiguous manner of expressing yourself mean these Fevers were all of the same Sort, or of different sorts?" he wonders before observing that to cure one fever twenty-five times is no warrant—as Berkeley implies that it is—for curing fevers of different sorts (32). Berkeley's admission that some patients were vomited prior to receiving tar-water, moreover, confounds any claim for tar-water's success in the case. It would require "exemplary Faith and Patience," Reeve sneers, to credit tar-water as Berkeley does (33).

This closing jab hits on just what frustrates *Siris*'s critics the most: Berkeley's demand that his readers exercise faith to achieve understanding. Charges of enthusiasm seek to demonize, and thus exorcise, just this claim, which *Siris*'s critics rightly see as central to the text. Porter has suggested that medicine and religion were not necessarily at odds in this period, but Berkeley's critics interpret his resistance to secular modes of explanation as pernicious to truth itself.[38] What is striking about the responses to *Siris* is their willingness to take Berkeley's call for interpretive humility as nothing more than enthusiastic dogmatism, thereby creating an opposition between faith and reason that implicitly asperses the former as coercive. The Bishop's failure to particularize, Risorius complains, means that "we are precluded from forming any Opinion ourselves, and [are] under a Necessity of acquiescing in his Judgment of the Distemper, which probably may be very erroneous" (5–6). Later, he objects that Berkeley writes as if "we had better give an implicit Assent to the Assertion" of tar-water's universal efficacy (22). "[H]owever glibly it may pass off with the Ladies," Jurin writes, "the *Ipse dixit* of your Lordship will not, with Men of Science, stand against Experience and well-founded Knowledge."[39]

The critics' frustration bears out Michel de Certeau's suggestion that modernity is marked by the desire "to *make the body what a society can write*"—to render the body transparent to knowledge and to produce thereby "an indefinite *progress* of the *body*."[40] The antagonism of Berkeley's critics bespeaks his critics' sense that a faith-based interpretive scheme threatens their own authority. Reeve is arguably the most explicit in opposing faith and reason. "[T]o imagine we should swallow all this Stuff on the mere obsolete Authority of *Verbum Sacerdotis*," he observes, "argues indeed, my Lord, such a monstrous Degree of Credulity as can be exceeded by nothing but our believing your Lordship" (9). Elsewhere, he insists that "I shall again require a more circumstantial Account of these Cures before I yield my Belief to them" (19). The embedded assumption here that belief is something to be conceded marks the distance between Berkeley and his critics. Berkeley's experimental method requires belief as an enabling condition of knowledge, rather than something granted—begrudgingly, it would seem—only after the facts have been established via what Reeve elsewhere calls "sober Experiment" (11). The pamphlet war over *Siris* is interesting not so much because it hinges on an opposition between science and faith but because the responses to Berkeley seem to create such an opposition as a way of constructing, and even conceiving, their own authority. For many of *Siris*'s medical readers, the residuum of mystery that Berkeley lets linger in the body represents an intolerable limitation of that authority, which they see no reason to concede.

Siris and Analogy

Figuring the body as a sign does not merely serve Berkeley's attack on mechanical physiology. It also serves as the starting-point for a more constructive account of how we acquire knowledge of the body and the cosmos it inhabits, an account in which analogy plays a central role. Berkeley's assumption that creation is a signifying text, which underwrites the substitution of faithful discernment for mechanism, leads him to propose analogy—a trope requiring such discernment—as a central way to interpret that text. "There is a certain analogy, constancy, and uniformity in the phenomena or appearances of nature," Berkeley writes, echoing similar statements in the *Principles*, "which are a foundation for general rules: and these are a grammar for the understanding of nature . . . so far forth as analogy obtains in the universe, there may be vaticination," of which scientific knowledge, or "*natural vaticination*," is only one sort (§252, 120).[41] *Siris* is a tissue of analogies: the sections that link tar-water's various cures are followed by ones in which tar-water is likened both to the superfine yet material "animal spirit" that "is the instrumental or physical cause both of sense and motion" in the human body (§153, 82), and to the "Vital Spirit of the World," which Berkeley casts as an animating "fire" or "Aether" (§152, 82).[42] The further likeness of the animal spirit and the aether is then established, paving the way for the climactic analogy between finite mind and divine Mind. Berkeley's reliance on analogy resists what Earl Wasserman sees as a "leveling and weakening" of the link between natural and moral realms that had played a key role in the mediaeval and Renaissance periods.[43] Rather than disclosing truth, analogy in the eighteenth century becomes merely the projection of human ideas onto a world not intrinsically matched to them, so that by century's end, as Wasserman tells us, "correspondences had become a phase of psychology, not ontology."[44] In *Siris*, analogy is a fruitful mode of inquiry because it highlights the ontologically real links between things. In particular, Berkeley implies that finite mind genuinely participates in the nature of divine Mind. While in the *Principles* and in *Alciphron* (1732) Berkeley advises a cautious use of analogy, in *Siris* he makes analogical reasoning central. *Siris* thus suggests Berkeley's increasing confidence in analogy, and the text's interlocking analogies allow him further to mark his distance from modernity and lay the foundation for his curious account of human agency.

As the previous section suggested, seeing the body as a sign facilitates Berkeley's ability to analogize from one case to another. Berkeley is clear that analogy is his preferred diagnostic method: "Analogy and probability prevail in medicine," he writes in one of his later letters on tar-water to his old school-fellow Thomas Prior; "these are the proper guides where experience hath not gone before."[45] Just as Berkeley's critics were frustrated by his inattention to the details of particular cases, they argue that in seeking similitude amongst cases he over-extends his reach. "Analogical Reasoning from fair Experiments I think safe and useful," Reeve notes, but Berkeley's analogies are falsely-grounded, merely "pretty" or decorative, and "ingeniously" crafted to support the notion of a panacea (18). Certain bodies, moreover, should not be linked to other bodies. The Bishop's panacea, Risorius observes, "may be better adapted to the Climate of Ireland . . . the prudent part would be, to leave it entirely to the *Irish*" (7). Even one of Berkeley's defenders concedes that tar-water likely suits only "poor People in *Ireland*, whose general Diet are potatoes and other vegetable Food, who perhaps live in Fenny and Woody Countries, and whose Constitutions are in some measure emaciated."[46] Other readers were made uneasy by well-publicized reports that tar-water cured a ship-load of Guinean slaves afflicted with small-pox.[47] Xenophobia is surely one reason for such complaints, but Berkeley's readers also seem to be resisting the richly analogical vision of the universe that *Siris* advances, a vision in which similitude takes priority over difference. Like symptoms and diseases, the critics imply, bodies must be distinguished from one another. Berkeley, though, treats the body as a common denominator, a means of joining rather than differentiating persons. Doing so paves the way for further analogies that depend on, rather than displace, those that link tar-water's various cures.

As *Siris* develops its claims, the chain of analogies gets extended from tar-water through the animal spirit to the aether and divinity. To forge the links of this chain, Berkeley emphasizes how, like tar-water, animal spirit and aether both produce diverse and sometimes contradictory effects, a similarity that allows him to begin to trace their common dependence on mind and Mind. The links are developed gradually. Building from his early claim that "a wonderful similitude or analogy [exists] between the mechanism of plants and animals" (§31, 41–42), Berkeley describes the essence of tar-water as an "extremely fine and subtle spirit," the vegetable analogue of the animal spirit in the human body (§121, 72). Widely-held in the eighteenth century, the idea of an animal spirit is often invoked to explain how, given the theologically orthodox view of matter as inert, an immaterial soul could communicate motion to the body.[48] The concept had sufficiently penetrated popular consciousness to earn mention in the *Spectator*, where Addison observes that "Women in their Nature are much more gay and joyous than Men; whether it be that their Blood is more refined, their Fibres more delicate, and their animal Spirits more light and volatile."[49] Analogizing tar-water and the animal spirit allows Berkeley to suggest that, like the animal spirit, tar-water's powers derive from an immaterial source while also letting him affirm the common-sense view that some "instrumental or physical cause" is required to mediate between immaterial and material realms (§153, 82). Only gradually does it become clear that Berkeley's treatment of this popular view is less than orthodox.

As Berkeley continues to discuss the topic of vital spirits, whether plant or animal, he begins to hint at the esoteric direction that *Siris* will take by invoking the Platonic and Stoic view that the world is itself an animal vivified by a spirit whose essence is fire, or aether. Scott Breuninger has suggested that the concept of a world-spirit functions in *Siris* to ground the chain-like structure of the text and to warrant the natural sociability on which its prescriptions depend.[50] The concept also functions to extend the chain of analogies in the text beyond material bodies. Operating in the body of the universe, the cosmic aether is akin to both tar-water and the animal spirit. As Timo Airaksinen notes, the figure of the cosmic body lets Berkeley's argument assume a God's-eye view of creation, underscoring the force of the connections he is drawing.[51] Tar-water's "volatile" essence is distilled from sunlight, and it conveys "a kindly genial warmth without heat" (§97,

64), circulating a version of the universal fire that is "the genial, cherishing, and vital flame of all living creatures" (§170, 88). Likewise, the animal spirit works in the individual body as the aether works in the cosmos: "In the human body . . . the animal spirit is supposed the immediate physical cause of . . . motion," Berkeley notes. "So likewise in the mundane system . . . the immediate . . . cause, that moves or animates all its parts, is the pure elementary fire or spirit of the world" (§161, 85). The animal spirit vitalizes the body's many functions in the same way that the aether produces "effects . . .[that] are very various, soft and cherishing, or violent and destructive, terrible or agreeable, conveying good and evil, growth and decay, life and death, throughout the mundane system" (§176, 90–91). The echo of the earlier claim that tar-water "suits all circumstances and all constitutions" reinforces the idea that proposing tar-water as a panacea is prologue to seeing the universe as divinely-ordered whole (§103, 65).

In order to arrive at divinity, Berkeley gives special attention to the analogy between the animal spirit and the aether. With its ambiguous ontological status—highly refined yet material, often described as a sort of inward flame—the animal spirit could be summoned to oppose secular, materialist accounts of thought and action, but crediting its existence did not necessarily betoken a religious outlook. [52] In *Siris*, though, the animal spirit is clearly understood as part of a divinely-ordered system: it links the individual to the cosmos and thence to God. "The . . . vital flame, animal spirit in man," Berkeley writes,

> is supposed the *cause* of all motions in the several parts of his body, whether voluntary or natural. That is, it is accounted the instrument, by means whereof the *mind* exerts and manifests herself in the motions of the body. In the same sense, may not *fire* be said to have force, to operate and agitate the whole system of the world; which is held together, and informed by one presiding Mind; and animated throughout by one and the same fiery substance, as an instrumental and mechanical agent? (§156, 83–84)

Berkeley returns to the analogy several times: "as the animal spirit of man, being subtle and luminous, is the immediate tegument of the human soul," he writes, "even so the spirit of the world, that active fiery ethereal substance of Light, that permeates and animates the whole system, is supposed to clothe the soul, which clothes the mind of the Universe" (§178, 91). Although the cosmology takes flight, the body is still implicitly present here. Rather than being transcended, the body remains present, tethering the text's increasingly esoteric claims.

The extent to which Berkeley relies on analogy in these sections of *Siris* is surprising given the only qualified endorsement analogy receives elsewhere in his work. On the one hand, he admits the productive philosophical role of analogy: in the *Principles*, he credits philosophers with "a greater largeness of comprehension, whereby analogies, harmonies, and agreements are discovered in the works of Nature, and the particular effects . . . reduced to general rules, . . . which . . . extend our prospect beyond what is present, and near to us" (§105, 141). Such rules are what we learn when we observe the important analogy between sense phenomena and language. On the other hand, Berkeley also simultaneously sounds a note of caution, remarking that "we should proceed warily in such things: for we are apt to lay too great a stress on analogies, and to the prejudice of truth, humour that eagerness of mind" that tempts us to think that we understand more than we can (§106, 141). His warning in *Siris* about "the proclivity of mankind to realize their notions" returns to this theme (§250, 119).

The ambiguity here seems to derive from competing definitions of analogy. In *Alciphron*, as Jules Law notes, Berkeley criticizes the slide from "proper" analogy, which "strictly signifies the Habitude or Relation of one Quantity to another" to analogy "in a looser and translated Sense" that "comes to signify all Similitude of Relations, or Habitudes whatsoever."[53] Proper analogies, such as those expressed by mathematical ratios, involve terms that share an intrinsic nature; "[l]ooser" analogy, notes Law, "involves orders or categories so incommensurable that any postulated relationship among them is a heuristic fiction rather than an objective representation of similar functions or structures."[54] Berkeley defends the possibility of proper analogy in *Alciphron*, but Law points out that the role of such analogy in his philosophy is limited.[55] Though they can be analogized to one another, visual experience and language, for example, are in Berkeley's view *non*-analogical forms of knowledge. Both involve merely arbitrary connections between signifiers, as his negative response to Molyneux's question shows.[56]

For critics who see *Siris*'s interest in tar-water as a way to lure readers into its metaphysics, Berkeley's analogies in this text would seem to be of the more relaxed variety. Peter Walmsley hints as much when he writes that, in this text, "[a]nalogy helps us to transcend apparent causes to find God."[57] But the pragmatic and embodied context of *Siris*'s analogies is not simply superseded as the text progresses, in Walpole's phrase, "from tar-water to the Trinity." The aether, as Berkeley explains, "is applied and determined by an Infinite Mind in the macrocosm . . . with unlimited power, and according to stated rules, as it is in the microcosm with limited power and skill by the human mind" (§154, 83). Here, Mind and mind vary in the extent of their "power" but seem to share the same instrument: "pure aether . . . is applied

. . . in the macrocosm or universe . . . as it is in the microcosm" (§154, 83). Not only does the body or microcosm remain in view, but its vivifying animal spirit is identified with the cosmic aether. The links of the chain seem solid. Furthermore, when Berkeley later returns to the relationship between mind and Mind, the point of connection is the integrity of the body, whether physical or cosmic. Just as "one presiding Mind gives unity to the infinite aggregate of things," he notes, so finite spirit unifies the body's members: "as life holds together the bodies of animals, the cause whereof is the soul,. . . even so the world is held together by harmony, the cause whereof is God" (§279, 131). "The mind," he reiterates, citing the Aristotelian commentator Themistius, "by virtue of her simplicity, conferreth simplicity upon compounded beings," namely the body, and in so doing "resembl[es] the Divine One by participation, and impart[s] to other things what itself participates from above" (§356, 160). The body is both where and how our likeness to God is realized.[58]

The language of participation here suggests that, though he never makes explicit a theory of analogy in *Siris*, Berkeley is imagining something like a causal relationship between mind and Mind. The nature of divinity, in other words, is communicated to that which it creates, and created beings can replicate this action by themselves transmitting this essence to their own effects. Such a relation also suits the overlapping nature of aether and the animal spirit, on the one hand, and tar-water, on the other. As Etienne Gilson has described it, the underlying metaphysics of causal analogy involves an intrinsic, participatory relationship between analogized terms: being is distributed from cause to effect, disseminating itself abroad in the universe.[59] Gilson focuses on the importance of causal analogy in the medieval period, but it is clear that *Siris* is frequently indebted to older modes of knowledge, prevalent from the classical era to the early modern, that modernity makes marginal.[60] "Such are the bright and lively signatures of a Divine Mind, operating and displaying itself in fire and light throughout the world," Berkeley muses at one point, drawing on the early modern view that the natural world is pervaded by resemblances between things, "that . . . all things seem full of divinities." (§173, 89–90). The use of causal analogy to characterize the relationship between God and human beings has historical precedent. Commenting on Aquinas's use of analogy in the *Summa Theologiae*, Battista Mondin observes that the "ontological ground of the analogy between God and other beings is the relation of efficient causality of these beings to God."[61] The specific ontology of causal analogy, moreover, seems implied in Berkeley's favorite scripture, the claim that in God "we live and move and have our being" (Acts 17:28 King James Version).[62] In amplifying this insight *Siris* retains an ontology structured by proper analogies in which body and soul matter equally.

Lyric Agency

Body matters in *Siris*, then, because it anchors both the text's attack on mechanical causality and the chain of analogies that Berkeley crafts in mechanism's place. And body plays a further role in the text: embodiment in *Siris* gives us knowledge of ourselves as agents. The paradox here is obvious for, as critics have noted, immaterialism seems to offer "no role whatever for . . . the production by human beings of changes in the external world."[63] If God is responsible for all we perceive, what is it that we do, precisely, when, as Berkeley insists, we direct the movement of our own legs? What concept of motion is in play here? In *Siris*, the same question arises when, in passages such as those quoted above, Berkeley alludes to the common belief that the "animal spirit in man is supposed the cause of all motions in the several parts of his body" (§156, 83). Citing this view without explicitly affirming it, Berkeley leaves room for a curious, elliptical account of agency that hovers in the background of *Siris* without ever being explicitly theorized. That account again relies on a use-based model of knowledge that brings us closer to God, for the analogy between finite and infinite spirit, Berkeley suggests, is further warranted by an intuition of power that embodiment affords us.

Sketchy as they are, Berkeley's remarks on agency have some affinity with G. E. M. Anscombe's claim that the selfhood denoted by the first-person pronoun "I" is not a thing or possession but, rather, a function of how the body is put to use.[64] This fact, Anscombe suggests, is neglected in modernity, where the self's embodiment tends to be forgotten or ignored. "I-thoughts," she writes, "are examples of reflective consciousnesses of states, actions, motions, etc., not of an object I mean by 'I,' but of this body."[65] To forget as much, Anscombe implies, is to presume—wrongly—that bodily life is only ever in service to, rather than a determinant of, the important work of the intellect. Consider Locke's claim that, should consciousness migrate to one's little finger, and that finger be amputated from the body, "'tis evident the little Finger would be the *Person*, the *same Person*; and *self* then would have nothing to do with the rest of the Body."[66] Though Jonathan Lamb reads this moment as an absurdist joke, Locke seems quite willing to dispose of the body as he advances his claim that "it is the consciousness . . . which makes the same *Person*, and constitutes this inseparable *self*. . . ."[67] By contrast, Berkeley argues in the *Principles* that the body is not amenable to such amputation. Denying the possibility of abstract ideas, Berkeley contends that we cannot have an idea of 'a human trunk': we can, he allows, selectively imagine "the trunk of a human body without the limbs. . . . But my conceiving or imagining power does not extend beyond the possibility of real existence or perception" (§5, 104). No matter how we might focus on particular parts of the body, a background sense of the whole is never lost. Because the idea of an abstract human trunk could not be the idea of a living human body, Berkeley denies the idea's possibility. For him, as for Anscombe, the body seems to represent a limit beyond which human thought cannot go. It counsels a sort of epistemic humility that accords with his view that we stand as mere readers of phenomena written by divine authority. In *Siris*, though—as his claim that we participate in God's nature through our experience of bodily integrity begins to suggest—the body is not only a limit but a resource, a site of identification with power.

Unfolding over several sections of *Siris*, the vision of human agency glimpsed in the text involves a distinction between phenomena that are signs from the creator and those that can be considered "effects of particular wills" (§258, 122). In arriving at that distinction, Berkeley is characteristically willing to reject commonplace assumptions about the body and its movements. Denying that involuntary and habitual bodily processes can be attributed to the fact "that unknowing nature can act regularly, as well as ourselves," he proposes that "[t]he true inference is—that the self-thinking individual, or human person, is not the real author of those natural motions" (§257, 122). Rather, because "what is done by rule must proceed from something that understands the rule," these motions are actions of "some other Active Intelligence" at work in our bodies (§257, 122). This surprising claim seems calculated to deflect the arguments of mechanists who might attribute agency to mere matter, but Berkeley puts mechanism in its place here only at the cost of the counter-intuitive suggestion that we assign some control of our bodies to another agent. A contemporary reader may well have recalled the far more plausible discussion in Locke's "Of the Association of Ideas," where Locke describes how "[c]ustom settles habits of thinking in the understanding, as well as of determining in the will, and of motions in the body: all which seems to be but trains of motions in the animal spirits, which, once set a going, continue in to the same steps they have used to. . . ."[68] Though less ironic in tone than Laurence Sterne, Berkeley nonetheless seems to anticipate his countryman's later objection, elaborated in the pages of *Tristram Shandy*, that such a view of the mind, though seemingly innocuous, can at an extreme reduce man to mechanism.[69] Berkeley's reclamation of agency from the specter of mechanism, though less flamboyant than Tristram's narrative shenanigans, may seem not much less idiosyncratic. Yet one compensation for the oddity of the claim that another thinking being circulates our blood is the intimacy it implies between that being and ourselves. That intimacy continues to develop as Berkeley introduces the important distinction between the actions of mind and Mind.

At first, Berkeley's argument seems unpromising, for his insistent immaterialism seems to limit the scope of human agency to a pinprick. "Instruments, occasions, and signs occur in, or rather make up, the whole visible Course of Nature," Berkeley maintains.

> These, being no agents themselves, are under the direction of One Agent concerting all for one end, the Supreme Good. All those motions, whether in animal bodies, or in other parts of the system of nature, which are not effects of particular wills, seem to spring from the same general cause with the vegetation of plants—an aethereal spirit actuated by a Mind. (§258, 122)

The moment arrives and dissolves in a flash, teasingly framed as a negative. All activity not willed by a finite agent is due to a divine one. The inference, though, remains: some activity can be attributed to finite agents. Yet if all that we perceive falls under Mind's purview, how exactly does such activity register? Berkeley seems to have in mind some sheer experience of embodiment, a self-experience of activity. By knowing how it feels to be enfleshed, generating activity in our own bodies, we come to believe in the efficacy of our own will.

If this account seems thin—and how can it not?—its stakes become apparent just a few sections later, when Berkeley implies that our experience of embodiment helps to warrant the analogy between finite and infinite Mind. Once again, the point is introduced to serve the larger claim that divinity orders the whole visible cosmos. In making that claim, though, Berkeley allows for a surprising moment of near-identity between macro- and microcosm, an identity routed in and through the body. "As in the microcosm," he writes,

> the constant regular tenor of the motions of the viscera and contained juices doth not hinder particular voluntary motions to be impressed by the mind on the animal spirit; even so, in the mundane system, the steady observance of certain laws of nature . . . doth not hinder but a voluntary agent may sometimes communicate particular impressions to the fine aethereal medium, which in the world answers the animal spirit in man. Which two, if they are two, although invisible and inconceivably small, yet seem the real latent springs whereby all the parts of this visible world are moved; albeit they are not to be regarded as a true cause, but only an instrument, of motion; and the instrument, not as a help to the Creator, but only as a sign to the creature. (§261, 123)

On the one hand, the analogy is between human agency operating on the animal spirit, and divine agency operating on the aether. Berkeley is imagining a human agency similar to that proposed a few paragraphs earlier. But he goes further this time, risking an identification of the instruments of mind and Mind when he wonders if they are entirely distinct. The potential identity between the animal spirit and the aether seems to make possible, just for a moment, a further range of action for the individual in the world, so that finite spirit too may make its mark on the cosmos. The chain of interlocking analogies, and the causal link between Mind and mind, make plausible the slight confusion here over just what sort of agent Berkeley is imagining, divine or finite. Even if the picture of the finite agent does not come wholly into focus, it remains true that the embodied experience of agency provides the paradigm for understanding the agency of Mind. We understand the action of an omnipotent agent via an intuition of power afforded by the body. The movement from tar to the divine, dizzying as it can be, does not leave the ordinary world, or the body, behind.

Just as the door opens to offer this glimpse of agency, though, Berkeley is careful to draw it almost shut again, not wishing to dislodge his claim about the signifying function of phenomenal experience. Neither the animal spirit nor the aether is a genuine cause; each functions only symbolically. Berkeley's reasons for citing rather than affirming the view that the "animal spirit . . . is supposed the *cause* of all motions" remain consistent (§156, 83). But however fleetingly, a door has been opened to some vision of human agency. It is agency of a curious sort. But is it really so uncharacteristic of Berkeley? The body's role in *Siris* harmonizes with his consistent claim that ordinary experience—use and practice—yields important forms of knowledge, as when we observe the regularities of experience in order to discern in them God's arrangement of the universe. Further, the emphasis Berkeley puts on perceiving our own embodiment fits with his view that to perceive is to participate in God's work—that, as John Richetti puts it, not only is it true for Berkeley that *esse est percipi*, but "*esse* is also *percipere*, participation . . . in the perception of the universe" as "a regular, beautiful, physicotheological spectacle."[70] We might thus say that to perceive ourselves as vital, embodied beings is to participate in the same activity that vitalizes the cosmos. By settling this perceptive power in the body, Berkeley anticipates Anscombe's claim that Enlightenment thought would do well to recall that "[s]elf-knowledge is knowledge of . . . the human animal that one is."[71] From another perspective, Berkeley may here reveal what the poet Susan Stewart has suggested is a uniquely lyric sensibility. Lyric forms, she proposes, have a special ability to convey "embodied consciousness" and "somatic conditions

[that] give us knowledge *how* and not only knowledge *of*."[72] Berkeley's interest in such knowledge—use-based, embodied, synthetic—pervades *Siris* and marks him as, in some sense, a highly poetic thinker. His text offers what might be seen as a lyric agency, simultaneously enabled by and realized in the prescription of the tar-water that links bodies to one another and to the Mind that informs somatic experience. Perhaps because *Siris* is in some sense a lyrical text, it is Yeats who can seem Berkeley's shrewdest critic, noting that "only in those speculations that seemed the lovable foible of a great man is he altogether real."[73]

Body matters in *Siris*, then, because it is the place where we both recognize our own agency and participate in an agency that surpasses us. Simultaneously the site of a poetic affirmation and a transcendence of subjective power, the body allows Berkeley to resist what he sees as the epistemological imperialism of the modern mechanists and reiterate his own view that faithful and humble interpretation of experience is our only route to knowledge. That the text hints at a sort of self-dissolution as the self threatens or promises to merge with the cosmic aether may further explain the outcry against its enthusiastic tendencies, for as Pocock, Lawrence E. Klein, and others have noted, such dissolution is a hallmark of enthusiastic discourse.[74] Yet *Siris* also offers a constructive if peculiar vision of the self as agent. Rather than retreat from philosophical argument in this text, Berkeley returns to and refines some earlier arguments, helping us understand a little better that gnomic early affirmation, "We move our Legs our selves."[75] In *Siris*'s closing paragraphs, his paradoxical dismissal and embrace of the body remains consistent. Though tempted by Plato's vision in the *Phaedrus* of a future state "free and unstained from those bodies, wherein we are now imprisoned like oysters," Berkeley argues, this time following the Plato of the *Theaetetus*, that "in this mortal state," we must work with rather than against the body. "While we sit still we are never the wiser," Berkeley writes, "but going into the river, and moving up and down, is the way to discover its depths and shallows. If we exercise and bestir ourselves, we may even here discover something" (§367, 164). In exercising his talents on behalf of tar-water, Berkeley improbably discovers a productive philosophical role for the body as a place where faith links with immediate experience to produce true understanding.

NOTES

1. *Gentleman's Magazine* 14 (June 1744): 327, and cited further as *GM.*

2. See Marjorie Hope Nicolson and G. S. Rousseau, "Bishop Berkeley and Tar-water," in *The Augustan Milieu: Essays Presented to Louis A. Landa*, ed. Henry Knight Miller, Eric Rothstein, and G. S. Rousseau (Oxford: Clarendon Press, 1970), 102–37. The authors quote Burke at 128–29 [from *The Correspondence of Edmund Burke*, ed. Thomas W. Copeland, 10 vols. (Chicago: University of Chicago Press, 1958), 1:26], writing to his good friend the Quaker poet Richard Shackleton.

3. *GM* 18 (March 1748): 119.

4. Henry Fielding, quoted from *The Journal of a Voyage to Lisbon, Shamela, and Occasional Writings* in the Wesleyan Edition of the Works of Henry Fielding, ed. Martin C. Battestin, 16 vols. (Oxford: Clarendon Press, 2008), 12: 564–65. See also Nicolson and Rousseau, "Bishop Berkeley and Tar-water," 135.

5. George Berkeley, *Farther Thoughts on Tar-Water*, in *The Works of George Berkeley, Bishop of Cloyne*, ed. A. A. Luce and T. E. Jessop, vol. 5 (London: Thomas Nelson, 1953), 219.

6. George Berkeley, *Siris: A Chain of Philosophical Reflexions and Inquiries concerning the Virtues of Tar-Water*, in *Works*, ed. Luce and Jessop, 5:74, §125. Hereafter cited parenthetically in the text by paragraph and page number. On the question of tar-water's North American origins, see Ian Tipton, "Two Questions on Bishop Berkeley's Panacea," *Journal of the History of Ideas* 30, no. 2 (1969): 203–14.

7. Peter Walmsley, *The Rhetoric of Berkeley's Philosophy* (Cambridge: Cambridge University Press, 1990), quotes Walpole at 144.

8. For many philosophical readers, *Siris* seems something of an embarrassment if not an outright cheat: Tipton writes of Berkeley's scientific speculations that "one cannot help wishing that the philosopher . . . had reserved just a little of his scepticism to apply to the concept of a panacea" ("Two Questions," 224) while, in "Berkeley's Style in *Siris*," *Cambridge Journal* 4 (1950–1): 427–33, Donald Davie complains that Berkeley indulges in so much metaphorical wordplay throughout *Siris* that "in the end, the reader has been inveigled into accepting an ambiguity as a meaning" (432). Stephen Leo Carr makes the most forceful case for Berkeley's "continued rhetorical duplicity," charging him with "disguising his ultimate goal" in order to appeal to readers; see "The Rhetoric of Argument in Berkeley's *Siris*," *University of Toronto Quarterly* 51, no.1 (1981): 47–60 (quoted at 54). Literary critics have tended to minimize the radicalism of Berkeley's challenge to epistemology by framing the key issue in *Siris* as a clarification or a refinement of the stance of the empirical observer. In *Philosophical Words: Locke, Berkeley, Hume* (Cambridge, MA: Harvard University Press, 1983), John Richetti discusses Berkeley alongside Locke and Hume and argues that Berkeley's aim is to restore humility to the practice of epistemology while also "rehabilitating the authority of the perceiving self" (129). Walmsley describes the text as a "drama of exploration" that depends on the method of inductive analogy as a means "to exceed the sensory" (*The Rhetoric of Berkeley's Philosophy*, 149, 172). In *The Rhetoric of Empiricism: Language and Perception*

from Locke to I. A. Richards (Ithaca: Cornell University Press, 1993), Jules David Law takes Berkeley's interest in language's rhetorical functions as at least partly exemplary of empiricist philosophy generally.

9. For a recent discussion of the tendency to overlook Berkeley's practical and religious projects in favor of his philosophical thought, see Scott Breuninger, *Recovering Bishop Berkeley: Virtue and Society in the Anglo-Irish Context* (New York: Palgrave, 2010), 1–14.

10. Michael Prince, *Philosophical Dialogue in the British Enlightenment: Theology, Aesthetics, and the Novel* (Cambridge: Cambridge University Press, 1996), 77.

11. Marina Benjamin has argued that we need to take seriously both the medical and theological aims of *Siris*, specifically its development of "a Trinitarian natural philosophy." See "Medicine, Morality, and the Politics of Berkeley's Tar-water," in *The Medical Enlightenment of the Eighteenth Century*, ed. Andrew Cunningham and Roger French (Cambridge: Cambridge University Press, 1990), 165–93 (quoted at 165). Breuninger draws attention to Berkeley's social and economic projects as an important and often-overlooked dimension of Berkeley's career; for his views on *Siris*, see *Recovering Bishop Berkeley*, 137–58.

12. In *The Religious Enlightenment: Protestants, Jews, and Catholics from London to Vienna* (Princeton: Princeton University Press, 2008), David Sorkin has argued that the reflexive opposition between religion and Enlightenment thought can be broken down once it is understood how religious belief actually supported aspects of the Enlightenment's development; his study focuses on individuals who promoted natural religion and a criterion of "[r]easonable belief [that] meant the coordination of reason and revelation" (12). In "Medicine, Morality, and the Politics of Berkeley's Tar-water," Benjamin ultimately describes *Siris* as an attempt to rationalize theology.

13. In *The Other Bishop Berkeley: An Exercise in Reenchantment* (New York: Fordham University Press, 2006), Costica Bradatan argues that Berkeley's philosophy must be assessed within a larger frame than enlightenment studies alone can offer and emphasizes Berkeley's debts to older intellectual traditions, from Platonism to alchemy and Catharism. Bradatan's fuller contextualization of Berkeley's work, however, does not significantly challenge standard interpretations.

14. J. G. A. Pocock, *Barbarism and Religion, Vol. 1: The Enlightenments of Edward Gibbbon, 1737–1764* (Cambridge: Cambridge University Press, 2001), 9. Pocock argues that the Enlightenment "occurred in too many forms to be comprised within a single definition and history . . ." (9). Roy Porter and Mikulas Teich's *The Enlightenment in National Context* (Cambridge: Cambridge University Press, 1981) is one earlier work that seeks to diversify Enlightenment studies; Jonathan Israel's *Radical Enlightenment: Philosophy and the Making of Modernity, 1650–1750* (Oxford: Oxford University Press, 2001) and *Enlightenment Contested: Philosophy, Modernity, and the Emancipation of Man* (Oxford: Oxford University Press, 2006) contest the focus on national studies to emphasize both the transnational character of Enlightenment and the importance of figures, such as Spinoza, previously considered marginal.

15. See J.G.A. Pocock, "Enthusiasm: The Antiself of Enlightenment," in *Enthusiasm and Enlightenment in Europe, 1650–1850*, ed. Lawrence E. Klein and Anthony La Vopa (San Marino, CA: Huntington Library Press, 1998), 7–28. For the interrelation of mainstream enlightenment culture and enthusiastic subcultures, see Paula McDowell, "Enlightenment Enthusiasms and the Spectacular Failure of the Philadelphian Society," *Eighteenth-Century Studies* 35, no. 4 (2002): 515–33, and Jon Mee, *Romanticism, Enthusiasm, and Regulation: Poetics and the Policing of Culture in the Romantic Period* (Oxford: Oxford University Press, 2003).

16. *Anti-Siris* (London: M. Cooper, 1744), 24. Hereafter cited parenthetically in the text.

17. On Berkeley's contemporary reputation for politeness, see for example A. A. Luce, *The Life of George Berkeley, Bishop of Cloyne* (London: Thomas Nelson and Sons, 1949). Luce notes that when Berkeley arrived in London in 1713: "His reception by the London wits was remarkable. He came and saw and conquered" (57). Berkeley established friendships of various intensities with Addison, Steele, Swift, Pope, and Arbuthnot. For his critical remarks on Shaftesburian politeness, however, see *Alciphron; Or, The Minute Philosopher* (Dublin: G. Risk, G. Ewing, and W. Smith, 1732), 1:123. Interestingly, Joseph Warton, who, writing in 1756, could be expected to be aware of the negative connotations of "enthusiasm" in the period, recounts a story he heard from Lord Bathurst about the "astonishing and animating force of eloquence and enthusiasm" with which Berkeley urged the Scriblerians to support his projected college in the Bermudas. See *An Essay on the Genius and Writings of Pope*, 4th ed., 2 vols., (London: J. Dodsley, 1782), 2:204.

18. Roy Porter, *Flesh in the Age of Reason* (New York: Norton, 2003), 26–27.

19. See Michel Foucault, *The Order of Things* (1970; repr., New York: Vintage, 1994), 71–77.

20. See Earl Wasserman, "Nature Moralized: The Divine Analogy in the Eighteenth Century," *ELH* 20, no. 1 (1953): 39–76. By "similitude," Wasserman has in mind a likeness that is imaginative rather than substantial (71).

21. George Berkeley, *Philosophical Commentaries*, in *Works*, ed. Luce and Jessop, vol. 1 (London: Thomas Nelson, 1948), 69, §548.

22. For one such reassessment, see Jonathan Sheehan, "Enlightenment, Religion, and the Enigma of Secularization: A Review Essay," *The American Historical Review* 108, no. 4 (2003): 1061–1080.

23. See Nicolson and Rousseau, "Bishop Berkeley and Tar-water," 116–28.

24. Thomas Reeve, *A Cure for the Epidemical Madness of Drinking Tar-Water Lately Imported from Ireland* (London: J. and P. Knapton, 1744), 4. Hereafter cited parenthetically in the text.

25. For the widespread ascription of enthusiasm in the period, see Michael Heyd, *"Be Sober and Reasonable": The Critique of Enthusiasm in the Seventeenth and Eighteenth Centuries* (Leiden: Brill, 1995). On enthusiasm's polemic stakes see, in addition to Klein and La Vopa, *Enthusiasm and Enlightenment in Europe, 1650–1850*, Jordana Rosenberg, *Critical Enthusiasm: Capital Accumulation and the Transformation of Religious Passion* (New York: Oxford University Press, 2011).

26. *A Letter to the Right Reverend the Bishop of Cloyne* (London: Jacob

Robinson, 1744), 31. For the attribution to Jurin, see Nicolson and Rousseau, "Bishop Berkeley and Tar-water," 118–19. For the *Analyst* controversy, see Geoffrey Cantor, "Berkeley's *The Analyst* Revisited," *Isis* 75, no. 4 (1984): 668–83.

27. For the charge of Quakerism, see *Anti-Siris*, 47; for Methodism, see *Anti-Siris*, 54 and Reeve, *A Cure*, 20.

28. George Berkeley, *A Treatise concerning the Principles of Human Knowledge*, ed. Jonathan Dancy (Oxford: Oxford University Press, 1998), 120, §50. (Hereafter cited parenthetically by paragraph and page number.)

29. Richetti emphasizes Berkeley's self-presentation in *Siris* as "a chastened perceiver who has experienced the humbling limits of ordinary perception" (*Philosophical Words*, 149).

30. On the role played by mechanical, materialist theories in the period, see John Yolton, *Thinking Matter: Materialism in Eighteenth-Century Britain* (Minneapolis: University of Minnesota Press 1983). For the way that mechanical theories mingled with older humoral accounts, chemical theories, and emerging vitalist discourses, see Lester S. King, *The Philosophy of Medicine: The Early Eighteenth Century* (Cambridge, MA: Harvard University Press, 1978), and Peter Hans Reill, *Vitalizing Nature in the Enlightenment* (Berkeley: University of California Press 2005).

31. See Benjamin, "Medicine, Morality, and the Politics of Berkeley's Tar-Water," 170–76.

32. George Berkeley, *Siris: A Chain of Philosophical Reflexions and Inquiries*, 2nd ed. (Dublin and London: W. Innys, C. Hitch, and C. Davis, 1744), 2.

33. King, *The Philosophy of Medicine*, 193.

34. *Siris in the Shades* (London: C.B. as printer; A. Dodd as bookseller, 1744), 13.

35. Risorius, *Remarks on the Bishop of Cloyne's Book, Entitled* Siris (London: J. Roberts, 1744), 16. Hereafter cited parenthetically in the text.

36. *Siris in the Shades*, 18.

37. Yolton, *Thinking Matter*, 185.

38. See Porter, "Medicine and Religion in Eighteenth-Century England: A Case of Conflict?" *Ideas and Production* 7 (1987): 4–17.

39. Jurin, *A Letter*, 18.

40. Michel de Certeau, *The Practice of Everyday Life*, trans. Steven Rendall (Berkeley: University of California Press 1984), 196.

41. For a discussion of this claim in the *Principles*, see for example §30–31, 113, and §107, 141–42.

42. Benjamin argues that the Berkeleian aether is material; see "Medicine, Morality, and the Politics of Berkeley's Tar-Water," 189.

43. Wasserman, "Nature Moralized," 44.

44. Wasserman, "Nature Moralized," 68.

45. George Berkeley, "A [Third] Letter to Thomas Prior, Esq., Concerning the Usefulness of Tar-Water in the Plague," in *Works*, ed. Luce and Jessup, 5:191.

46. Philanthropos, *The Bishop of Cloyne Defended; Or, Tar-Water Proved Useful* (London: J. Rivington, 1744), 17–18.

47. See Berkeley, *Farther Thoughts*, 210. The case was mentioned in *The Gentleman's Magazine* in March 1745.

48. See Yolton, *Thinking Matter*, 153–89.

49. Joseph Addison, *Spectator* 128 (27 July 1711) in *The Spectator*, ed. Donald F. Bond (Oxford: Clarendon Press, 1965), 2:8.

50. Breuninger calls the "*pneuma*," or world-spirit, "the first step in the process of *oikeiosis*—the outward bond of sociability between humans" on which *Siris* insists, and which complements the text's "'upward' movement toward intellectual improvement." See *Recovering Bishop Berkeley*, 151.

51. See "The Chain and the Animal: Idealism in Berkeley's *Siris*," in *Eriugena, Berkeley, and the Idealist Tradition*, ed. Stephen Gersh and Dermot Moran (Notre Dame: University Press of Notre Dame, 2006), 224–43. Airaksinen notes that the idea of a world-spirit is "the strangest and the most archaic of" Berkeley's metaphors in *Siris*, "something which looks almost ridiculous to a modern reader" (226).

52. Although willing to entertain a materialist and implicitly secular account of thought, Locke agreed with most of the principles of the theory of animal spirits (see Yolton, *Thinking Matter*, 157–60).

53. Berkeley, *Alciphron*, 160–61; see Law, *Rhetoric of Empiricism*, 101–4.

54. Law, *Rhetoric of Empiricism*, 103.

55. In *Alciphron*, Berkeley says that a proper analogy can be drawn between human and divine qualities, opposing those, such as William King, who would claim "that we cannot frame any direct or Proper Notion . . . of Knowledge or Wisdom, as they are in the Deity" (162). For details of the controversy on this point, see Luce, *The Life of George Berkeley*, 44. Wasserman notes that Berkeley seems to have "accepted an . . . analogical relationship, ontological rather than epistemological" in his early essays for the *Guardian* ("Nature Moralized," 57).

56. Berkeley denied that a formerly blind man would, upon regaining his sight, be able to connect his new visual impression of three-dimensional shapes with the physical sensations with which he was already familiar; see Marjolein Degenaar, *Molyneux's Problem: Three Centuries of Discussion on the Perception of Forms* (Dordrecht: Kluwer, 1996), 26–38.

57. Walmsley, *Rhetoric of Berkeley's Philosophy*, 168.

58. Richetti emphasizes the importance for Berkeley of "the synthesizing wholeness of the mind or the understanding," but he does not touch on the role of the body as a site for such synthesis (*Philosophical Words*, 150).

59. See Etienne Gilson, *The Spirit of Mediaeval Philosophy* (New York: Scribner's, 1940), 84–107.

60. See Bradatan, *The Other Bishop Berkeley*, 40–56. Bradatan suggests that Berkeley sees philosophy as a "palimpsest" and that "the intellectual faculties one needs . . . are not the capacity of invention or innovation, nor the capacity of discovering new things or formulating new hypotheses, but only the hermeneutical faculties: memory, the capacity of association, interpretation, and storytelling" (55).

61. Battista Mondin, *The Principle of Analogy in Protestant and Catholic Theology* (Hague: Martinus Nijhoff, 1963), 34.

62. The saying has been attributed to the Greek philosopher Epimenedes; see

H.J. Lawlor, "St. Paul's Quotations from Epimenides," *The Irish Church Quarterly* 9, no. 35 (1916): 180–93. Throughout *Siris*, Berkeley's theological vision is highly dependent on classical sources.

63. C. C. W. Taylor, "Action and Inaction in Berkeley," in *Essays on Berkeley: A Tercentennial Celebration*, ed. John Foster and H. Robinson (Oxford: Clarendon Press, 1985), 211–225, quoted at 211.

64. G. E. M. Anscombe, "The First Person," in *Mind and Language*, ed. Samuel Guttenplan (Oxford: Clarendon Press, 1975), 45–65, quoted at 59.

65. Anscombe, "The First Person," 62.

66. John Locke, *An Essay concerning Human Understanding*, ed. Peter H. Nidditch (Oxford: Clarendon Press, 1979), 341.

67. Locke, *Essay*, 341. See Jonathan Lamb, "Locke's Wild Fancies: Empiricism, Personhood, and Fictionality," *Eighteenth Century Fiction* 48, no. 3 (2007): 187–204.

68. Locke, *Essay*, 396.

69. For Sterne's response to Locke, see the opening chapter of *Tristram Shandy*, in which Tristram describes the individual as a mere clockwork mechanism, his "animal spirits . . . cluttering like hey-go mad," forming a path "smooth as a garden-walk, which, when they are once used to, the Devil himself sometimes shall not be able to drive them off it." Laurence Sterne, *The Life and Opinions of Tristram Shandy*, ed. Howard Andersen (New York: Norton, 1980), 1–2.

70. Richetti, *Philosophical Words*, 181.

71. Anscombe, "The First Person," 62.

72. Susan Stewart, "What Praise Poems are For," *PMLA* 120, no.1 (2005): 235–45, quoted at 235.

73. William Butler Yeats, introduction to *Bishop Berkeley: His Life, Writings, and Philosophy*, by J. M. Hone and M. M. Rossi (London: Faber, 1931), i–xxix, quoted at xvii.

74. See Pocock, "Enthusiasm: The Antiself of Enlightenment"; Lawrence E. Klein, "Sociability, Solitude, and Enthusiasm" in *Enthusiasm and Enlightenment in Europe, 1650–1850*, 153–77; and Jason Frank, "'Besides Our Selves': An Essay on Enthusiastic Politics and Civil Subjectivity," *Public Culture* 17, no. 3 (2005): 371–92.

75. Berkeley, *Philosophical Commentaries*, §548, 69.

Sarah Fielding's *Lives of Cleopatra and Octavia*: Anecdote and Women's Biographical Histories

APRIL LONDON

The proliferation of anecdotal writing over the course of the eighteenth century offers an interesting pathway to questions of genre adaptation in the period. Lionel Gossman's argument—that from their European advent, these "highly concentrated miniature narratives" were "closely related to history, and even to a kind of counter history"—identifies anecdote with the most prestigious of contemporary forms.[1] But anecdote was also important to other, so-called lesser strands of historiography, and in particular to modes such as biography, reshaped in the decades following the 1750s by a new attention to private experience and personality. Sarah Fielding's *Lives of Cleopatra and Octavia* (1757) appears at this critical juncture. Described by its author as a Plutarchan "Biography" infused with "some Mixture of Romance," and by modern critics variously as biography, orientalist text, historical fiction, satire, novel, and didactic tale, the work has a categorical indeterminacy ideally suited to exploring the relation between biography's emergent focus on inwardness and the English tradition of anecdotal writing that stretches from the late seventeenth century to the Romantic period.[2] While *Cleopatra and Octavia* did not exert any observable influence on its successors, Fielding's inventive adjustments to the anecdotal secret histories she inherited illuminate the spate of early nineteenth-century biographical histories, particularly those written by women. Comparison of *Cleopatra and Octavia* with Elizabeth Hamilton's *Memoirs of the Life of Agrippina* (1804), Elizabeth Benger's comments on that work in her 1818 *Memoirs of the late Mrs. Hamilton*, and Lucy Aikin's reflections on her own *Memoirs of the Court of Queen Elizabeth* (1819) suggests that by realigning Fielding's unstable genre mix these later writers articulated a version of anecdotal biographical history that was deemed appropriate for women in ways that political history was not.

The emergence of anecdote as a distinct mode following the 1674 translation of Procopius' *Anekdota* as *The Secret History of the Court of Justinian*, combined with its subsequent ubiquity, makes it a particularly useful guide to genre transformation. Initially Whiggish in orientation, English secret histories retailed scurrilous anecdotes about court culture in an effort to expose monarchical abuses of "power, privilege, and prerogative" and thereby make the case for "limited constitutional monarchy."[3] Subsequent Tory polemicists, most notably Delarivier Manley, retained their predecessors' emphasis on sexual intrigue and on the suspect motivations of private individuals who sought to direct affairs of state to their own benefit. While Isaac D'Israeli's *Enquiry into the Literary and Political Character of James the First* (1816) condemned the nineteenth-century reprinting of these early secret histories, dismissing them as "garbage" that "would have perished in their own merited neglect" had they not been "dragged from their lurking holes," his contemporaries clearly relished both older and more recent exercises in political defamation.[4] D'Israeli himself made extended use of existing anecdotal secret histories when writing his *James the First* and *Commentaries on the Life and Reign of Charles the First, King of England* (1828), and Sarah Green's *The Private History of the Court of England* (1808) revives the techniques of the *romans à clef* when she sets her narrative in the period of Henry VI, finding in assumed names and a remote period a cover for her satire on Regency corruption.

For many writers before mid-century, including Jonathan Swift in *Gulliver's Travels*, "*Anecdotes*, or secret History" were very nearly transposable terms.[5] But as anecdotal modes proliferated, the initial identification with secret history loosened and new narrative possibilities emerged. Evidence of changes in the representational functions of anecdote can thus be seen not only in the continuing interest in the secret histories that Eve Tavor Bannet denominates "a self-conscious genre of historical, political, and life-writing" reaching from Delarivier Manley, Aphra Behn, Daniel Defoe, John Oldmixon, and Henry Brook through to Walter Scott's nineteenth-century two-volume compilation on the Jacobean court, but also, more generally, in anecdote's evidential importance to developing professions, including law and medicine; its late-century authorizing as a rich source of quasi-antiquarian material for social and political historians; and in its centrality to new modes of writing about domestic life, both privately, in memoirs, novels, and biographies, and socially, in Table Talk, conduct manuals, conversation guides, and collections of bon mots.[6]

Anecdote in fact becomes so inclusively a feature of contemporary writing that it cuts across many of the categorical divisions customarily used to discriminate narrative kinds, making its appearance in genres from the most prestigious and conventionally structured (history and belles lettres) to the least reputable and idiosyncratic (journalistic essays and novels), and appealing in the process to a widening range of reading audiences. Within this broad history of expansion, moments of particularly focused development tend to coincide with periods of generic instability, suggesting that anecdote's mediatory functions acquired new efficacy in accordance with the devaluing of received modes. The publication of Sarah Fielding's *Cleopatra and Octavia* in the experimental decade of the 1750s offers a test of this conjecture, since her highly inventive deployment of anecdote proves critical to unpicking the twists of competing genres to which the work tacitly refers: secret history, romance, history, antiquarianism, historical fiction, novel, memoir, and biography.[7] The rapidly evolving mid-century literary field seems to have encouraged writers habitually to turn to anecdote in part because it offered a concentrated narrative structure—the exemplarity Joel Fineman claims "produces the effect of the real"—but also because it enabled appraisal of contiguous, often competing, forms.[8] From this perspective, the eighteenth-century penchant for anecdote fits with Enlightenment skepticism about established or privileged genres, a skepticism that encouraged both the Scottish conjectural, philosophical, and literary histories of Hume, Ferguson, Millar, and Robertson and the matching obtrusion of the novel into the domain of history.[9] As new modes positioned themselves athwart traditional history writing, they also worked hard to appropriate the cultural authority of their perceived adversaries. This emulative instinct is anticipated in the alertness of early eighteenth-century secret histories to the shift in power from Stuart court elites to Hanoverian constitutional monarchy: the crude voyeurism and borderline pornography of Delarivier Manley's depiction of Whig grandees in the *New Atalantis*, for instance, recede from view with the consolidation of the Whig oligarchy.

Commentators gradually register this change and in the process attest to anecdote's indexical functions: Ephraim Chambers's *Cyclopaedia, or, An Universal Dictionary of Arts and Sciences* (1778–1788), for instance, does not (like Manley's works) foreground the element of sexual scandal when it defines anecdote as "a term used by some authors, for the title of

Secret Histories; but it more properly denotes a relation of detached and interesting particulars."[10] The expansion of Samuel Johnson's sense of the mode's connotations in successive editions of his *Dictionary* provides further compelling evidence of its responsiveness to cultural change. The 1755–6 edition retains the classical understanding in its designation of anecdote as "something yet unpublished, secret history." But the fourth 1777 edition reveals the growing importance of quotidian experience by adding: "It is now used, after the French for a biographical incident: a minute passage of private life."[11] Together, Johnson's definitions look back to late seventeenth-century secret history and forward to the early nineteenth-century domestication of politics in biography.

It is principally in this latter biographical sense that anecdote threads its way through Sarah Fielding's novels, translations, and histories: from her (probably) first print appearance in the letter from Leonora to Horatio in the interpolated "History of Leonora, or the Unfortunate Jilt" in Henry Fielding's *Joseph Andrews*; through the "Life of Anna Boleyn" in *A Journey from This World to the Next* (1743), focused on a woman who, like Cleopatra, carefully dispenses with her rivals (at least temporarily) through her manipulation of a powerful male; *David Simple* (1744) and *Volume the Last* (1753); *The Governess* (1749); *The Cry* (1754); the *Lives of Cleopatra and Octavia* (1757); the *History of the Countess of Dellwyn* (1759); the *History of Ophelia* (1760) with its concentration narrative, the imprisonment of Ophelia in the Marchioness of Trent's Gothic castle; and the translation of Xenophon's *Memoirs of Socrates* (1762). Many of these works, through their stress on the performative aspects of character—whether for reasons of deceit as in *Volume the Last* or for more virtuously prudential ones as in *Ophelia*—seem intrinsically suited to the dramatic potential of anecdote and its epigrammatic tendencies. But for Fielding, didacticism is also of critical importance, and here the affective power of anecdote served the additional function of enlisting audience sympathies. The nature and sophistication of that audience, of course, influence which aspects of the mode will be emphasized. At one extreme, *The Governess* presents its juvenile readers with brief, improving exempla designed to reinforce appropriate behaviour for girls. At the other extreme, *Cleopatra and Octavia* elicits (and amends) anecdote's conventional association with scandalous secret history as part of a comparative evaluation of biography, novel, romance, and history writing.

The Introduction to *Cleopatra and Octavia* praises "Biography" because it "engagingly tempts [the Mind] to look into and know itself"(54), an invitation to self-scrutiny closely tied to biography's unsurpassed capacity to move the reader:

> . . . the famous Amours of *Anthony* and *Cleopatra*, having a true Foundation, will more effectually impress the fatal Consequences of a mad, intoxicated Lover, and a false insinuating Woman, than may be expected from the most admired or accomplished Novels; and the Distresses of a virtuous *Octavia* will excite a more lasting Sensibility of Pity or Relentment, than can be indulged from the most pathetic Descriptions of Romance (55).

Drawing on detachment and engagement as evaluative principles, Fielding argues that, to a far greater degree than novels or romances, biography encourages the suspension of disbelief critical to literature's moral efficacy. "The Life of Cleopatra" further widens the gap between biography and novel by aligning Fielding's chosen criteria of temporal distance and emotional proximity with historiographic practice: "Hard is the Task you have imposed on me," Cleopatra begins, "not only to recount with Impartiality and Faithfulness the History of my own Life, but likewise to reveal those secret Motives of my Actions, which were once so little known to myself, that I was almost as much the Object of my own Deceit, as were either of my powerful Lovers" (56). Two strands of history writing, more often represented in the period as incompatible, are here drawn together: on the one hand, "Impartiality" and "Faithfulness" connect Cleopatra's "Life" with the conventions of classical historical narrative; on the other, the attention to "secret Motives" and "powerful Lovers" invokes the customary tropes of secret history.

Fielding, however, makes an important adjustment to the norms of scandal chronicles. While individual testimony is a signature of early eighteenth-century secret histories, Cleopatra's phrase "once so little known to myself" introduces a variation on first-person speech—the fiction of posthumous communication popularized in Elizabeth Rowe's 1728 *Letters from the Dead to the Living*—that detaches her account from the immediacy of contemporaneous narration.[12] Throughout her biography, phrases such as "had I once thought" or "now I am sensible" sustain a retrospective vantage point that culminates in her recognition that "the Indulgence of my Ambition, and the cultivating in myself the Spirit of Pride and Vanity, had produced more Misery than Happiness"(125). From a kind of speaking 'middle distance' distinct from her role as agent in Anthony's downfall, Cleopatra pronounces the moral of the piece, a moral that will shortly be confirmed by the alternative direction of Octavia's "Life": "Thus I breathed my last, sadly imposing on myself, and fell a wretched Sacrifice to that Treachery and Ambition, wherein I had so long placed my chief Delight; and of whose fatal Consequences, I shall be, to all future Ages, a perpetual and disgraceful Monument"(125).

The double perspective supplied here by narrated and narrating selves—sequential description and chastened regret—is echoed in the bifurcation of the text itself, where the testimony of Octavia follows Cleopatra's. These individual life stories are organized as a chronological series of events, with occasional references to past circumstances. But the distinct accounts at the same time form an integrated narrative of *paired* figures. The coupling invests the *Lives* with a non-sequential dynamic that cuts across the progressive unfolding of the separate biographies by introducing the counter motif of repetition, with its invitation to compare and contrast. Repetition had shaped much of Fielding's earlier writing, perhaps most strikingly in *David Simple* and *Volume the Last* where it appears in numbers of different guises: in minor characters (Splatter/Varnish), in major groupings (David and Camilla/Cynthia and Valentine or the sibling units of the Simples and Camilla and Valentine), in anecdotes like that of the Tilson family where the novel's themes of charity, avarice, and story-telling are distilled, and in the very nature of *Volume the Last* as a sequel reworking an original text. In *Volume the Last*, as in *The Governess*, the structural device of repetition emphasizes the devaluing of worldly concerns relative to unchanging, spiritual matters, and aids in training the reader to engage with the text both laterally through comparison and developmentally through the unfolding of the plot.

In these novels, repetitions of paired figures are internally constituted: invented characters and situations are shaped to didactic purposes at the author's will, a trait well-suited to Fielding's inclination to develop the "Methods of Fable and Moral" over those of realist evocation.[13] When rendered in the speculative historiographical terms of *Cleopatra and Octavia*, repetition acquires another layer of potential in the form of revisionist deliberation on past events, realized psychologically through Cleopatra's retrospective consciousness and politically through her domestication of imperial exploits. Sarah Fielding's choice of subject and deployment of illustrative anecdote continue, however, to infuse this revisionism with a moral intent that is underscored by the formal differences between Cleopatra and Octavia's narratives. As Christopher D. Johnson has documented, Fielding's knowledge of classical sources is both extensive and sophisticated.[14] But not only does she amend the practice of Plutarch, her most obvious antecedent in the pairing of biographical subjects, when she substitutes first-person for his third-person point of view, she also *naturalizes* her scholarship, abstaining from the display of learning that might have legitimated her title to the voice of magisterial historian soon to be claimed by Catharine Macaulay, the first volume of whose *History of England* would be published in 1763. We might interpret Fielding's choice of personalized biographical history as an instance of a woman author's anxieties about decorum trumping her expertise. It is also possible, however, to see it more purposively as one of the many challenges to narrative history in what Mark Phillips describes as a mid-century turn to the sentimental and affective.[15] From this perspective, revisionism emerges as a crucial principle on a number of different fronts, including the unsettling of genre categories, the education of readers, and the wish to contemporize historically distant figures.

While Fielding clearly assumed her readers' close knowledge of her topic, anecdote helps to give a more particularized and genre-specific edge to the large-scale revisiting of familiar territory. She exploits the conventional associations of anecdote with sexual scandal by restricting it to the "Life of Cleopatra" where it helps to set her subject's ambitious and scheming nature apart from Octavia's self-effacing and conciliatory one. Cleopatra testifies to her passion for manipulation (the defining trait of Delarivier Manley's Duchess of Marlborough) in the four extended anecdotes she includes in her individual *Life*: first, the staging of her introduction to Anthony, second, the "prevailing on him to put to Death my Sister *Arsinoe*"(65), third, the fishing trick in which she exposes him to humiliation and then artfully channels his anger through egregious flattery, and fourth, her inducing him to beat almost to death a servant she thought "put on a scornful Sneer at the Anticks I played to divert his Master"(69).[16] Each of these concentrated episodes graphically inverts an accepted period virtue: in the first encounter with Anthony, manipulation of appearances triumphs over transparency; in the execution of her sister, sibling rivalry over familial love, in the disparaging of Anthony's fishing skills, social power over personal loyalty; in the reaction to the servant's putative scorn, tyranny over tolerance.

But unlike the anecdotes in earlier eighteenth-century secret histories, Fielding's do not use sexual intrigue to allude to present-day political chicanery (unless we are willing to take a cue from Henry Fielding's *Tom Jones* and see the slippage from Egyptian to gypsy as evidence that Cleopatra represents Jacobite absolutism). Instead, they are directed explicitly to displaying an individual woman's proscribed behavior and implicitly to suggesting the gender reversals that make her untoward dominance possible. Cleopatra's *Life* offers up a case study in susceptibility to negative influence, attraction to luxury, "greedy Love of Pleasure"(65), changeability, and sensuousness: all vices traditionally ascribed by misogynist writers to women, but applied here, of course, to Anthony. The known female authorship of the *Lives* would presumably give additional force to this emphasis on Anthony and Cleopatra's *mutual* contravention of gender codes and might perhaps be seen to contribute to the defence of the wider cultural purview of biographical, relative to political, history, especially in regards to the former's capacity to test the role of private conduct in matters of state.

The first anecdote, in which Cleopatra describes the staging of her introduction to Anthony, sets the terms for the reader's understanding of all subsequent ones as narrative encapsulations that are both historically focused and ethically resonant. To encourage an analytical response, Fielding ascribes to Cleopatra, as Linda Bree notes, a "flatness of tone" consistent with an account that "leaves little or nothing to the imagination; it lays bare the contrivance behind the mystery."[17] This strategy of diminishment through the stripping away of both rhetoric and behavioural deceit recalls the use of revelatory anecdotes in secret history. From this perspective, the trickery to which Fielding's account directs our attention encompasses both the real-life Cleopatra's manipulation of Anthony and, intertextually on the grounds of its equivocal ethics, earlier dramatic representations by Dryden and (possibly) Shakespeare.[18] Her own didactic use of invented detail is channelled into exposing the sexual duplicity that enables Cleopatra's emasculation of Anthony. The music, the cavalcade of beautiful women, Cleopatra's "plac[ing] herself in a pensive Posture" to observe Anthony while giving the impression that he is screened from her view, the slip of the foot, "as it were by Accident" that causes her to fall "on her Knees" and then respond to his raising her with the supposedly impromptu comment that she "hoped this Accident, at our first Interview, was a good Omen, that by his Strength he would support a Woman's Weakness, and defend a Queen who resigned herself to his Power" (62): all of these fabrications depend for their success on Anthony's blinkered assumptions about women's debility, the same reflex that makes him immune to Octavia's genuinely loving attempts to help him recover his virtue. The martial metaphor Cleopatra uses to describe her line of attack, "I had Art enough to be sensible on what Trifles sometimes depend a Woman's gaining or losing a Conquest" (61), completes the series of ironic reversals that culminates in the submission of the conqueror to the conquered. The symmetry of the anecdote—it opens and closes with Cleopatra's description of the perspective from which Anthony will view her—enhances its coherence as a micro-narrative and our willingness to read the pattern of behaviour described in it as predictive. The historical personages in turn acquire contemporary ethical relevance as the mannish woman and womanish man are equally disparaged through contrast with Octavia, the recognizably mid-eighteenth-century model wife and mother.

This anecdote and those following are clearly designed to condemn their subject. Yet the revisionist energy they stimulate, both formally and conceptually, foregrounds Cleopatra's status as an historical agent who warrants sustained analysis. Octavia's virtuous endurance is, by contrast, conveyed without recourse to anecdote and her narrative is allotted only a quarter the space of her rival's. The imbalance between the ambitious

Cleopatra and the anodyne Octavia, between loquacity and brevity, between directive power and ineffectuality, substantiates Joel Fineman's contention that anecdote is "the literary form that uniquely *lets history happen* by virtue of the way it introduces an opening into the teleological and therefore timeless narration of beginning, middle, and end."[19] In *Cleopatra and Octavia*, anecdote's capacity at once to disrupt and authenticate historical enquiry also casts into sharp relief the work's contemporary literary contexts: on the one hand, exemplary history—in Bolingbroke's summary, "philosophy teaching by example"—on the other, its more speculative Enlightenment variants. Fielding's "Introduction" to the *Lives* aligns her work with exemplary history by way of an evaluative contrast between biography's focus on "Persons who have really made their Appearance on the Stage of the World" and the lesser form of romance or the novel: "in the latter the Reader seldom so far forgets himself, as not to recollect that the Characters are imaginary and feigned; whereas the former, like Mirrours, reflect the real Images of . . . [the historical] Persons" (55). In practice, however, Fielding's anecdotes disturb the reflective clarity of the "Mirrour." Anecdote—with its incitement to re-think the past, its attention to psychological complexity, its metanarrational tendencies—moves the *Lives* away from the "real Images" that classical narrative histories claim to produce and toward manners and opinions as appropriate objects of historical enquiry.

In *Cleopatra and Octavia*, the grounds on which biography might reconcile exemplary and philosophical or conjectural history remain largely undeveloped. A number of linked late-century developments enabled later writers to extend Fielding's use of anecdote in precisely these reconciliatory terms: first, the disciplinary distinction of novel, biography, and history; second, as Isaac D'Israeli proposes in *Dissertation on Anecdotes* (1793) and then realizes in his *Enquiry into the Literary and Political Character of James the First* (1816) and *Commentaries on the Life and Reign of Charles the First* (1828), the acceptance of secret histories as legitimate source material for historiographers; and third, the incursion of women into genres formerly the preserve of men, followed in the early nineteenth century, by a gendered redefinition in which the writing of biographical histories (that is, not political ones in the mode of Catherine Macaulay's) came to be seen as appropriate for women.[20] All three come into play in the sequence of representative texts with which this essay concludes. The reception of my first example, Elizabeth Hamilton's 1804 *Memoirs of the Life of Agrippina*, reveals the dangers of holding to the mid-century genre hierarchies that privilege biography through contrast with the lesser form of the novel; the comments of my other, slightly later, examples, Elizabeth Benger and Lucy Aikin, suggest conversely that biography achieved a new legitimacy once it was advanced as history's complement rather than the novel's adversary.

Writing in 1804, Elizabeth Hamilton, like Fielding, strategically locates her *Life of Agrippina* as an "agreeable medium" between overtly "didactic" literature and the too "interesting" novel. In doing so, she departs from the precedent of Sarah Scott whose *History of Gustavus Ericson, King of Sweden* (1761) had focused on "the texture of public history" rather than the details of private life.[21] Hamilton does make some adjustments to Fielding's claim that biographies consistently rouse more powerful emotions than novels. The latter's principal defence of biography rested, as we have seen, on its providing "true Mirrours" of historical persons, "real Images" that would immediately "impress" and "excite" the reader and more enduringly incite a "lasting Sensibility of Pity or Relentment" beyond "the most pathetic Descriptions of Romance."[22] Hamilton initially appears to concede to fiction the advantage of affective directness, but does so in order to distinguish between emotionally-facile and intellectually-engaged modes of reading: "in sitting down to peruse the memoirs of a fellow-being . . . the . . . emotions produced will . . . probably [be] less vivid [than the novel], but the interest will be deeper; while the impression made upon the mind, by a belief in the reality of the scene will give a peculiar force to whatever is calculated to operate either as a warning or an example."[23]

A half-generation later, Elizabeth Benger's 1818 *Memoirs of the late Mrs. Hamilton* suggests that Hamilton's casting of the novel as biography's foil had a profoundly negative impact on her subsequent literary reputation. After back-handed praise of Ellis Cornelia Knight's *Marcus Flaminius* as a work that "possesses great merit . . . [but] is [merely] a novel," Benger asserts that *Memoirs of the Life of Agrippina* "is preposterously classed with novels; and an opinion has been commonly entertained that it is, in reality, a sort of biographical romance. No idea could be more unfounded. The author, directed by her learned friends, was indefatigable in collecting documents and procuring materials for an authentic work. Through the medium of translation, she had been conversant with the best historians, annalists, poets, and orators of ancient Rome; and she was guided by the most esteemed writers on the subjects of antiquities, laws, and usages."[24] In the opening pages of *Agrippina*, Hamilton herself had outlined in precisely these terms the scholarly researches Benger holds up for praise; but the latter's rejection of *any* contiguity between history, novel, and biographical romance is decidedly the product of her later moment. Lucy Aikin provides further evidence of this shift in genre affiliations in the nearly exactly contemporary comments on her own *Memoirs of the Court of Queen Elizabeth*. In an August 1816 letter to Mrs. Taylor, written while she was working on the *Court of Elizabeth* (published in 1819), Aikin makes no references to the novel as a contrastive or competitive form. Instead, she defines her stance by alluding to an historiographical grid in which an unappealing barebones narrative history is flanked by the two extremes of antiquarian detail and conjectural theorizing in the Scottish Enlightenment mode. "Any historian", she asserts,

> who undertakes to narrate the events of centuries must necessarily neglect the illustration of their literature, their biography, the manners, and domestic morals; but are not these to the great body of readers, at once the most instructive, and the most amusing branches of the knowledge of past ages? On the other hand, the mere antiquarian presents all the minuter parts of this knowledge in a detail which is often dry and disgusting; he is frequently destitute of all powers of writing, and almost always void of that philosophical spirit which combines, which generalizes, and infers. Yet the writer of essays on the progress of civilization, on manners, &c. is still worse; he is generally a Scotch or French metaphysician, who sets out with a system; if the former, he gives you facts so exaggerated, so embellished, or so distorted, that you would give the world to get clear out of your head all the error he has put into it."[25]

Aikin's alternative is a version of cultural history, in which as the Preface to her *Memoirs of the Court of Elizabeth* asserts, "biographical anecdotes" provide the source material that helps to evoke the "manners, opinions and literature of the reign," mediating for the "great majority of readers" the arcane reaches of gentlemanly and professional historians.[26]

In 1773, Samuel Johnson remarked to Boswell, ". . . I love anecdotes, I fancy mankind may come, in time, to write all aphoristically, except in narrative; grow weary of preparation, and connection, and illustration, and all those arts by which a big book is made."[27] This skeptical response to the principle of the "big book" offers yet another point of entry to the shifting status of biographical writing relative to political historiography in the period. Johnson's slightly ironic judgment anticipates the late-century emergence of anecdote as a powerful vehicle of counter history in the work of such writers as Isaac D'Israeli and Lucy Aikin. As this paper has argued, however, their accomplishments are predicated on a mid-century re-orientation of anecdote away from its then-dominant association with prurient scandal, a re-orientation anticipated in Sarah Fielding's work. Her biographical history enlists the pointed exemplarity of anecdote for moral ends by curtailing the form's customary links with the sexually explicit detail and partisan politics of earlier scandal chronicles and by contrasting

Cleopatra's self-aggrandizement with Octavia's reticent domesticity. In doing so, she prepares for the late-century turn in women's biographical writing to anecdote as a hybrid mode that combines novelistic affect with claims to documentary truth. While her work may not have been acknowledged as a direct influence in this adaptation of anecdote, her sophisticated handling of its potential for qualifying current genre hierarchies, for engagement of the reader through skilful management of the techniques of distance and proximity, for encouraging sociability through conversation, and for gender-inflected analysis makes her—at least from a modern perspective—a pivotal figure.

NOTES

1. Lionel Gossman, "Anecdote and History" *History and Theory* 42 (May 2003): 149, 152. Gossman details variations on the classic anecdote with its "strikingly dramatic three-act structure consisting of situation or exposition, encounter or crisis, and resolution the last usually marked by a 'pointe'or clinching remark, often a 'bon mot'," including the "relatively unstructured short narratives of particular events, such as the miscellaneous murders, trials, and natural catastrophes recorded in Smollett's late eighteenth-century *History of England from the Revolution to the Death of George II*, as a kind of addenda to the principal political events,. . . the *faits divers* reported in the newspapers," and the late eighteenth- and early nineteenth-century "species of historical writing that deliberately eschewed large-scale 'narrativization'" (149–50). Annabel Patterson, *Early Modern Liberalism* (Cambridge: Cambridge University Press, 1997) argues for anecdotal secret history as a quintessentially Whiggish genre, a claim disputed by Rebecca Bullard in *The Politics of Disclosure, 1674–1725: Secret History Narrative* (London: Pickering & Chatto, 2009) who documents the emergence of Tory alternatives. David Simpson provides trenchant analysis of anecdote and conversation in Romantic literary culture and beyond in *The Academic Postmodern and the Rule of Literature: A Report on Half-Knowledge* (Chicago and London: University of Chicago Press, 1995). Paul Keen discusses anecdote's relation to the "miscellaneous style of writing" that emerged in response to the "excesses of modern literature" in *Commerce and the Spectacle of Modernity, 1750–1800* (Cambridge: Cambridge University Press, 2012), 111. Anecdote also provided contemporary novelists with the means to adjudicate the competing claims of romance, satire, and history. See, for example, Charlotte Lennox, *The Female Quixote Or the Adventures of Arabella* ed. Margaret Dalziel, intro. Margaret Anne Doody (Oxford: Oxford University Press, 1989), 261–73.

2. Sarah Fielding, *The Lives of Cleopatra and Octavia* ed. Christopher D. Johnson (Lewisburg: Bucknell University Press, 1994), 54, 55, and cited further

in the text. Kathleen M. Oliver, "Sarah Fielding's *Lives of Cleopatra and Octavia* and the British Historical Novel" in *Masters of the Marketplace British: Women Novelists of the 1750s* ed. Susan Carlile (Bethlehem, Pennsylvania: Lehigh University Press, 2010), 87–107, sets the work in the evolving tradition of historical fiction; Sara Gadeken, "Gender, Empire, and Nation in Sarah Fielding's *Lives of Cleopatra and Octavia*" *Studies in English Literature 1500–1900* 39, no. 3 (1999): 523–538, describes it as Fielding's "only historical novel" and, building on the analysis of *David Simple* and *Volume the Last* in her "Sarah Fielding and the Salic Law of Wit" *Studies in English Literature 1500–1900* 42, no. 3 (2002): 541–57, as an important satire of commercial modernity. While Timothy Dykstal does not refer directly to *Cleopatra and Octavia* in his "Provoking the Ancients: Classical Learning and Imitation in Fielding and Collier" *College Literature* 31 (2004): 102–22, his argument that Fielding and Jane Collier draw on neo-classical contexts to attack modern readers is germane. See also, for an account of Fielding's as an exemplary mid-century career, Betty Schellenberg, *The Professionalization of Women Writers in Eighteenth-Century Britain* (Cambridge: Cambridge University Press, 2005).

3. Eve Tavor Bannet, "'Secret History': Or, Talebearing Inside and Outside the Secretorie," 367–388 in *The Uses of History in Early Modern England,* ed. Paulina Kewes (San Marino, California: Huntington Library, 2006), 376.

4. Isaac D'Israeli, *An Inquiry into the Literary and Political Character of James the First* (London, J. Murray, 1816), 161–62.

5. Jonathan Swift, *Gulliver's Travels,* ed. Herbert Davis, intro. Harold Williams (Oxford: Basil Blackwell, 1965), 199.

6. Bannet, "Secret History," 368. For the relation between secret history and cognate genres, see Robert Mayer, *History and the Early English Novel: Matters of Fact from Bacon to Defoe* (Cambridge: Cambridge University Press, 1997), Michael McKeon, *The Secret History of Domesticity: Public, Private, and the Division of Knowledge* (Baltimore: The Johns Hopkins University Press, 2005), Melinda Alliker Rabb, *Satire and Secrecy in English Literature from 1650 to 1750* (New York: Palgrave Macmillan, 2007), and William Beatty Warner, *Licensing Entertainment The Elevation of Novel Reading in Britain, 1684–1750* (Berkeley: University of California Press, 1998).

7. This mid-century moment also saw the eclipse of seventeenth-century romances, the conduit through which classical texts had previously reached wider audiences, by a new fascination with the medieval, the inspiration for Thomas Leland's *Longsword Earl of Salisbury* and Horace Walpole's *Castle of Otranto*, the 1760s novels Anne H. Stevens identifies in *British Historical Fiction before Scott* (New York, Palgrave Macmillan, 2010) with the emergence of the historical novel and its subsequent development in Sophia Lee's *The Recess* and Clara Reeve's *Old English Baron*. In Stevens's account, romance and antiquarianism provide the formal features of historical fiction, and the success of Hume's and Robertson's histories, its financial incentive. The concurrent extension of anecdote's modal range might be considered an additional and significant impetus to the consolidation of late-century historical fiction.

8. Joel Fineman, "The History of the Anecdote: Fact and Fiction" in *The New Historicism,* ed. H. Aram Veeser (New York and London: Routledge, 1989), 60.

9. On genre competition and its narrative consequences, see Karen O'Brien, "History and the Novel in Eighteenth-Century Britain," 389–405, *Uses of History in Early Modern England,* ed. Kewes (San Marino, California: Huntington Library, 2006), Mark Salber Phillips, *Society and Sentiment: Genres of History Writing in Britain, 1740–1820* (Princeton: Princeton University Press, 2000), and April London, *Literary History Writing, 1770–1820* (Houndmills, Basingstoke: Palgrave Macmillan, 2010).

10. Ephraim Chambers, "Anecdote" in *Cyclopaedia, or, An Universal Dictionary of Arts and Sciences Volume I* (London: 1778–1788).

11. Samuel Johnson, *A Dictionary of the English Language . . . Second Edition* (London: 1755–1756), I.160; Samuel Johnson, *A Dictionary of the English Language . . . The Fourth Edition Revised by the Author* (London: 1777), I. 170.

12. Fielding's marriage of the eighteenth-century 'letters from the dead' mode and Plutarchan biography allows her to sidestep one of the most damaging of the attacks on secret history: its specious claims to historicity. By having Cleopatra and Octavia speak in the first person, Fielding also resolves the problems implicit in another of its genre conventions, the witness— individuals whose direct access to the private affairs of the principals may verify their reliability as accessories, but whose disloyalty in communicating secrets simultaneously taints the incriminating information. The publication of Montagu and Lyttelton's *Dialogues of the Dead* in 1760 suggests continuing interest in the form.

13. Sarah Fielding, *The Governess; or, The Little Female Academy,* ed. Candace Ward (Peterborough, ON: Broadview Press, 2005), 45.

14. Johnson, "Editor's Introduction," *Cleopatra and Octavia*, 20–24.

15. Phillips, *Society and Sentiment.*

16. The anecdote relaying the failed attempt to seduce Herod (with its playing out of the female rivalry theme) and the one in which Cleopatra "dissolved [a pearl] in Vinegar, and drank it off" in order to win a wager with Antony that she could consume a dinner "more than the Value of Six Million Sesterces"(107) repeat the characteristic feature of the unprincipled pursuit of control.

17. Linda Bree, *Sarah Fielding* (New York: Twayne Publishers, 1996), 113.

18. As Frans de Bruyn documents, Dryden's *All for Love* was "preferred over Shakespeare's original throughout the eighteenth century, which explains the small number of performances of the original text (only six, using Garrick's adaptation). *All for Love* was performed 136 times between 1701 and 1800." See "Reference Guide to Shakespeare in the Eighteenth Century," in *Shakespeare in the Eighteenth Century* ed. Fiona Ritchie and Peter Sabor (Cambridge: Cambridge University Press, 2012), 385.

19. Fineman, "History of the Anecdote," 60.

20. For women's engagement with the writing of history across a range of genres over the long eighteenth century, see Devoney Looser, *British Women Writers and the Writing of History, 1670–1820* (Baltimore and London: Johns Hopkins University Press, 2000). Late-century women-authored anecdotal histories were

often framed in apologetically gendered terms, as in Susannah Dobson's prefatorial declaration that she can "only humbly recommend [her book] to the perusal of the most leisure hour [sic]: may they [readers] have the candour to excuse the inability of one whose sex and want of knowledge, prevented her from performing it in a better manner." See her *Historical Anecdotes of Heraldry and Chivalry, Tending to Show the Origin of Many English and Foreign Coats of Arms, Circumstances and Customs* (Worcester, Hall and Brandish, 1795), 2-b.3. Isaac D'Israeli's contemptuous rendering in the *Dissertation on Anecdotes* of Catherine Macaulay as a petty defacer of books might be seen as typical of many contemporary attempts to undermine women's claims to seriousness as political historians. See Isaac D'Israeli, *Literary Miscellanies: Including A Dissertation on Anecdotes* (London: Murray and Highley, 1801), 56–57.

21. Karen O'Brien, *Women and Enlightenment in Eighteenth-Century Britain* (Cambridge: Cambridge University Press, 2009), 207.

22. Fielding, *Cleopatra and Octavia*, 55.

23. Elizabeth Hamilton, *Memoirs of the Life of Agrippina, The Wife of Germanicus*, 3 vol. (Bath and London: R. Cruttwell for G. & J. Robinson, 1804), 1: xxvi. Hamilton accepts that her lack of classical training and hence her reliance on translations and "modern histories" mean that the "learned reader" will not "find any accession to his knowledge with regard to facts," but does claim that the *Memoirs* may "give rise to reflections that did not before occur: nor will he be displeased to re-peruse even those trifling anecdotes, which, by delighting the youthful fancy, had served to sweeten the labours of his school-day hours. In a work intended only for the learned, these might with propriety have been omitted; but as there are many readers of her own sex, who are only acquainted with the outline of Roman history, every minute circumstance which tended to render the scene familiar to the imagination, was essential to the author's plan. In this respect, advantage might undoubtedly have been derived from the assistance of the artist; but by the author who aspires at having a book approved on other grounds than the merits of its adventitious embellishments, such decorations will be rejected, as, while they do not essentially enhance the value of the work, add materially to its price." (1: xxvii–xxx)

24. Elizabeth Ogilvy Benger, *Memoirs of the Late Mrs. Elizabeth Hamilton. With a Selection from her Correspondence, and other Unpublished Writings* (London: Longman, Hurst, Rees, Orme and Brown, 1818), I.160, 161–2.

25. Lucy Aikin, "To Mrs. Taylor, August 1816" in *Memoirs, Miscellanies and Letters of the Late Lucy Aikin* ed. Philip Hemery Le Breton (London: Longman, Green, Longman, Roberts & Green, 1864), 142.

26. Lucy Aikin, *Memoirs of the Court of Queen Elizabeth* (London: Longman, Hurst, Rees, Orme, and Brown, 1818; reprinted Cambridge University Press, 2010), iv, v.

27. James Boswell, *Journal of a Tour to the Hebrides, with Samuel Johnson* (London: Henry Baldwin for Charles Dilly, 1785), 32.

Rewriting the Family Romance: Prostitution and Revolution in Restif de la Bretonne's *Le Palais Royal*

RORI BLOOM

In *Le Pornographe*, published in 1769, Restif addresses the problem of prostitution in an essay within a series of essays entitled *Les Idées singulières*.[1] This particular project proposes a general systemic reform in which prostitutes would be controlled by the state, housed apart, and sheltered from abuse so that in turn society would be shielded from the ills associated and sheltered with unregulated debauchery. In his article "Restif de la Bretonne and the Reform of Prostitution," David Coward assesses *Le Pornographe* as progressive, explaining that Restif does not condemn prostitutes for their vice but views them as victims of poverty who merit sympathy and social protection.[2] When Restif revisits the subject of prostitution in his 1789 work *Le Palais Royal*[3] at the very moment when fundamental social change was occurring all around him, one would imagine that he would return to his position of social activism with a renewed call for laws to regulate the practice of prostitution. However, as Peter Wagstaff has observed, Restif's writing during the Revolution presents a retreat from his previous projects for social reform into a personal world of sexual fantasies,[4] and *Le Palais Royal* is exemplary of this movement from general to particular solutions, from hope for a different future to a retreat into the familiar and familial past. In his interviews with the prostitutes he meets in the *allée des soupirs*, Restif is not interested in discovering and documenting their everyday experience but in delving into their origins, asking them to recount their early life from the circumstances of their birth to their entry into the sex trade. Significantly, the majority of the women he features are from families with means, and their entry into prostitution is often less a result of economic need than of the perversion of a parental figure; accordingly, in this text, Restif situates the causes of prostitution not in general socio-economic factors but in psycho-sexual problems particular to each family. Moreover, at the end of many of the stories, if Restif proposes a solution for prostitution, it is not a general proposition for institutional reform but a personalized rescue of the individual prostitute in a return to virtue through a reunion with her family. In *Le Palais Royal*, Restif facilitates the *affabulation* of a family romance for the girls he meets, one that sometimes features the elevating claim of noble parents but just as often the degraded image of sexually perverted ones. At the same time, the exploration of family relations in the prostitutes' stories allows Restif to oscillate between his dual views of the family as both the site of moral salvation and the nexus of sexual corruption. In his constant return to family origins, Restif shows not only an inability to abandon his own strange family values but also an incapacity to truly believe in the power of the Revolution to offer new solutions for society.

Family Romances

In *The Family Romance of the French Revolution*, Lynn Hunt defines the Freudian paradigm in this way:

> By 'family romance,' Freud means the neurotic's fantasy of 'getting free from the parents of whom he now has a low opinion and of replacing them by others who, as a rule, are of higher social standing.'[5]

While the historian Hunt applies the Freudian concept to the collective unconscious, literary critics have used it to study the story an individual tells about his or her own family: Marthe Robert has established that the *roman des origines* is at the origin of the nineteenth-century French novel,[6] and Jan Herman has recently adapted Robert's ideas by reading the eighteenth-century French novel as a *récit généalogique*.[7] In examining Restif's own autobiography, *Monsieur Nicolas*, Peter Wagstaff has identified the presence of a Freudian family romance in Restif's ambivalence toward his father and his superiority to his surroundings.[8] As well, the obviously invented genealogy in *Monsieur Nicolas* which traces the author's ancestors back to emperors of ancient Rome exemplifies the Freudian neurotic's claim to noble origins as a confirmation of his own importance.[9] When Restif solicits the girls of the *Palais Royal* not for their sexual favors but for their stories, he is clearly interested in their *histoires* in the sense of personal and family histories. In story XIII he propositions Dorine in this way: "[V]oilà six francs: donnez-moi le seul plaisir que je suis capable de goûter avec vous: c'est à dire causons et racontez-moi votre histoire" (80). The stories told by the girls are not meant to be an exact substitution for a sexual act; Restif does not ask to hear a night in the life of a prostitute or even a particularly perverse highlight of her career; rather, he returns to his personal obsession with the past by asking the prostitute for the story of her origins.[10] This interest in origins is clearly stated in story IX, for when he first sees Cécilia he expresses his desire to discover her parentage: "Cette fille n'est pas née du sang grossier d'un homme et d'une femme obligés au travail" (57). In *Le Palais Royal*, Restif helps several of his heroines elaborate their own family romances by tracing the origins of the girls he meets to rich, important, or even noble parents. Filumène is the daughter of a bishop, Bouton de Rose of a rich man, Cécilia's father is a decorated police inspector and her mother a countess, Zaïre is the sister of "un homme très connu" (73), Adélaïde is the daughter of "un artiste célèbre" (76), Isabelle believes she is "fille [naturelle] du Duc de D** P**" (176), and Cunégonde is "reconnue pour sa fille naturelle par le prince de N***" (201). If, according to David Coward, Restif's writing in *Le Pornographe* removed some of the moral stigma from prostitution by attributing its causes to the overwhelming poverty of the majority of the French population,[11] his return in *Le Palais Royal* to the idea that many of the prostitutes he meets come from noble or at least socially and economically advantaged backgrounds moves the reader away from a focus on the general, social causes of prostitution and into a fantasy world where the abandoned girl dreams of aristocratic parents who will return to rescue her from the ignoble circumstances into which she has fallen.

In *Le Palais Royal*, the last two stories are the most exemplary of the Freudian family romance; in each, the heroine as a child feels that she is somehow born for better things and later as a young woman finds her happy ending through a reunion with the higher born parents of her childhood dreams. Although in story XXXI, the heroine's resemblance to the princess is striking while the appearance of the princess's daughter recalls that of a particular house servant, Rosière grows up thinking herself to be the daughter of the prince's Swiss guard. The story's protestations that the children have not been switched only cause the reader to suspect the truth, especially since Rosière possesses all of the physical and moral qualities of a princess while the young princess herself is both ugly and ill-tempered, as Rosière explains: "Frédérique-Eléonore de S* était fort laide, & un peu méchante. En jouant, elle me pinçait, me maltraitait, me disait que j'étais une fille de basse naissance [. . .] vile roturière, fille de domestiques" (181–82). Following the Freudian paradigm for the family romance, the seemingly lowborn girl can only wish that one day the royal couple will be revealed to be her own parents and that her special qualities will be recognized to the humiliation of her childhood tormentor. Similarly, in story XXXII, although Polhimnie was raised by peasants, she has every reason to suspect her own high birth, a fantasy that allows her to dream of an escape from past abuse and present degradation: "Vous savez que j'étais élevée à la campagne, sous le nom de fille de mon nourricier & ma nourrice: mais quoique ces gens m'appellassent leur fille, je m'apercevais qu'ils riaient toujours un peu en me donnant ce nom. Enfin, une nuit, je les entendis qui se disaient: —On a biau faire! Alle est toujou's d'moiselle! [. . .] Souvent aussi dans nos jeux, mes prétendus frères & soeurs, m'appellaient *petite bâtarde, Demoisillon*" (192). Restif, of course, recognizes in both of these stories the obvious indications of the girls' true identities and takes it upon himself to investigate Polhimnie's case in particular: "Nous lui demandâmes la permission de faire des informations sur ce qu'était devenue la méchante femme de chambre qu'elle croyait sa mère" (196). Fortunately, a well-informed *abbé* appears on the scene to reveal the girls' parentage, indicting the house servant for having replaced the baby princess with her own daughter by placing the true princess with peasants: "Voici la vraie Princesse; c'est Polhiminie, qu'elle mit secrètement à la campagne [. . .] & la prétendue Princesse, laide comme cette femme & comme le gros C—in son père, a été substituée au véritable sang des S* & des W***" (197). He also announces that when the firstborn child of the Swiss guard died, this same housekeeper had stolen the first baby princess and given her to the Swiss family, revealing Rosière to be a princess and Polhimnie's sister as well. The story ends in this family reunion complete with caresses and cries of joy, the two former prostitutes rescued by their rightful family from which circumstances have separated them. In this fairy-tale which concludes *Le Palais Royal*—this fulfillment of the fantasy of the family romance—Restif proposes a solution to prostitution that seems not only far from addressing reality but also far from "revolutionary" in the sense that the happy ending here features a return to a superior social status as the girls are made whole in their elevation from whore to princess.[12]

Family Reunions

Even when the prostitutes of the Palais Royal are not revealed to be princesses poised to reclaim their royal rank, Restif reflexively returns to each girl's past in his efforts to offer her a better future through a reunion with her family. In this, *Le Palais Royal* differs markedly from the plans for institutional change proffered in *Le Pornographe* and approaches the sort of individualized interventions seen in many episodes of *Les Nuits de Paris* where Restif rescues damsels in distress.[13] In the preface to *Le Palais Royal*, Restif may address government officials, urging them to create state solutions by writing: "Hommes publics! Nous vous dévoilons les abus: notre tâche est remplie; c'est à vous seuls qu'il appartient de les corriger" (8). Nevertheless, in many of the stories, Restif will not wait for state action but intercedes personally to return the wayward girl to her parents' protection.[14] In the story of Eléonore, Restif's efforts to reunite the prostitute and her parents end in the girl's punishment: "[N]ous la suivîmes et le même soir, nous avons mis ses parents à portée de la reprendre. Elle est au couvent" (101). In other cases, however, Restif's efforts achieve a happy return to virtue as in the story of Mélanie, where he reunites a kidnapped girl with her uncle:

> Elle nous parut fort triste! Nous lui en demandâmes la raison? Elle venait d'entrevoir son oncle. Ceci nous a donné l'idée de la servir. Nous avons averti M. Naya le dimanche 20; & le lundi 21, il avait retiré Mélanie du désordre. (37)

Another happy reunion results when Restif tells the story of Rosemonde at a dinner party and her mother recognizes the tale of her lost daughter; Restif immediately takes her to Rosemonde's room where her mother cries: Ma chère, ma pauvre fille! En quel état je te trouve!" (44) Rosemonde quits prostitution on the spot to return home with her mother and sister. In the case of Agnès, Restif is again active in rescuing the girl from prostitution by appealing directly to her estranged father and recalling him to his paternal responsibilities: "Nous nous sentions disposés à servir [. . .] Agnès [. . .] Aussi, dès le lendemain, nous allâmes chez le chanoine [son père . . . et] nous convînmes avec le chanoine de ce qu'il y avait à faire pour sa fille, qu'il a placée dans une maison honnête" (151). When he finds that Dorothée's libertine father is recently deceased, Restif is happy to work to recoup the girl's inheritance and reunite her with her brother. Similarly, at the end of the story of Corisandre, Restif locates the girl's estranged mother and reestablishes both family ties and legal claims to an inheritance from her mother's late husband:

> Nous avons découvert à Madame *** le sort de sa fille. Son mari est mort, dans ces entrefaites, & nous avons réclamé l'état légal de Corisandre, née à Paris d'une mère vivant sous le même toit que son époux. Les co-héritiers n'ont pas plaidé. (158)

Restif is again the advocate for these girls in their return to decent society via a reunion of the girl and her family.[15]

In other cases, Restif does not directly contact the family but imagines that his stories will be so successful that they will be read by a relative who will recognize and reclaim a lost daughter. This is stated at the end of the first story, where Restif expresses the hope that Filumène's married sister will read his account of her and potentially come to the prostitute's aid: "On dit qu'elle ignore le sort de sa soeur. Elle l'apprendra par cette historiette: car, vu la célébrité de notre nom, nous espérons qu'elle sera lue de tout le monde" (29). At the end of the next tale, Restif expresses an even greater confidence in the power of his writing to push the girl's parents to reclaim her: "Nous espérons que le père de Rosette, après avoir lu cette histoire, viendra au secours de son infortunée fille! . . . Sa mère au moins la réclamera" (33). When Cécilia expresses her desire to go to the courts to make her father support her and allow her to escape the Palais Royal, Restif urges that she await the publication of his story, persuading her to rely on the power of his published work to appeal to her parents and move them to help their estranged offspring. He concludes her story thus :

> Puisse la publication de cette histoire faire trembler Deremhi et le contraindre à rendre promptement ce qu'il doit à sa fille naturelle! Puisse la mère qui est plus riche encore, connaître par nous le sort de Cécilia! (62–63)

Similarly in the case of Cécile and Rosette, Restif's story calls upon the parents, whose names are disguised, urging them to help their daughters by threatening that he'll reveal their identities if they do not: "Si Ovide et Ninette ont de l'âme, ils viendront au secours de leurs filles [. . . Q]u'ils les sauvent et les adoptent; ou, quelque jour, nous les ferons rougir de leur indignité" (70) The story of Fayelle also contains a general appeal to family members that emphasizes the urgency of her need. She is the prey of brutes and faces "un effrayant avenir, à moins que quelqu'un de sa famille vienne à son secours"(52). Finally, when Jeanne expresses the desire to be saved from her less than honorable estate, declaring "Ha! Que j'aurais de la reconnaissance pour l'homme ou la femme qui me tirerait de ma triste situation" (147), Restif steps into his favored role as savior and finds her a maternal benefactress, coincidentally named Mme la Mère, certain that his writing has the power to found a new family and confident that he can convince Mme la Mère to become the adoptive mother of the disgraced Jeanne and her orphaned siblings: "Nous ne doutons pas que ce récit extraordinaire que nous allons lui faire lire sur l'épreuve ne l'intéresse, et qu'elle ne déploie sa bienfaisance sur Jeanne, sur ses soeurs et sur son frère" (147). Restif not only emphasizes his active agency in these personalized reformations of prostitutes but congratulates himself on the happy endings he has brought to his stories and their lives: "Telle et l'heureuse tournure que nous sommes parvenus à faire prendre aux choses, à force de soins & d'attentions" (153).[16] And he concludes this story with a statement that sums up his role as the savior of prostitutes through his involvement in their family affairs: "Que de bien ferait un homme puissant & bon, qui pénétrerait dans l'intérieur de toutes les familles!" (158–159). Without pushing for an overtly sexualized reading of the verb "pénétrer," it is clear here that Restif is advocating an intimate contact between the reformer and the prostitute, foregoing state-based solutions for prostitution and favoring individualized interventions.

Originary Perversion

Restif's best solution for prostitution, it would seem, would be to return the girl to her origins, to fulfill the fantasy of the family romance he has provided. However, while these stories often end with Restif's appeal to parents to reclaim their disgraced daughters and save them from further ignominy, the family is not always the preserve of sexual innocence but the scene of originary perversion.[17] Chouchou's mother is raised in a strict home from which strangers are barred, but she is seduced and impregnated by a visiting cousin under her parents' own roof (53). Although Cécile's father and mother seem to be excellent parents "remplis de la lecture de Jean-Jacques Rousseau," her father eventually succumbs to the charms of his daughter's nanny and proceeds to impregnate the young Rosette as Cécile's mother breastfeeds their baby in the same room. "Retirez-vous: votre présence troublerait mon lait," this philosophical mother admonishes the copulating couple (66). In the story of Eléonore, the young heroine initiates an accidental orgy in a darkened room of the family home where Eléonore is paired with her uncle, her mother with a stranger, and her aunt with her father. When the lights go on and the unintended couples discover their shame, Eléonore flees her family's censure by running off to become a prostitute in the Palais Royal. Restif concludes this very immoral tale with a moral lesson, warning parents not to leave young girls alone with male family members: "[O]n laisse prendre trop de familiarité avec des jeunes filles . . . par des beaux-frères, de beaux-oncles, des cousins mêmes [. . .] Oui nous connaissons trois filles publiques qui le sont devenues par leurs beaux-frères, maris de leurs soeurs [. . .]" (102). The family here is not the haven of virtue into which young girls who have strayed into vice may return but instead the very source of debauchery.

In this conjugation of family and sexuality, Restif is likely not just recording stories as recounted to him but reinventing them to satisfy his own often incestuous fantasies.[18] In tracing the origins of two exotic prostitutes, Restif reconnects with the prevalent European fantasies of incest as typical of African and South American societies. In the story of Zilia, whose name recalls the heroine of Mme de Graffigny's *Lettres d'une péruvienne* in which the heroine is set to marry her brother before Europeans invade their Incan idyll, the heroine's mother was betrothed to a cousin until she fell in love with a visiting Frenchman. The African Esther is a child of a polygamous family who is sold into slavery when her widowed mother refuses to marry her deceased husband's eldest son although this "frère aîné, par les lois du pays, a le droit de prendre ses belles-mères pour femmes" (124). Incestuous activities are not however limited to Restif's romanticized account of these exotic societies since incest is characteristic of the families of many of Restif's Parisian prostitutes. While Mélanie's mother was seduced and impregnated by a priest but then taken in by her brother, most visitors to Mélanie's home take her to be the child of an incestuous union between the brother and his sister. Agnès is the product of an incestuous relationship between another clergyman and his young niece, whom he first takes in her sleep and then rapes repeatedly despite her tears. When Agnès's mother dies, her father's housekeeper, a sort of evil step-mother sells young Agnès into prostitution and marries her handsome young brother. In the story of Jeanne, the girl admits that her parents were brother and sister and explains their incest as the cause of her current state as a sex worker: "Je suis fille d'un Boucher, & . . . de sa soeur. Ainsi, vous voyez que je ne pouvais être avouée dans la société; il fallait que je devinsse ce que je suis" (143). Corisandre is equally "honteuse d'exister à cause de son origine [. . .] Elle doit le jour à sa grand'mère" (155) since her mother abandoned an illegitimate son who later returns to rape her. Her step-father will sell her into prostitution to rid the family of this disgrace.

The family then is not the haven to which errant girls may return but rather the source of their perversion, and often parents themselves are the first to prostitute their daughters.[19] In the story of the four sisters, their mother's decision to prostitute her daughters is presented not as an inevitability but as a choice: abandoned by her husband, Mme Ogret has the talent to support herself by giving lessons but chooses instead sell her daughters' favors: "[E]lle quitta son enseignement [...] s'établir aux environs du Palais Royal" (104). Likewise, Rosette (mother of Bouton de Rose), Filumène, and Bienfaite are sold to rich men by their widowed mothers. While this paradigm could confirm the cause of prostitution as the parents' penury, here the stories of the child's sale into prostitution often insist not on the family's desperation but rather on their corruption. Aglaé is sold by her father to pay his gambling debts (38) as is Dorothée whose father sees her beauty as a source of income: "[S]on exécrable père [. . .] la trouva jolie; & et comme il avait tout dissipé il lui vint dans l'idée de se faire une ressource de sa fille" (140). Zaïre is sold by her journalist brother to his depraved friends, including the doctor who cures him of various venereal diseases (74). In Restif's stories, psychological motives rather than financial ones often determine parents' decisions to prostitute daughters. Although Adélaïde's mother is left with the debts of her recently deceased libertine husband, she prostitutes herself and her daughter not so much out of need but out of a desire for revenge against her faithless husband, declaring: "Adélaïde, il faut nous venger [. . .]. Tu ressembles à ton père, ton amant est un infâme . . . [E] lle voulut [l]'avilir pendant que son âme en serait témoin" (77–78). Baby Cécilia is abandoned by her policeman father into the arms of a woman he imprisons, and this adoptive mother avenges herself against him years later by selling the twelve-year old Cécilia to her own father: "Elle savait que l'exempt qui l'avait arrêtée était le plus libertin [. . .] des hommes: elle me para voluptueusement: et comme j'étais grande pour mon âge elle me fit trouver sous les yeux de cet homme, amateur des fruits verts et d'un goût dépravé. L'effet répondit à ses vues [. . .] et je lui fus livrée pour satisfaire des fantaisies atroces" (61). Rosemonde is the daughter of a doctor whose mistress is jealous of the girl's beauty and sells her virginity to a rich man in order to degrade her. The beautiful Sofie's favors are sold by her jealous stepmother for similar reasons. While the fairy-tale endings of some of the stories transform prostitutes into princesses reclaimed by their royal families, other stories begin with the fairy tale figure of the evil step-mother who persecutes the heroine or the cruel parent who abandons the child in the dark of night to the hungry wolves of the Palais Royal.

Brothel as Home

In stories that end with the prostitute returned to her family or those that begin with the family pushing the heroine into prostitution, Restif's narratives in *Le Palais Royal* demonstrate the interpenetration of the public sphere of the *fille publique* and the private sphere of family life. And just as he reveals the sexual nature of family relations, he also reveals the existence of family structures in the world of prostitution. In fact, the last sixteen prostitutes in Restif's thirty-two portraits are organized in family groups around a motherly madam so that the girls see each other as sisters. Dorothée, Jeanne, Agnès and Corisandre affectionately call the madam who manages them "Maman" (140–41) and describe her as a motherly figure. Gertrude, (171), Isabelle (176), Rosière (185), and Polhiminie (194) all call Madame Cunégonde "maman" and extol her maternal kindnesses, exclaiming: "Jugez comme nous la devons aimer!" (194). Explaining her relationship to her co-workers, Agnès also evokes familial feelings: "[N]ous nous aimons comme soeurs" (156). In the brothel run by another motherly madam, Mme Ogret, four real sisters are joined by the foreign-born prostitutes Esther and Zilia who are accepted not just into the business but welcomed into a family. Madame Ogret says of Zilia: "[M]es filles [. . .] l'ont aimée comme une soeur" (135); Esther expresses her gratitude to the family, explaining: "Vous m'avez traitée en soeur; votre mère m'en a servi" (127). The brothel is thus described by Restif as an oasis of maternal, filial, and sisterly affection. When a young merchant falls in love with one of the sisters, he brings his respectable mother to meet her, and this future mother-in-law's impression of the family transforms the whorehouse into the home of virtue: "Voilà une jolie famille! [. . .] C'est tout mérite dans cette heureuse maison" (113). Somehow Restif's description of prostitutes has rejoined his sentimental idealization of girls from good families, those "jeunes & touchantes beautés dont les attraits naissants ont encore le charme inexprimable de l'innocence" to whom he has dedicated his first published work, *La Famille vertueuse*.[20]

In *Le Palais Royal*, Restif does not address prostitution as a public concern in need of state-sponsored solutions but instead imagines that the problem may be resolved on a small scale by domesticating sexual desire, incorporating it into family life by means of marriage. Instead of the Parthenions of *Le Pornographe*—large-scale structures for keeping prostitution outside of the city—the brothel is transformed into a bourgeois home where whore becomes wife. In a recent article on *Le Pornographe*, James Steintrager examines the often ignored frame narrative which contains Restif's reforming project—an epistolary novel which ends with a reformed libertine marrying a virgin—in order to argue that Restif's proposition for state-sponsored reform of prostitution is to a certain extent subverted by the novel's sentimental storyline: "This intensification of intimacy can be thought of as the counterpart to the policing power of the state apparatus." However, Steintrager continues by explaining that "Rétif did not explicitly propose family intimacy as a functional solution to the shifting organization of society,"[21] since the central conceit of *Le Pornographe* offers an institutional solution to prostitution. Restif's reconsideration of the plight of prostitutes in *Le Palais Royal* moves sentimental ideas about marital love expressed in the margins of the *Le Pornographe* into the center of this later text by advancing the return to family life as the remedy for prostitution, pushing girls from the public space of the Palais Royal's arcades into the domestic enclosure of the family home.[22] A model for making a house of ill repute into a proper family home is manifested in the architecture of Mme Ogret's brothel, with its "porte dérobée" for the entry of clients interested in prostitution and its "porte honnête" for the entry of bourgeois visitors. When one of the Ogret daughters is seen at the theater by a young man, he follows her home through the "porte honnête et bourgeoise" (111) indicating his honorable intentions. In the end, each of Mme Ogret's daughters is married out of prostitution and into bourgeois life:

> Angélique est dévote avec sa belle-mère, dont elle est chérie et qui la vante à tout le monde, comme un modèle . . . & sa manière de se mettre est si différente de ce qu'elle était au Palais-royal, que personne ne peut la reconnaître à Paris. Adèle est dans le pays étranger [avec son mari allemand]. Sofie est montée dans la magistrature [avec son mari magistrat]. Pour Zéfire, idole de

> son mari, elle le suit dans les garnisons, & lui est scrupuleusement fidèle. (122)

According to this new model, clients come in and husbands come out, transforming harlots into homemakers

While Restif calls for state-sponsored solutions until the last paragraph of the volume—"Puissions nous en peignant les désordres qui existent, engager les augustes Législateurs nationaux, à exécuter un plan de réforme" (201)—he continues until the end to rely on individualized solutions for rescuing the prostitutes of the Palais Royal, the most personal initiative being his own marriage to Gertrude. When he meets this girl, whose favors are offered to him by a madam, she has been made up to look like a young cousin he had been forbidden to marry years before: at the heart of Parisian debauchery, Restif experiences a return to the innocence of young love. Although Gertrude lives in a brothel among prostitutes, she inspires not lust but love; she is "le touchant objet de notre premier amour" (171) whose virginity offers him the privilege of entering "dans le temple du bonheur" (172) resulting in a "tendre attachement" (190) for the "adorable Gertrude" (189) so that "notre cousine [. . . est] devenue notre épouse" (200). Restif here seems to be reenacting the frame narrative of *Le Pornographe*, reforming his own libertine tendencies through a return to sentiment, rescuing a lost girl by reuniting her with her family and saving a virgin from a life of vice with the offer of marriage.[23]

Refusing Domesticity

If a new ideology of intimacy is an implicit solution for prostitution in *Le Pornographe* and an explicit one in *Le Palais Royal*, the later text also admits a limit on the possibility of domesticating sexuality. Interestingly, the limit is not that of the unchecked desire of men but rather on the refusal of some women to accept Restif's offer to facilitate their return to family life. When Dorine sees her sister married and pregnant, she decides to become a prostitute to escape the fate of bourgeois family life: "Son mariage ne me donna pas envie de suivre son exemple: toujours grosse, toujours faisant des enfants. Je m'informai à une femme qui me servait s'il y avait un moyen d'avoir un amant sans devenir mère" (81). And so Dorine, armed with the knowledge of contraception decides to become in her own words not a *mère de famille* but "une femme de plaisir" (80). The young Coquine, ignorant of methods for preventing pregnancy, is horrified to find herself with child and despairs: "grosse à mon âge . . . non, non, je ne veux pas l'être" (86). She delivers her baby in secret and tosses it into the latrines in order to continue a life of pleasure; when the baby's father saves it and six months later presents their daughter to Coquine, she stabs the child through the heart with a hairpin and runs off to Paris to hide among the prostitutes of the Palais Royal. Elise is a woman who has rejected family life, having read Ninon de Lenclos and Madame Geoffroy, she would rather be surrounded by multiple men than be married to one: "Elise se trouvant sa maîtresse, déstestant le mariage, un seul mari, des enfants, etc. crut voir le bonheur dans la condition de son aieule [. . .] Là voilà catin" (92). Although childless, Elise buys children from the poor families of the neighborhood, dragging them with her on her nightly walks to give her clients the air of being properly *en famille*; these children, however, are walked until they drop dead, so that Elise's seemingly maternal gesture is also a murderous one. In the world of prostitution that Restif describes, maternity is most often perverted, even in the professional terminology whereby young prostitutes are managed by women called *matrulles*, a deformation of the word matron that implies a deformation of the maternal figure. In fact, many of the girls he meets have one goal: escaping from the domination of this bad mother to live independently. The stories of Bouton de Rose, Aglaé, Chouchou and others end with the explanation that "elle s'est mise à elle." While Restif is worried about the vulnerability of the prostitute alone in the world without her family, several of the prostitutes explain that it is in their best interest to escape the exploitation of the controlling *matrulle* but also the patriarchal structures that Restif would like to re-impose upon them, preferring professional autonomy in the Palais Royal.[24]

Restif and Revolution

Restif's writing is often considered a sort of proto-realism, a document of his day from the point of view of the man on the street. In *Le Palais Royal*, however, Restif is less concerned with representing the everyday struggles of prostitutes than with fantasizing about their past and determining their future. The idea that Restif gives voice to the otherwise underrepresented under-classes of Old Regime France is also problematic when applied to *Le Palais Royal* since while his heroines seem to speak, their discourse is a sort of ventriloquism by which Restif gives expression to his own obsessive fantasies. Finally, while Restif has been described as a socially progressive reformer on the side of the Revolution, his socio-political stance in this text seems remarkably reactionary. While Lynn Hunt explains the Revolution's family romance as a rejection of disappointing parents in favor of a new society founded on fraternity,[25] Restif questions the family only to reaffirm its patriarchal order either by proposing a return of each girl to her family of origin or by encouraging her to found a new family through marriage. In this way, prostitutes are reintegrated into society not through institutional change that would regularize their profession but through a return from public life to the private sphere of the family. In cases where parents are not available to rescue their estranged offspring, Restif calls upon rich benefactors to adopt these lost girls, relying on aristocratic patrons to rectify social problems instead of looking to the Revolutionary government. While in the preface to volume two he condemns "une aristocratie corruptrice" (II,7) for the problems of society, he shows a real nostalgia for the rule of the Royal Family when he recounts their arrival in Paris on October 6, 1789, noting: "Nous avions senti couler nos larmes, en comtemplant le petit Dauphin saluer les Français" (71). While he is touched by the hardships of the Royals, he is also frightened by the violence of the Revolutionary mob a few nights prior "[C]ette soirée-là les Filles du Palais Royal étaient le jouet de la jeunesse indisciplinée qui les entourait, les troussait, et les fouettait" (14). In his epilogue to volume 1, Restif attributes the corruption of the Palais Royal to the degeneracy of the Old Regime and explains his work as a justification for Revolutionary change: "A notre manière, nous montrons combien [la Révolution] était nécessaire" (202). In the preface to the second volume when he tries to envision how the Revolution will remedy prostitution, he cannot—despite his own earlier projects—imagine any real institutional change but only a sort of mystical elevation of souls by which all citizens of the Republic will return to virtue: "Nous posons en fait que si notre admirable Révolution se consolide [. . .] elle élevera tellement l'âme que dans dix ans, on ne trouvera plus de filles publiques" (II:7–8). In *Le Palais Royal*, Restif does not offer revolutionary solutions for prostitution but instead proposes a retreat from the turmoil of the Revolution, admitting: "[T]out en attaquant les abus [nous avons entrepris] de présenter quelquefois l'attrait du plaisir" (7). In the end it would seem Restif is not so much trying to save these girls but to save their stories, so that in the face of a new future, this visionary turns nostalgic in order to preserve memories of pleasures that are soon to be relegated to the pre-revolutionary past.[26]

NOTES

1. Nicolas-Edme Restif de la Bretonne, *Le Pornographe ou idées d'un honnête homme sur un projet de règlement pour les prostituées propre à prévenir les malheurs qu'occasionne le publicisme des femmes* (Londres [i.e. Paris?] : chez Jean Nourse, 1769).

2. David Coward, "Restif de la Bretonne and the Reform of Prostitution," *Studies on Voltaire and the Eighteenth Century* 176 (1979): 357-8.

3. Restif de la Bretonne, *Le Palais Royal* (Londres [i.e.Paris?], 1792). Subsequent references to this work will be cited in parentheses within the text.

4. In reference to Restif's *Nuits révolutionnaires,* Wagstaff notes: "[I]n the background, the history of France is being made, while in the foreground the history of Rétif takes pride of place" (*Memory and Desire: Rétif de la Bretonne, Autobiography and Utopia* [Amsterdam: Rodopi, 1996],10). In reference to another of Restif's works from the Revolutionary period, Wagstaff remarks: "The emotional narcissism and incestuous undertones that characterise later works such as *La Dernière aventure d'un homme de quarante-cinq ans* betrays a reluctance to come to terms with a reality which is inevitably temporal, changing, and uncertain"(14).

5. Lynn Hunt, *The Family Romance of the French Revolution* (Berkeley: University of California Press, 1992), xiii.

6. Marthe Robert, *Roman des origines et origines du roman* (Paris: Grasset, 1972).

7. Jan Herman, *Le Récit génétique au XVIIIe siècle* (Oxford: SVEC, 2009).

8. Peter Wagstaff, "The Childhood of Monsieur Nicolas: Rétif de la Bretonne and the 'Family Romance," *British Journal for Eighteenth-Century Studies* 9, no. 1 (1986): 61–71.

9. Restif de la Bretonne, "Ma Généalogie" in *Monsieur Nicolas* (Paris: Gallimard, 1989), 6–14.

10. The stories of the girls of the Palais Royal differ in this respect from the whore's confession as defined by Kathryn Norberg in which "the heroine briefly describes her parents and her adolescence before launching into the real substance of her [story: . . . a] series of sexual encounters" ("The Libertine Whore: Prostitution in French Pornography from Margot to Juliette" in *The Invention of Pornography,* ed. Lynn Hunt [New York: Zone Books, 1996], 229–30). In the introduction to his edition of *Le Palais Royal* (Paris: Manucius, 2009), Pierre Testud confirms that "[c]e qui suscite la curiosité du narrateur envers les trente-deux filles de l'Allée des Soupirs, c'est leur passé, et non leur présent" (23).

11. Coward: 358–59.

12. Restif nevertheless addresses the political incorrectness of these two tales which show the noble girls as virtuous heroines deserving of admiration while the daughter of servants is reviled as the villainess, declaring: "Loin de nous l'idée de prêter de l'élévation aux sentiments à raison de la naissance ! mais la fausse Frédérique-Eléonore, étant née d'une méchante femme & d'un C—in [. . .] elle avait & les vices de sa conception, effet du libertinage, & ceux du caractère de ses parents [. . .] Nous voilà suffisamment justifié du préjugé frivole de la naissance" (199).

13. Restif de la Bretonne, *Les Nuits de Paris (*Londres, 1788 [–1789]).

14. This reunion of the prostitute with her family is antithetical to the reforms proposed in the earlier *Pornographe*, which prohibits contact between the prostitute and her family: "Les jeunes filles [. . .] devront être recues sans informations sur leur famille[. . .] il sera expressément defendu par les Administrateurs aux Gouvernantes de s'en instruire, & aux filles de le confier meme à leurs compagnes"

(116). Moreover, according to *Le Pornographe*, parents will be prevented from rescuing their prostituted daughters: "[L]es parents ne pourront en retirer leur fille malgré elle: ils ne pourront même lui parler, si elle le refuse [. . .] on les fera sortir dès qu'elle les aura reconnus" (117).

15. This proposed reintegration of the prostitute into social and familial life differs markedly from that of *Le Pornographe* in which prostitutes are considered marked by "une tache ineffaçable" (133) and are prevented from rejoining society in the Pathenions from which "une fois entrées elle ne devaient jamais sortir" (236).

16. In a footnote to his story, Restif applauds the Revolution for eradicating one of the root causes of sexual perversity in French society by eliminating the celibacy of priests and thus making impossible the repetition of the story of Agnès's father the chanoine, who was only driven to sire illegitimate children because he was unable to channel his sexual appetites into the licit channels of bourgeois family life: "Sans le célibat, imposé trop indifféremment à tous les Ecclesiastiques, l'infortuné Chanoine aurait-il mené une vie coupable toujours pressée entre le crime & la peine?. . . Ha! Concitoyens! La Motion de l'Abbé Cournand est un chef d'oeuvre de la raison, & les sots, les Aristocrates, peuvent seuls la condamner ou s'en mettre en colère!" (153).

17. This oscillation between positive and negative representations of the family illustrates what Pamela Cheek has called "one of Restif's signature moves [. . . that is :] he will not let purity, or indeed value, stay reliably in one place" ("The Festival of Incest in *Le Paysan perverti*," *Symposium* 60, no. 3 [Fall 2006]: 135).

18. In her analysis of incest in *Le Paysan parvenu*, Cheek acknowledges Pierre Testud's detailed documentation of Restif's incestuous relationship with his own daughters (in *Rétif de la Bretonne et la création littéraire* [Geneva: Droz, 1977]) before exploring the elaboration of an "eroticized 'family'" in Restif's fictional work (Cheek, 141).

19. Whereas in *Le Pornographe* parents of prostitutes are described as "honnêtes mais inattentifs [. . .] les dupes de la confiance qu'ils ont en leurs enfants" (84), in *Le Palais Royal*, the family has a much more important role to play as the cure for prostitution but also as its cause.

20. Restif de la Bretonne, *La Famille vertueuse* (Paris: Duchesne, 1767), v.

21. James Steintrager, "What Happened to the Porn in Pornography? Rétif, Regulating Prostitution, and the History of Dirty Books" *Symposium* 60, no. 3 (Fall 2006): 196.

22. According to Bradford Mudge, Daniel Defoe's anti-prostitution tract presents prostitution as a threat to the institution of marriage and thus to the population of a prosperous nation, opposing illegitimate and legitimate sexual practice (*The Whore's Story: Women, Pornography, and the British Novel 1684–1830* [Oxford: Oxford University Press, 2000], 54), Restif's thoughts on prostitution mitigate this opposition since in *Le Pornographe* prostitution can contribute to the state when illegitimate offspring are trained to be productive members of society while in *Le Palais Royal* the pleasures of prostitution are integrated into domestic life with the rehabilitation of prostitutes through marriage to their clients.

23. *Le Pornographe* clearly has as its object the protection of men from the

threat of prostitution, since "l'honnête homme séduit paie de sa santé" (92). In *Le Palais Royal*, it is no longer the male client but the girl prostitute herself whom the reformer strives to save.

24. Although Kathryn Norberg has argued that "[f]or Restif de la Bretonne and many authors thereafter the prostitute is fundamentally good [. . .] a hapless victim, an impoverished working class child who is dominated and abused" (228), some of the prostitutes of *Le Palais Royal* are actually rather bad: closer to Norberg's "libertine whore" than her "virtuous courtesan," they refuse the role of victim and Restif's offers of assistance to pursue their profession and the measure of independence it affords. While *Le Palais Royal* is informed by a Rousseaustic ideal of femininity which orients Restif's ultimate aim to relegate prostitutes back to the private sphere of family life, the fact that some prostitutes reject rescue, preferring to remain in the public sphere as *filles publiques,* demonstrates a certain resistance to new notions of womanhood.

25. Hunt, xiv. Paradoxically, it is not the 1789 *Palais Royal* but the 1769 *Pornographe* which reforms prostitution in a way that reaffirms the value of fraternity, since under the proposed system of the Parthenions, the children of prostitutes become wards of the state, loyal not to a private family but to the public good: "ils n'ont pas de parents, ni de liaisons, leur père c'est l'Etat" (*Le Pornographe,* 227).

26. *Le Palais Royal* may not in the end even be of the same genre as *Le Pornographe*, a utopian project calling for reform, but instead closer to *Les Contemporaines*, stories meant to convey Restif's Parisian present. Moreover, in *Le Palais Royal*, Restif returns to the impulses that inspire his *Inscripcions*, a diary based on his inscriptions on the stone walls of the île Saint-Louis, an expression of his desire to preserve the past in view of an uncertain future. My reading thus confirms the conclusion of Pierre Testud's introductory essay of his edition of *Le Palais Royal* where he writes: "Dans le fracas d'un monde qui s'écroule, l'écrivain doit encore jouer sa partie, *converser* pour *conserver*" (30).

Lazzaro Spallanzani's Hybrid Ruins: A Scientist at Serapis and Troy

SABRINA FERRI

The Hybridity of Ruins

Ruins are fundamentally hybrid things. Architectonic objects originally defined by human intentionality, but disfigured and deprived of their function by time and the elements, they are mixtures of nature and culture.[1] The definition of ruins as hybrids is not entirely new. In a well-known 1911 essay, "The Ruin," Georg Simmel presented the ruin as a product of the action of nature on the works of man. He described the precarious balance of ruins between human intentionality and nature's downward force as a return to the earth: "the ruin," he wrote, "orders itself into the surrounding landscape without a break, growing together with it like tree and stone."[2] Simmel's reflection hinted at the ruin as a hybrid; his definition, however, presented it as an unstable form, subject to two opposing forces— man and nature— but actually defined by neither. The ruin was read as a metamorphic object, in a state of becoming suspended between form of art and form of nature, between the past and the present. Ultimately, Simmel dissolved the complexity of the hybrid by recognizing that the tensions deriving from the contrasting elements that make up the ruin—human will, nature, past, and present—contribute to a "unity of external image and internal effect."[3]

From another perspective, but in a way that similarly weakens the epistemological potential of the hybrid, art historian Paul Zucker also described ruins as "aesthetic hybrids." In a 1966 article, Zucker identified three categories that could be applied to ruins and that defined the way in which they could be understood: 1) the ruin as a vehicle to evoke a "romanticizing mood;" 2) the ruin as a document of past architectonic practice or style; 3) and, finally, the ruin as a model or source of inspiration for new constructions.[4] These possible roles that the ruin can play are not mutually exclusive and, in fact, they often overlap and depend on one another. Thus, according to Zucker's interpretation, the ruin is an impure architectonic object defined by the combination of its possible functions. The latter, however, are all defined in terms of "aesthetic attitudes"[5]: whether the ruin functions as an archive of tradition, as a proleptic image of future construction, or both, its hybrid nature remains confined within the field of artistic expression, while the many other possible ways of reading its mixed form fade into the background. Neither the interpretation of Simmel nor that of Zucker succeeds fully at recognizing the complexity of the hybrid network that makes up a ruin's essence.

The idea of the ruin as a hybrid, in fact, is conceptually enticing precisely because it raises the issue of the ontological status of the hybrid considered in its most basic form, that of a mixture of nature and culture. Hybrids, as Bruno Latour points out in *We Have Never Been Modern*, challenge our belief systems and simplified apprehension of reality because they defy any clear-cut attempt at categorization: "Where are we to put these hybrids? Are they human? Human because they are our work. Are they natural? Natural because they are not our doing."[6] For Latour the question of the hybrid, of its status and significance, is at the heart of the critical self-reflection of modernity. The hybrid, which for Latour is not necessarily an object or an individual organism but is produced by the intersection of networks that human and non-human entities share, represents the irreducible entanglement of culture and nature. The critical stance of modernity is characterized by a relentless attempt at reducing this entanglement to a straightforward dualism, or, as Latour puts it, at "purifying" the hybrid by creating "two entirely distinct ontological zones: that of human beings on the one hand; that of non-human on the other."[7] In the process of purification, the scientist—whether social, political, or natural—plays a key role in separating the worlds of nature and culture, because in the act of critique, or analysis, he/she isolates the object of study from the complex environment that defines its identity and boxes it into carefully separated disciplinary domains.[8]

From this point of view, the approach to the study of monumental ruins of Lazzaro Spallanzani (1729–1799)—an eighteenth-century naturalist who is nowadays considered one of the fathers of modern biology[9] —is especially interesting precisely because it illustrates both the question of the hybrid and the implicit link between purification and modern science. Ruins are recurrent objects of discourse and description during the eighteenth and early nineteenth centuries—suffice it to think of Giovanni Battista Piranesi's (1720–1778) etchings of Roman antiquities, in which ancient buildings and monuments rise in decrepit elegance, subdued by nature, but somehow made more beautiful—of a terrible and awe-inspiring beauty—by their organic transformation.[10] In the eyes of Spallanzani, as of many eighteenth-century artists and writers, the sublime, unsettling power of ruins as images of decay lies in the coming together of nature and culture under the same predicament of finitude. Ruins stir the imagination by evoking the sense of an ending: In a metaphorical shift from the historical to the biological, the dissolution of a civilization—embodied by decaying buildings—comes to prefigure the end of human life.

Even if Spallanzani, as we shall see, recognized the stirring power of this aesthetics of decay, his perspective on ruins was eminently scientific. He applied to ruins the same analytical method that he used to study natural phenomena and organisms. His scientific observations on ruins indicate an idea of the hybrid that cannot be reduced to a simple convergence of aesthetic categories or to an object in transition from the artificial to the natural. Unlike Zucker's hybrid ruins, Spallanzani's ruins are not defined merely by their aesthetic functions, nor, like Simmel's, are they transitional objects that escape any categorization. The ruins that are the object of Spallanzani's attention are hybrids in so far as they are initially apprehended as ontological units in which the natural and the artificial, the organic and the inorganic, apparently coexist without ever being mutually exclusive, and without ever displacing one another. What we might call the "natural component" of ruins enables Spallanzani to study them as natural organisms; under the scrutiny of the scientific method, however, the ruin—a natural and cultural hybrid—is purified and paradoxically incorporated exclusively into nature. Seeming to follow Latour's narrative of disciplinary compartmentalization and purification, Spallanzani transforms what are works of man—albeit caught in a process of organic transformation—into things of nature that, precisely because they are momentarily abstracted from their cultural context, can become objects of scientific knowledge. The entanglement of nature and culture, however, is not easy to extricate and, at the dawn of modernity, Spallanzani's example shows not only the extent to which each thing is embedded in a network of cultural significance, material forces, scientific and social practices, but also the tensions and convergences between different disciplinary methods that eventually lead to the emergence of new objects of knowledge.[11]

Disciplining Ruins

A naturalist, an experimental scientist, and a tireless traveler, Spallanzani can be considered the prototype of the modern scientist: "the foremost naturalist in Europe," as Voltaire put it.[12] He was one of the main exponents of an approach to natural philosophy grounded in direct experimentation that would eventually redefine the natural world as a field of scientific enquiry rather than of mere philosophical conjecture. Spallanzani conducted research on animal regeneration, digestion, blood circulation, and respiration, but he is most often remembered for his contributions to the study of reproduction and artificial insemination and for how, with his experiments, he disproved the theory of spontaneous generation—that is, the idea that organic life could spontaneously generate from inanimate matter.[13]

Driven by a relentless scientific curiosity, Spallanzani worked within the framework of the scientific method, basing his studies on first-hand observation and direct experimentation. He traveled extensively to observe and study *directly* natural phenomena and to collect scientific specimens that would eventually become part of the collection of the Museum of Natural History in Pavia, one of the first modern scientific museums.[14] That the main purpose of Spallanzani's travels was scientific is attested by his detailed travelogues, in which he meticulously recorded his scientific observations on fields of enquiry as diverse as zoology, botany, mineralogy, and meteorology.[15] Although his primary concerns were the biology and geology of the places he visited, Spallanzani's annotations about topics such as languages and customs, social and material culture, ancient objects and remains of past civilizations, reveal his wider interests in human history and antiquarianism.[16] In this respect, Spallanzani's interest in archaeological ruins is one of the instances in which his naturalistic and antiquarian interests converge.

By merging the methods of the natural sciences and antiquarianism, Spallanzani applied his knowledge of biological processes and organisms to the study of architectonic ruins, both in order to shed light on natural phenomena and to ascertain the chronology of the monuments themselves. He approached monumental ruins as material documents of the past that were just as much *artificial* things, attesting to the vicissitudes of human history, as they were *natural* things, testifying to the transformations of the natural world. In fact, the idea of the ruin as a hybrid that defies ordinary ontological classification emerges from the convergence of the methods of the natural sciences and antiquarianism that, during the course of the eighteenth century, redefined the historical method as an empirical approach to concrete materials.

Eighteenth-century antiquarians, with their attention to a panoply of different things—both organic and inorganic—and with their philological method of description and analysis, paved the way for an approach to the study of history based on the interpretation of material sources.[17] Similarly, natural scientists relied on material evidence such as biological samples, fossils, minerals, and terrain strata to investigate the nature and modifications of the organisms and phenomena they studied. Eventually, antiquarianism and the natural sciences would converge to provide innovative tools and methods for the interpretation of history and the material past, leading to the invention of archaeology in the early nineteenth century.[18] Between the mid- to late-eighteenth century, however, a clear shift of historical perspective and method had already taken place. The new historical approach took as a point of departure the material objects of the past, both natural formations and artifacts of human construction. One of the crucial modifications was the way in which eighteenth-century scholars, of both the humanities and the sciences, came to view both works of nature and especially man-made objects as temporal crystallizations—as temporal objects that contained a story. The different attitude towards the past had to do with the slow acquisition of a new temporal sensibility, and with the idea that material objects carry within them the visible signs of change and decay and are in fact essentially "historical."[19]

The hybridity of the ruin, thus, is linked to the historicization of the objects of scientific enquiry—that is, the idea that anything, from an animal specimen to a coin, had a temporal depth, or rather that things contained several time-layers that could elucidate the past development of natural and historical events.[20] Eighteenth-century natural scientists and antiquarians shared methods and approaches to their objects of study and even the same vocabulary of ruination. French naturalist Georges Cuvier (1769–1832), for example, equated naturalists and antiquarians in their common endeavor to reconstruct the history of the past through ruins and fragments, since

> it will be necessary for physicists to do for the history of nature what antiquarians do for the history of the techniques and customs of peoples; the former will have to go and search among the ruins of the globe for the remains of organisms that lived at its surface, just as the latter dig in the ruins of cities in order to unearth the monuments of the taste, the genius, and the customs of the men who lived there. These antiquities of nature, if they may be so termed, will provide the physical history of the globe with monuments as useful and reliable as ordinary antiquities provide for the political and moral history of nations.[21]

Cuvier intentionally applied the vocabulary of antiquarianism to the field of natural sciences. His comment suggested that both "the ruins of the globe" and "the ruins of cities" shared the same status as fragmentary evidence of past events and could consequently perform the same function as historical archives. The system of metaphors used by Cuvier implied a transfer of methods from the field of antiquarianism to that of natural science: Naturalists, or more precisely proto-geologists, should approach the study of nature in the same way as antiquarians, by excavating ancient towns and studying their artifacts, reconstructed the events and monuments of past civilizations. By adopting a deductive antiquarian method, based on the use of concrete evidence, the former would be able to examine nature and its transformations according to rigorous temporal paradigms and produce an actual "history" of natural events, an empirical narrative of the changes that the natural world had undergone over time.[22]

Spallanzani's observations on ruins, as I will show in the following pages, indicate a transfer of methods that goes in the opposite direction: he adopted scientific techniques to study ancient monuments and transposed concepts and procedures from the field of biology and botany to that of human history, anticipating the methods of modern archaeology. The methodological transposition is made possible by the very essence of ruins, which the scientist describes as a compenetration of nature and artifice, but is also based on a process of purification. In the moment when he analyzes the ruin as natural evidence, Spallanzani disentangles it from the human context in which it came to be and to which, to a certain extent, it still belongs. His readings of ancient ruins, as we shall see, suggest that the status of material remains depends on whether the attention of the observer is fixed on the natural or on the cultural component, and more precisely on whether the narrative that is being constructed concerns human society or natural history.[23] The temporal valence of the ruin, however, opens the possibility of overcoming the separation between the two contexts or perspectives by establishing new connections between them. The material remains of the past tell a story in which humanity and nature are inextricably intertwined.

Networking Ruins: Between Natural History and Human History

A few examples from Spallanzani's travel observations will help illustrate the essence of his approach to ruins and the tensions deriving from the challenge posed by the hybrid. In particular, I will focus on his visits to two important archaeological sites that became the object of careful scientific observations recorded in his travel journals, the six-volume *Viaggi alle*

Due Sicilie e in alcune parti dell'Appennino (1792–1797)[24] and *Viaggio a Costantinopoli*, an unedited collection of notes, journal entries, and letters.[25] In 1788, Spallanzani traveled across the Kingdom of the Two Sicilies with the main objective of studying the seismic and volcanic activities that had affected the area for centuries.[26] Along the coast of Campania, in Pozzuoli, he visited the site of the ancient *macellum*, or marketplace, of the city, which was then believed to be a temple dedicated to Egyptian god Serapis—a site of crucial importance, as we shall see, both in the history of archaeology and in the development of geological research.[27] A few years earlier, in 1785, Spallanzani had embarked on a one-year journey that led him from Venice to Pula, Corfu, Cythera, and finally to Constantinople. In Asia Minor, he visited the area of Alexandria Troas, which, following a brief reference in Vergil's *Aeneid*, many believed to be the site of the Homeric city of Troy.[28] Both the Troad and the so-called "Temple" of Serapis have a rich cultural history in which advancements in scientific research and historical knowledge intersect. The two sites are places of disciplinary convergence and exchange, where local past and physical geography bring together different fields of knowledge and enquiry—history, literature, geology, architecture, and art history—in unexpected and yet fruitful configurations.

The first example that I would like to consider is that of the Temple of Serapis, whose hybrid form, as we shall see, generates different interpretations, or narratives, depending on the interpreter's point of view and on the intersection of natural and cultural elements. The pages of Spallanzani's Sicilian travelogue dedicated to the Temple clearly show how his scientific reading of the ruin simplifies the hybrid and "constructs" it as an object of naturalistic enquiry: the monumental remains are apprehended under the category of nature. Since its excavation in the 1750s, the supposed temple had attracted numerous visitors among naturalists and antiquarians, including scholars such as William Hamilton and John Soane: It was a stop that Spallanzani could not miss during his journey. The ruins of the Temple stood in the Phlegraean Fields, an area surrounding the city of Pozzuoli that was well known for its geological features but that was also rich in ancient sites and monuments; the recently excavated Herculaneum and Pompeii were not too distant. As the news of the discovery spread, and more and more travelers reached the area, the Temple revealed a number of enigmatic features and soon became what one of the first visitors, British architect Joseph Woods, aptly—and with remarkable foresight—described as "a standing puzzle for antiquaries and naturalists."[29] And indeed, the Temple represented an enigma for the scholars of both antiquity and the natural world. From an architectonic point of view, while the building was easily recognizable as a Roman construction, its overall features appeared to be unique and eluded any known architectural style or classification.[30] Moreover, a statue of Serapis, which was found on the site during the excavations, convinced scholars that the structure had been a temple dedicated to the Egyptian deity—a *serapeum*. Another interesting feature of the monumental remains pertained to the field of the natural sciences: the three columns of the Temple that were still standing exhibited two large dark bands, on their lower mid section, which appeared to have been formed by marine mollusks that had perforated the surface and eaten their way through the marble. This seemed to suggest that the sea level of the area had been subject to dramatic changes since antiquity. The ancient ruins bore on themselves traces of physical changes that had profoundly affected the morphology of the area. Architecture and Nature, human will and natural forces had come together in a single location to offer unique evidence of the close link between the history of nature and the history of man.

During the first part of his "vulcanico viaggio," or "volcanic journey," to Southern Italy, Spallanzani spent a month in Naples, from where, accompanied by Scipione Breislak (1750–1826), one of the pioneers of volcanology, he visited Pompeii, Herculaneum, and the area of the Phlegraean Fields. Breislak, a professor of physics at the "Nunziatella" Military Academy and director of a sulfur refinery at the Solfatara crater, had provided one the most complete accounts of the natural phenomena connected to the Temple.[31] Like many others before him, he had tried to advance an explanation for the traces of erosion on the columns and, given Spallanzani's fame as a scientist, he was eager to have his opinion on the matter.

In his journal, Spallanzani recounts how he and Breislak reached the Temple after surveying the area of the Solfatara. Before describing in detail the architectonic remains, he notices: "If this building can interest the lover of the mimetic arts because of its architecture, at the same time, it never ceases to feed the naturalist's curiosity."[32] This introduction alerts readers to the double nature of the object under examination: the three columns that are the standing remains of the Temple are identified as belonging both to the category of art—because of their intrinsic aesthetic value as architectonic remains—and to that of nature, because they fall within the realm of naturalistic enquiry. The paragraph that follows, however, opens with a description of the material composition of the ruins, noting that they are made of cipollino marble, a limestone sediment found at the bottom of the sea that slowly metamorphosed into marble over thousands of years. Spallanzani immediately delimits his field of research and shows that his primary concern resides with natural history, and more precisely, as we shall see, with specific aspects of geology and lithology. He focuses his attention on the eroded rings that surround the columns:

> Only at the height of approximately nine feet from the ground, each column begins to be worn away on the surface, and the wear proceeds upward and around the circumference of the column it forms a rough horizontal band; it is uneven, and more than two feet high, whereas the rest of the marble is smooth and clean. This band is pocked all over by a kind of rock-piercing clam: and some of the holes contain even now their shells, either whole or broken.[33]

While Spallanzani correctly explained the erosion as having been caused by mollusks—or what he calls "little marine animals"[34]—that had drilled holes into the marble, he did not understand that the perforations were the result of the raising of the sea level caused by a periodical surging and/or recession of the ground surface, a phenomenon now known as bradyseism.[35]

On the basis of the presence of marine organisms on the columns, however, he hypothesized that the marble of which the columns were made must have been submerged beneath water for a certain period of time:

> Perhaps someone will object that it seems strange that those columns, though they stood straight up, had been soaked at length by marine waters on that band, and not in the parts below it. But isn't it possible that before ending up in that building, they had been buried at the bottom of the sea, so that only that band, covered with marine shells, touched the water? And even if others do not find this hypothesis sufficient, and do not find another more satisfying, I will return to the evidence, unconcerned that I cannot explain it.[36]

Spallanzani was not too distant from the solution of the mystery. A few years later, in 1830, British geologist Charles Lyell (1797–1875) would correctly identify the phenomenon as the result of uniform movements of the earth's surface both upwards and downwards. The columns, which had been built above the level of the sea, were later submerged by water when the land sank, and, after an extended period of time underwater—long enough for the process of erosion to leave deep marks—they emerged again when the movement of the terrain reversed.[37]

Spallanzani's approach makes it clear that while the three ruined columns are perceived as a unity brought about by the mixture of aesthetically organized inorganic matter and naturally occurring living organisms, for the purpose of the scientist's investigation it is necessary to restrict one's point of view to a single aspect. The stance of the observer, thus, is in and of itself an epistemological choice—one that defines and "constructs" the object of study. In this case, the choice is made possible by the hybrid status of ruins, which offers an endless possibility for redefinition and reinterpretation. By looking at ruins exclusively as natural evidence, Spallanzani puts in place an interpretive distortion that enables him to carry out a systematic and coherent scientific assessment of the natural processes of which the Temple is evidence. This distortion reconfigures the status of the monumental remains and subsumes them under the category of a natural document.

A passage by contemporary Swiss geologist Jean-André de Luc (1727–1817) perfectly captures the ambiguous epistemological categorization of ruins and the ontological shift that is dependent on the choice of a specific field of enquiry. In a letter addressed to German naturalist Johann Friedrich Blumenbach (1752–1840), de Luc describes the Roman ruins near the city of Koblenz, which had been submerged for centuries beneath the sediments of the Rhine, and explains how such antiquarian evidence can be a reliable source for reconstructing the physical geography of a given area:

> Now the place [*place*] which these Roman monuments occupy in this mass of transported matter (an accumulation which could have begun only at the birth of our continents) transforms these historical documents into geological monuments; it is an example of the chronometrical scales to be found in the course of all rivers, agreeing with each other, and with every other kind . . .[38]

De Luc's explanation implies a transformation or metamorphosis of one thing into another that calls into play the perspective of the investigator. This transformation is facilitated by the fact that "the monuments of the Romans" have been slowly absorbed into the natural world to the point where they have become concrete evidence of nature's modifications, such as erosion, sedimentation, and flooding. The two different categories of the ruin as either a "historical document" or a "geological monument" are not mutually exclusive, but rather they depend on the "place," as de Luc calls it, that they occupy.

I understand de Luc's term "place" to indicate both the context within which the ruin finds itself and that within which it is placed in order to be interpreted. The way in which the ruin is read depends on its contingent position in a specific temporal or cultural moment, within a given geographical environment, or in the framework of a certain interpretive paradigm or system. For instance, the ruins to which de Luc refers as an example of "geological monuments" can be considered as such because of their physical position along the river Rhine, where they were found lying beneath an eight-foot sand stratum. Their significance as "chronometric scales" is also determined by a number of other interrelations, such as the fact that the time scale they show is consistent with other evidence from the area. A series of interrelated factors and conditions that add to the interpretive mediation of the observer, contribute to "transform" the historical monument into a geological document. Analogously, Spallanzani's experience at the Temple of Serapis shows how the status of the ruin is determined by a constellation of events, phenomena, and circumstances, i.e. by a network of human and non-human elements. The proximity to the area of Herculaneum and Pompeii gave the Temple greater prominence and contributed to make it internationally known. Its aesthetic features, as Spallanzani suggests with his reference to the "lover of the mimetic arts," attracted the attention of artists and antiquarians. The presence of mollusks on its columns and its location in an area subject to intense geological instability opened up the possibility for a scientific reading such as the one that Spallanzani himself offers. Moreover, the debate that developed around the geological phenomena linked to the Temple mobilized scholars to account for them. Just as time and the action of natural forces transformed the monument into a ruin, new conditions and relations, and any subsequent study modified what the Temple was.

De Luc's observation, however, suggests as well that what the ruin is depends not only on its "place" in a network, but also on whether the story that is being told concerns the human world, the vicissitudes of its peoples, the development of architectonic styles and aesthetic principles, or rather geological transformations, biological changes, and physical revolutions. It is, in other words, a matter of narrative, of how the different elements in the network are organized and connected into a field of relations from which they acquire meaning. In the case of the Temple of Serapis, Spallanzani constructs a narrative of naturalistic observations and tells a story of material transformation and animal erosion. His is a narrative of purification, if you will, that disaggregates the hybrid and assigns it to a single ontological zone, that of nature. The plurality and diversity of interpretations that the Temple itself produced over time, however, shows that the hybrid network of relations that the ruin gathers around itself resists the creation of a narrative that is entirely pure. In the story of Serapis, the two components of nature and culture are closely interrelated. For Charles Lyell, for instance, Serapis offered the material proof of his uniformitarian theories,[39] since the marks of erosion on its columns showed that the earth's surface had been subject to cyclical small-scale modifications over long periods of time. The evidence born by the ruins, however, also demonstrated that the physical changes that had shaped the earth had been taking place during historical times and were still occurring in the present. Nature and human beings appeared beneath the same temporal contingency. Significantly, Lyell chose an engraving of the Temple,[40] a human construction and a token of classical antiquity, as a frontispiece for the first volume of his seminal book on the sciences of the earth, *Principles of Geology*. For the British geologist, the ruin was, as Martin J. S. Rudwick has put it, "a highly effective epitome of his argument. It linked the human world with the natural, human history with geohistory, classical scholarship with scientific research . . ."[41] The Temple showed that natural revolutions and human history had a synchronous historicity.

The interpretive vicissitudes of the ruins of the Troad follow a similar narrative in which human developments and natural history are seen to intersect. Analogously to what happens with the ruins of Serapis, Spallanzani analyzes the ruins of Alexandria Troas as natural evidence. His reading, as we shall see, transforms the ruins into temporal markers of the earth's changes. This reflection on the temporality of nature, however, inevitably implicates a reassessment of the temporality of human things.

When Spallanzani set sail for Constantinople, a voyage that he had been planning for years, he regarded the visit to Troy as an essential part of his journey. Troy and the Homeric epic had always had a strong hold on the Western imagination and, while the area of the Troad had attracted visitors since classical times, since at least the end of the sixteenth century a growing number of travelers from the western world, convinced of the historical truth of Homer's account, had voyaged to Asia Minor to see the remnants of the ancient city and the site of the Trojan War. The exact location of Troy, however, was very much a matter of conjecture and by the eighteenth century, when the scientific study of the Homeric geography of the Troad began, it was still a source of intense debate among learned travelers.[42] The ancient Homeric city lay on the hill of Hisarlik, where Heinrich Schliemann would excavate in 1870, but many early travelers identified it with Alexandria Troas, a Greek city founded in 300 BC along the coast opposite the island of Tenedos. As Vergil had written: "[From Troy] Tenedos is in sight, a famous island that was replete with riches as long as Priam ruled."[43] Over the years, many, such as Ruggero Giuseppe Boscovich (1711–1787), an Italian astronomer and mathematician who visited the region of the Troad in 1761, had raised doubts as to whether Alexandria Troas was in fact the actual Troy.[44] The British traveler Robert Wood (1717?–1771), who was among the first to attempt a topographical study of the area in 1742 and 1750, had concluded that since the geographical features of the region must have radically changed since Homer's times, it would be impossible to locate the site of Troy, and that, in any case, the very ruins of the city had been completely erased: "Of the true and famous Troy there have been no traces for ages: not a stone is left, to certify, where it stood."[45] Prompted by Wood's conclusions, between 1785 and 1787 French diplomat and antiquarian Jean Baptiste Lechevalier carried out the first systematic topographical survey of the Trojan plain. In 1785, during his first trip to the Troad, Lechevalier, who was a member of French Ambassador Choiseul-Gouffier's research team, located the city on the heights of the village of Bunarbashi, near the supposed source of the river Scamander. Despite considerable controversy, Lechevalier's theory would remain dominant until the 1860s.[46]

The story of the search for the vestiges of Troy is one that links people and things—scientists, antiquarians, and amateur scholars, fiction and historical reality, landscape and ruins—in a tight network of causality and chance. Spallanzani's experience at the ruins of the Troad is a perfect example of this intricate web of connections and exchanges. When the naturalist embarked for Constantinople, in Venice, he was on the same vessel that carried Lechevalier to the East. Because of a travel delay, the two did not visit the Troad together, but during the journey they had the opportunity to share their research and to discover common passions:

> That Minister [. . .] had likewise taken on board the celebrated Dr. Spallanzani, one of the most ingenious Naturalists of the present age, whom Emperor Joseph II dispatched to the Levant, in order to enrich the Science of Nature by new discoveries. Amidst the shining qualities which distinguished my respectable companions in this voyage, I soon discovered a passion for the monuments of Antiquity similar to that which I myself entertained.[47]

Spallanzani certainly shared the same fascination for the monuments of antiquity as his French fellow-traveler,[48] and yet he declared that his first interest, in visiting the ruins of Troy, was that of a naturalist: "The famous island of Tenedos, and the even more famous ruins of Troy were two things that I could not leave unexamined, but not as an antiquarian in that destroyed city of Asia, but simply as a naturalist who considers the quality of the marble, of the granite, and of the other stones that make up those ruins."[49] Once again, on the subject of ruins, Spallanzani was careful to define his approach as a scientific enquiry.

From the point of view of a naturalist, the ruins of Troy represented one of "the most surprising and [the] strangest" phenomena that Spallanzani had observed during his journey to the East:

> But, in my opinion, the two most difficult to understand, most surprising, and strangest phenomena are those that I observed; the first years ago in the Western Riviera of Genoa [. . .] the other phenomenon, which I recently observed both in Troy and in Constantinople, is that the immense ruins of the first city, and the streets, the aqueducts, and most of the buildings of the second city, are made of a whitish marble, which was generated by nothing other than petrified mollusks. There is certainly no small wonder that these three grandiose and illustrious cities were constructed from animal remains! [50]

When compared to the "organic nature" of the remnants of Troy, the issue of the location of the Homeric city lost relevance in Spallanzani's eyes. Like many other travelers of the time, Spallanzani did in fact visit the site of Alexandria Troas, but upon surveying the ruins, he agreed with Boscovich, whose account of the journey in the East he repeatedly cites in his travel notes, that the remnants could not have possibly been those of the Trojan city:

> These pieces of granite are clearly burned on the outside, and to some extent also on the inside. I would therefore be inclined to believe that these were some of the actual remains of the ancient Troy burned by the Greeks, on top of which in much later times the Roman Troy was built. It is all too clear, as the cited Authors [Lycon, Martiniere, and Boscovich] remark, that the buildings still present are too grandiose in their architecture, too noble in their workmanship, and too fine for one to call them work of the Trojans. [51]

These cursory references to the debate surrounding the location of Troy and to the hypothesis on the actual nature of the ruins that he visits,[52] show Spallanzani's keen antiquarian tastes and reveal an attention to architectural and aesthetic features which remains otherwise unexpressed. The allusions to the fire that destroyed the city and to the characteristics of its architecture, which are undoubtedly based on a thorough knowledge of the Homeric text, suggest that at the origin of Spallanzani's visit to Troy was a profound historical curiosity stimulated by his literary imagination.[53] As Schliemann's enterprise would confirm, the archaeological story of the Troad is defined by such an intersection of fiction and history.[54] Although Spallanzani's analysis of the ruins focuses on the organic "quality of the marble, granite, and rocks" of which they are made, the same sense of historical and cultural awareness informs his visit to the area.

Spallanzani, however, did not linger on the problem of the actual site of the Homeric Troy, but he returned to the topic of the ruins and their composite nature several times both in his travel notes and in letters addressed to friends and colleagues. Writing to Count Giovanni Giuseppe di Wilzeck, he wondered: "Who would have ever said that such a noble and spacious city was composed of nothing other than animal substances?"[55] And in his travel journal, he noted: "Who would have said that Troy had been made of fossil shells, or rather of shells from a single species!"[56] Spallanzani's sense of marvel seems to suggest a selective attention that gives relevance to the unusual nature of the material that makes up the ruins—the so-called lumachella marble, a sedimentary limestone containing fossil shells. In fact, what struck the scientist was first and foremost the unusual accumulation of marine fossils of the same species in the rocks of an elevated area. What could explain such a large presence of petrified organisms? Spallanzani considered the possibility of a universal catastrophe, but also seemed open to different readings of the phenomena:

> After so many long disputations, we are still left in humiliating uncertainty as to whether it was a general actual cause that buried beneath the ground, almost all at once, this prodigious quantity of men, quadrupeds, fish, and other marine and terrestrial animals; or more probably if several specific causes came together, at different times and in different ways, to produce such memorable effects. We only know, because our experience clearly shows it, that this principle, whether single or multiple, caused the greatest upheavals of our planet [. . .] But we ought to confess without blushing that we do not know at all if these revolutions, if these violent movements of animals into new regions, were the result of some universal cataclysm, whether earthquakes, or volcanoes, or some other equally tumultuous agent.[57]

As it emerges from this passage, Spallanzani sees the ruins of Alexandria Troas—or Troy, as he always refers to it—as cross-sections of natural history. The remnants of human civilization, as in the case of Serapis, prove useful to explore the developments of physical revolutions in such a way that, once again, nature and human history appear closely intertwined. In studying the ruins, Spallanzani carries out a close inspection of their material composition, "simply as a naturalist," as he had set out to do.

This approach, a true "autopsy" that relies on proof provided by experience, falls within the research field indicated by the scientist. In a way, however, it also prefigures the methods of modern archaeological research, and not only because of the empirical, scientific analysis of the ruins that Spallanzani performs. Archaeological thought requires the investigator to establish a link between the present and the past through the examination of material evidence and to situate the thing into a meaningful network of association, contrast, and understanding. To use Michael Shanks's definition, archaeology might be thought of as a "history of things."[58] To think of material residues historically, as evidence that can provide access to the past, requires a concrete conception of time, one that has depth and thickness. In other words, it is necessary to think of time in its materiality. One may consider Michel Serres's suggestive concept of the "percolation of time" in order to better grasp what it means to see things as temporal archives and to think of time as matter. Serres proposes a different way to consider temporality and the passage of time, one that takes into account our perception of time and the way in which we experience it in relation to material things. Time—he explains—does not flow, rather it saturates people and objects. Each object is temporally layered and carries within itself the traces of different moments and eras: "An object, a circumstance, is thus polychronic, multitemporal, and reveals a time that is gathered together, with multiple pleats."[59]

Spallanzani's analysis of the architectonic remnants of Alexandria Troas shows such a polychronic awareness of time. Like a series of geological strata in a quarry, the ruins of the ancient city are multitemporal: They bear witness to a great civilization that existed at a certain moment in time, but they also contain fossil remains that point to a different temporal layer.[60] Interestingly, this polychrony merges together the life of a cultural artifact with the life of nature, showing that there is no solution of continuity between nature and culture. When Spallanzani speculates about the possible causes for the fossil accumulation in the ruins of Troy, he proposes a series of conjectures—earthquakes, volcanic eruptions, a universal cataclysm—that transport him and his readers to a time before the construction of the city itself—when some kind of natural revolution trapped large numbers of animals and people under mud and sediments, and the marble that would eventually make up the ruins began to form. Thus, the observation of the ruins, accompanied by an exercise of analytical imagination, enables Spallanzani to contemplate a deeper version of time, one that extends far back into the past, possibly even before the beginning of history. The techniques of natural history applied to a human artifact produce, in this sense, a paradoxical effect: the span of human history— represented by the ruin that subsists as an architectonic form —becomes part of the larger cycle of natural history. Despite the temporal distortion that relegates human history to a negligible parenthesis—a moment comprised between natural disasters and material decay—Spallanzani's scientific response to the ruin blurs the boundary between nature and culture, which appear as belonging to the same chronostory, or historical narrative —as was the case with Lyell's reading of the natural phenomena of Serapis.

The ruins of Troy become the expression of the temporal relation between humanity and nature. The sense of marvel expressed by Spallanzani, therefore, cannot be linked exclusively to his scientific curiosity. If the ruin is the hybrid form par excellence—that merges nature and culture in a shared process of decay—then the ruins of Alexandria Troas, with myriads of marine mollusks embedded in their marble, represent the expression of the ruin in its purest and most revealing form. Architectonic construction is a form of subjugation of nature, as epitomized by the "organic" marble out of which Constantinople and Alexandria Troas are shaped, but in the process of ruination, nature takes the upper hand and reclaims what, in the beginning, belonged to it. The hybridity of the ruins of Troy is defined by this convergence between the life of natural things and the life of artifacts that ultimately emerges from Spallanzani's scientific approach: *artificialia* and *naturalia* are both caught in a cycle of continuous transformation of matter that renders ontologically pure categories imprecise at best. Embodying the indissoluble bond between nature and culture, the hybrid ruin resists any narrative of purification.

Conclusions

I began this essay with a reflection on the inherent hybridity of the ruin, making the claim that Lazzaro Spallanzani's scientific perspective on monumental ruins illustrates the interpretive and classificatory issues posed by the hybrid, at the same time as it offers a paradigmatic example of how the essence of a thing—in this case the Temple of Serapis and the remains of Troy— is defined and transformed by an interlocking network of forces and conditions. Geography and landscape, literary fascination, history, human interest, and natural events come together to shape and define the stories of places such as Serapis, Troy, and their ruins. Spallanzani's methodological approach to ruins remains firmly rooted within a scientific framework—which may be read as a practice of purification of the hybrid—but, as I hope to have shown, the narrative of biological and chemical transformation that he tells is much more complex. In fact, Spallanzani's observations on Serapis and Alexandria Troas show that there is a biology of decay expressed by ruins that is just as meaningful as the aesthetics of decay analyzed by theorists of the ruin, such as Georg Simmel and Paul Zucker.[61]

Spallanzani's approach to the remains of the Trojan city and to the ruined Temple of Pozzuoli is defined by the convergence of antiquarian taste—which manifests itself in his fascination with the material record of the human past—and naturalistic curiosity. In both cases, Spallanzani focuses on the processes of organic transformation that have affected the ruins and the marble of which they are made. Even if his scientific description shifts the focus away from the ruins as cultural formations, his analysis of their organic materiality, as we have seen, is carried out contextually with a reflection on temporality, long duration, and large-scale changes. The ruin as a whole, thus, is placed in a temporal continuum in which natural events and human enterprises unfold together and in which material decay becomes a feature of biological change— whether it is the process of erosion brought about by rock-boring mollusks or the sedimentation of animal remains into marble. By reading a cultural artifact as a chronological record of natural change, Spallanzani shows how nature becomes inscribed on human history and how the latter is shaped as much by human agency as it is by contingent extra-human factors such as natural catastrophes. Even more suggestively, his approach implies the inherent organicity of human processes and constructions. Building, for example,—as the analysis of the ruins of Troy shows—appears as a process of transformation of organic substances into purposeful structures. As suggested by Spallanzani's reading, and as the interpretive stories of Serapis and Troy demonstrate, the hybrid form of the ruin comes to embody this assimilation of natural history and human history that is at the basis of new disciplines such as geology and archaeology, both of which take shape between the end of the eighteenth century and the mid-nineteenth century. Thus, as seen through the eyes of a late-eighteenth-century naturalist whose research intersects with the beginnings of modern science, the ruin delivers the image of a world in which man and nature are perceived as in constant interaction and exchange, indissolubly joined, as belonging to one and the same temporal flow.

NOTES

1. Ruins are a continuous source of theoretical reflection and the literature on the topic is extensive. I have found particularly useful the following approaches to ruins that deal with the nature-culture nexus and modernity: Marc Augé, *Le temps en ruines* (Paris: Galilée, 2003); Robert Ginsberg, *The Aesthetics of Ruins* (Amsterdam; New York, NY: Rodopi, 2004); Julia Hell and Andreas Schönle, eds., *Ruins of Modernity* (Durham: Duke UP, 2010); Roland Mortier, *La poétique des ruines en France. Ses origines, ses variations de la Renaissance à Victor Hugo*

(Geneva: Librairie Droz, 1974); Alois Riegl, "The Modern Cult of Monuments: Its Character and Its Origin," trans. Kurt Forster and Diane Ghirardo, *Oppositions* 25 (1982): 21–51; Georg Simmel, "The Ruin," trans. David Kettler, 379–85, in "Two Essays: The Handle, and The Ruin," *Hudson Review* 11, no. 3 (Autumn 1958), 371–85; Jean Starobinski, "Melancholy Among the Ruins," in *The Invention of Liberty,* 1700–1789, trans. by B.C. Swift (Geneva: Skira, 1964), 179–81; Starobinski, "Le rovine," *Il menabò di letteratura* 7 (1964): 253–56; Paul Zucker, "Ruins. An Aesthetic Hybrid," *The Journal of Aesthetics and Art Criticism* 20, no. 2 (Winter 1961): 119–30; as well as the special issue *Estetica delle rovine*, special issue of *Rivista di estetica*, 21, no. 8 (1981).

2. Simmel, "The Ruin," 383.
3. Ibid., 385.
4. Zucker, "Ruins," 120.
5. Ibid.
6. Bruno Latour, *We Have Never Been Modern*, trans. Catherine Porter (Cambridge, MA: Harvard University Press, 1993), 50.
7. Ibid. 10–11.
8. Latour mentions two distinct practices that define modernity: "translation" and "purification." The former is the creation of networks (see note 12), or, as he puts it, "mixtures between entirely new types of beings, hybrids of nature and culture," whereas the latter is the separation of the hybrid by "the modern critical stance" (ibid). According to Latour, the history of modern science is a process of purification that nonetheless produces a series of new hybrids, created by new disciplines and technologies. He is interested in redefining the study of modern science, whereas I am engaging with his theories in order to better understand how an early modern scientist addressed the issues raised by the encounter of nature and culture.
9. On Lazzaro Spallanzani's role in the birth of modern biology, see: Ernesto Capanna, "Lazzaro Spallanzani: At the Roots of Modern Biology," *Journal of Experimental Zoology* (*Mol. Dev. Evol.*) 285, no. 3 (1999): 178–96. On Spallanzani's activities as a scientist and the historical and scientific context in which he worked, see Walter Bernardi and Marta Stefani, eds., *La sfida della modernità: Atti del Convegno Internazionale di Studi nel bicentenario della morte di Lazzaro Spallanzani* (Florence: Olschki, 2000); Bernardi and Paola Manzini, eds., *Il cerchio della vita: Materiali di ricerca del Centro Studi Lazzaro Spallanzani di Scandiano sulla storia della scienza del Settecento* (Florence: Olschki, 1999); Giuseppe Montalenti and Paolo Rossi, eds., *Lazzaro Spallanzani e la biologia del Settecento. Teorie, Esperimenti, Istituzioni scientifiche* (Florence: Olschki, 1982); and J. Rostand, *Les origines de la biologie expérimentale et l'abbé Spallanzani* (Paris: Fasquelle, 1951).
10. On Piranesi and ruins, see Richard Wendorf, "Piranesi's Double Ruin," *Eighteenth-Century Studies* 34, no. 2, *Antiquarians, Connoisseurs, and Collectors* (Winter 2001): 161–180; and Andreas Huyssen, "Nostalgia for Ruins," *Grey Room* 23 (Spring 2006): 6–21, rpt. in Hell and Schönle, *Ruins of Modernity*, 17–28.
11. My use of the term "network" throughout is in dialogue with actor-network

theory, and especially with Bruno Latour's instantiation of it. Latour thinks about the network as a way of relocating agency, so that the essence of things resides in a concomitance of human and non-human agents that cannot be reduced to a single perspective. In terms of the present essay, Latour's network theory has been useful, first, in that it has helped me to describe how ruins (hybrids) resist interpretation and narratives of purification, assuming agency within their own histories; and second, in that it has allowed me to define places like Serapis and Troy in terms of a confluence of multiple factors, agents, and perspectives. The literature on network theory is wide-ranging, but I have found especially fruitful the following works: Latour, *We Have Never Been Modern*; Latour, "Networks, Societies, Spheres: Reflections of an Actor-network Theorist," *International Journal of Communication* 5 (2011) *Network Theory*, accessed 15 August 2012, http://ijoc.org/ojs/index.php/ijoc/article/view/1094/558; Michel Serres and Bruno Latour, *Conversations on Science, Culture, and Time* (Ann Arbor: The University of Michigan Press, 1995); and Graham Harman, *Prince of Networks: Bruno Latour and Metaphysics* (Melbourne: re.press, 2009).

12. "Le premier Naturaliste de l'Europe." "Voltaire a Spallanzani, à Ferney par Genève 6 Juin 1776," in Spallanzani, *Carteggi*, ed. Pericle Di Pietro, 12 vols., in *Edizione Nazionale delle opere di Lazzaro Spallanzani*, part 1, (Modena: Mucchi, 1989), 11:131. Translations in the text are my own unless otherwise stated. Voltaire and Spallanzani began to correspond in 1766, when Spallanzani was in the process of experimenting on the regeneration of snails. Voltaire was able to reproduce the results of his experiment. On this see, Marguerite Carozzi, "Bonnet, Spallanzani, and Voltaire on Regeneration of Heads in Snails: A Continuation of the Spontaneous Generation Debate," *Gesnerus* 42 (1985): 265–88.

13. Spallanzani disproved the theory of spontaneous generation in his *Saggio di osservazioni microscopiche concernenti il sistema della generazione de' signori Needham e Buffon* (1765). For Spallanzani's importance in this area of research, see Charles E. Dinsmore, "Lazzaro Spallanzani: Concepts of Generation and Regeneration," in *A History of Regeneration Research: Milestones in the Evolution of a Science*, ed. Dinsmore (Cambridge: Cambridge University Press, 1991), 67–90. Spallanzani's work on artificial insemination is contained in the *Dissertazione sopra la fecondazione artificiale in alcuni animali*, published as a part of his *Dissertazioni di fisica animale e vegetabile* (1780).

14. On Spallanzani's private collection and work for the natural history museum in Pavia, see Maria Franca Spallanzani, "Le 'camere di storia naturale' dell'Istituto delle Scienze di Bologna nel Settecento," in *Scienza e letteratura nella cultura italiana del Settecento*, ed. Renzo Cremente and Walter Tega (Bologna: Il Mulino, 1984), 149–83; M.F. Spallanzani, "La collezione naturalistica di Lazzaro Spallanzani," in Montalenti and Rossi, *Lazzaro Spallanzani*, 589–601; and M.F. Spallanzani, *La collezione naturalistica di Lazzaro Spallanzani: I modi e i tempi della sua formazione* (Reggio Emilia: Comune di Reggio nell'Emilia, 1985).

15. On scientific travels in the eighteenth century, see Marco Ciardi, "Dalla scoperta del nuovo mondo all'esplorazione dell'atmosfera: Le origini del viaggio scientifico," in *Esplorazioni e viaggi scientifici nel Settecento*, ed. Ciardi (Milan:

BUR, 2008), 7–107. Significant portions of Ciardi's anthology are dedicated to Spallanzani's travels. On Spallanzani's scientific travels in general see, Giacomo Pighini, *Viaggi ed escursioni scientifiche di Lazzaro Spallanzani. Con documenti inediti ed illustrazioni e testi di Lazzaro Spallanzani* (Bologna: L. Capelli, 1929); M.F. Spallanzani, "'Filosofiche escursioni.' I viaggi naturalistici di Lazzaro Spallanzani," in L. Spallanzani, *Pagine scelte dalle opere*, ed. C. Castellani and M.F. Spallanzani (Reggio Emilia: Comune di Reggio Emilia-Civici Musei); and M.F. Spallanzani, *I viaggi naturalistici di Lazzaro Spallanzani. Immagini per una ricerca* (Reggio Emilia: Amministrazione Provinciale, 1981).

16. In this convergence between antiquarian interests and naturalist research, Spallanzani followed the example of Italian astronomer and mathematician, Ruggero Boscovich (1711–1787) and French botanist and physician, Joseph-Louis Pitton de Tournefort (1656–1708), both of whom had written scientific journals with antiquarian strains: respectively, *Giornale di un viaggio da Costantinopoli in Polonia dell'Abate R.G. Boscovich, con una sua Relazione delle rovine di Troia* (Bassano, 1784) and *Relation d'un voyage au Levant fait par ordre du Roy* (Lyon, 1717). Spallanzani cites them both in his own travelogues. See Ciardi, "Spallanzani, Lechevalier e le rovine di Troia: Un capitolo delle relazioni tra storia della scienza e storia dell'archeologia," in Bernardi and Stefani, *La sfida della modernità*, 241–62.

17. See Arnaldo Momigliano, "Ancient History and the Antiquarian," in Momigliano, *Contributo alla storia degli studi classici* (Rome: Edizioni di Storia e Letteratura, 1955), 67–106. See also Mark Salber Phillips, "Reconsiderations on History and Antiquarianism: Arnaldo Momigliano and the Historiography of Eighteenth-Century Britain," *Journal of the History of Ideas* 57, no. 2 (1996): 297–316.

18. While not all naturalists were antiquarians, their respective practices were not always necessarily separate, as Maria Toscano has shown in *Gli archivi del mondo: Antiquaria, storia naturale e collezionismo nel secondo Settecento* (Florence: Edifir, 2009). She describes the figure of the "naturalist-antiquary" as a "convinced defender of the methodological and epistemological continuity between the scientific and humanistic disciplines and of the centrality of visible and experimental data" (10). The circumscribed phenomenon of naturalist-antiquarianism in the late eighteenth century, in fact, shows the "compenetration between the sciences and the *humanitates*" (9) that in a certain way foreshadowed modern archaeology. To use the words of Matthew R. Goodrum, in "Recovering the Vestiges of Primeval Europe: Archaeology and the Significance of Stone Implements, 1750–1800," *Journal of the History of Ideas* 72, no. 1 (2011): 51–74: "Antiquarianism . . . had close links with natural history during this period and many antiquaries employed methods and a mode of reasoning drawn from the sciences. By the late eighteenth century, antiquarianism itself was changing and a new science of archaeology was emerging and defining its own professional identity" (52). On the creation of the discipline of archaeology see Suzanne L. Marchand, "From Antiquarian to Archaeologists? Adolf Furtwängler and the Problem of 'Modern' Classical Archaeology," in *Momigliano and Antiquarianism: Foundations of the*

Modern Cultural Sciences, ed. Peter Miller (Toronto: University of Toronto Press, 2007), 248–85 and Alain Schnapp, *The Discovery of the Past* (New York: Harry N. Abrams, 1997). On early archaeology in Italy, see Giovanna Ceserani, *Italy's Lost Greece: Magna Graecia and the Making of Modern Archaeology* (Oxford: Oxford University Press, 2012).

19. The idea of cultural and natural objects as temporal archives is linked to the development of "temporalization," or the understanding of natural and human change in terms of historical processes, on which see, Reinhart Koselleck, *Futures Past: On the Semantics of Historical Time*, trans. K. Tribe (New York: Columbia University Press, 2004) and Koselleck, *The Practice of Conceptual History: Timing History, Spacing Concepts*, trans. T. S. Presner et al. (Stanford: Stanford University Press, 2002). See also Michel Foucault, *The Order of Things. An Archaeology of the Human Sciences* (New York: Vintage Books, 1973); Koselleck, ed., *Gli inizi del mondo moderno* (Milan: Vita e Pensiero, 1997); Wolf Lepenies, *La fine della storia naturale* (Bologna: Il Mulino, 1991); and Arthur O. Lovejoy, *The Great Chain of Being* (Cambridge, MA: Harvard University Press, 1964). On the idea of the historicization of nature and culture during the eighteenth century in the context of Spallanzani studies, see Dietrich v. Engelhardt, "Storicizzazione della natura nel Settecento," in Bernardi and Stefani, *La sfida della modernità*, 3–15. My own work on Spallanzani is connected to a book in progress on conceptions of time and ruination in Italy between the mid-eighteenth and early-nineteenth centuries.

20. The main idea, as we shall see, is that objects such as the ruins of Alexandria Troas or the columns of the Temple of Serapis were seen as exhibiting visible signs of change over time that pointed back to different chronological moments – events such as a fire, in the first example, or a flood in the second one, that had taken place at different points in the past. Whereas the focus was certainly on understanding objects within a certain temporal context, I would argue that objects themselves were implicitly seen, as shown by Spallanzani's observations below, as containing various detectable traces of past events, or what I define as "time layers."

21. Cuvier, *Extract from a memoir on an animal of which the bones are found in the plaster stone around Paris, and which appears no longer to exist alive today*, in *Georges Cuvier, Fossil Bones, and Geological Catastrophes. New Translations and Interpretations of the Primary Texts*, ed. and trans. Martin J.S. Rudwick (Chicago: The University of Chicago Press, 1997), 35–41 (35). ". . . il faudra que les physiciens fassent pour l'histoire de la nature, ce que les antiquaires font pour l'histoire des arts et des mœurs des peuples ; il faudra que les uns aillent chercher dans les ruines du globe les restes des êtres animés qui vivaient à sa surface, comme les autres fouillent dans les ruines des cités, pour y déterrer les monuments du goût du génie & des coutumes des hommes qui les habitaient. Ces antiquités de la nature, si on peut s'exprimer ainsi, fourniront à l'histoire physique du globe, des monuments aussi utiles & aussi certains, que les antiquités ordinaires en fournissent à l'histoire politique et morale des nations." Georges Cuvier, *Extrait d'un Mémoire sur un animal dont on trouve les ossements dans la pierre à plâtre des environs de Paris, & qui paraît ne plus exister vivant aujourd'hui*, in *George Cuvier*, ed. and trans. Rudwick, 285–91 (286). This paper was delivered at the

Institut de France on October 6, 1798.

22. The idea of producing a history of natural events is linked to the process of temporalization, on which see note 19 above. On this topic and on the transferal of methods between antiquarianism and the natural sciences, see Rudwick, *Bursting the Limits of Time: The Reconstruction of Geohistory in the Age of Revolution* (Chicago: The University of Chicago Press, 2005) and Rudwick, *Worlds Before Adam: The Reconstruction of Geohistory in the Age of Reform* (Chicago: The University of Chicago Press, 2008).

23. The tension between culture and nature is still present in contemporary theoretical reflections on the interpretation of archaeological remains. For example, Vassilis Lambrinoudakis notes: "A characteristic example is the dilemma faced in the restoration of the temple of Zeus in Olympia: The drums of most of the columns of this building still lie as they fell. Restoring them would have produced a much more complete image of the original form of the building, which was a *human creation*. On the other hand, though, the condition in which the ruin is found forms part of its history, even if this condition, caused by an earthquake, forms part of its *natural history*. Which of these two poles is the more significant? A balanced compromise was chosen: one of the columns was re-erected, giving again the sense of height and grandeur of the original building, while the rest were left on the ground, testifying to its later fate." Lambrinoudakis, "Rediscovering, Reconstructing, Using the Past: Archaeology of the Classical World," *Athens Dialogues* (2010), Stories and Histories, Period One, accessed August 15, 2012, http://athensdialogues.chs.harvard.edu/cgi-bin/WebObjects/athensdialogues.woa/wa/dist?dis=68.

24. Lazzaro Spallanzani, *Viaggi alle Due Sicilie e in alcune parti dell'Appennino*, ed. Ezio Vaccari, 2 tomes, in *Edizione nazionale delle opere di Lazzaro Spallanzani*, part 4, vol. 6, *Opere edite direttamente dall'autore* (Modena: Mucchi, 2006–07). His travelogues record a series of research trips during the summers and falls between 1788 and 1790. Besides the works cited in note 15, see M.F. Spallanzani, "Lazzaro Spallanzani 'viaggiatore filosofo'," in *La regione e l'Europa. Viaggi e viaggiatori emiliani e romagnoli nel Settecento*, ed. Elvio Guagnini (Bologna: Il Mulino, 1986), 173–223. According to Paolo Mazzarello, these travel diaries were widely read even outside of the scientific community. He cites the example of Victor Hugo, who mentions Spallanzani's work in *Le Dernier Jour d'un Comdamné* (1829). See Mazzarello, "Spallanzani in Oriente," in *Viaggio a Costantinopoli, in Edizione nazionale delle opere di Lazzaro Spallanzani*, part 5, vol. 3, *Opere edite non direttamente dall'autore* (Modena: Mucchi, 2012), 11–63 (14 n.9).

25. Spallanzani was never able to publish the travelogue of his voyage to Constantinople. Part of it was published posthumously by Naborre Campanini, as *Viaggio in Oriente di Lazzaro Spallanzani ordinato e compilato su i giornali di viaggio e su altri manoscritti inediti* (Turin: Bocca, 1888). In 1934, Benedetto Biagi transcribed a more complete collection of the documents associated with the voyage, as *Viaggio a Costantinopoli, in Le opere di Lazzaro Spallanzani*, ed. Filippo Bottazzi and Mariano L. Patrizi, vol. 5, part 1 (Milan: Hoepli, 1934). More recently, the first complete edition of the manuscripts of Spallanzani's travelogue

in the East has been completed by Paolo Mazzarello, as *Viaggio a Costantinopoli, in Edizione nazionale delle opere di Lazzaro Spallanzani*, part 5, vol. 3, *Opere edite non direttamente dall'Autore* (Modena: Mucchi, 2012). I have cited the older Bottazzi-Patrizi edition throughout because it is more widely available and it contains not only Spallanzani's manuscripts, but also the correspondence he maintained during the voyage. On this trip, see Mazzarello, *Costantinopoli 1786: La congiura e la beffa. L'intrigo Spallanzani* (Turin: Bollati Boringhieri, 2004); Mazzarello, "Spallanzani in Oriente;" and M.F. Spallanzani, "Lazzaro Spallanzani 'viaggiatore filosofo'," 204–10.

26. On Spallanzani's interest in the geological sciences, see Vaccari, "Lazzaro Spallanzani and his Geological Travels to the 'Due Sicilie': The Volcanology of the Aeolian Islands," in *Volcanoes and History: Proceedings of the 20th INHIGEO International Symposium 19–24 September 1995*, ed. Nicoletta Morello (Genoa: Brigati, 1998), 621–52; Vaccari, "I *Viaggi alle Due Sicilie* e il contributo di Spallanzani alle scienze geologiche del Settecento," in Spallanzani, *Viaggi alle Due Sicilie*, 1:9–28; and Vaccari, "Spallanzani e le scienze geologiche del Settecento: Un percorso interpretativo tra carteggi e diari di viaggio," in Bernardi and Stefani, *La sfida della modernità*, 293–317.

27. For an exhaustive account of the significance of the "Temple" of Serapis in the history of science, archaeology, and art, see Luca Ciancio, *Le colonne del Tempo: Il 'Tempio di Serapide' a Pozzuoli nella storia della geologia, dell'archeologia e dell'arte (1750–1900)* (Florence: Edifir, 2009).

28. The confusion regarding the location of Troy is discussed in note 41 below.

29. Joseph Woods, *Letters of an Architect from France, Italy, and Greece*, 2 vols (London, 1828), 1:194.

30. The architectonic and topographical analysis that definitively identifies the "Temple" of Serapis as the *macellum* appears in Charles Dubois, *Pouzzoles antique; histoire et topographie* (Paris, 1907), 286–314. See Ciancio, *Le colonne del Tempo*, 8 n.8.

31. Along with Alberto Fortis, Breislak was one of the pioneers of volcanology and geology in Italy and wrote the first manual of geology in Italian, *Introduzione alla geologia* (Milan, 1811). His account of the Temple appears in *Essais minéralogiques sur la Solfatare de Pouzzole* (Naples, 1792), 167–78. See Spallanzani, *Viaggi alle Due Sicilie*, 2:125 n.1.

32. "Questo Edifizio se per l'architettura può interessare l'amatore delle Arti imitatrici, non lascia insieme di pascere la curiosità del Naturalista." Spallanzani, *Viaggi alle Due Sicilie*, 1:136.

33. "Solamente all'altezza di 9 piedi circa da terra ogni colonna comincia ad essere superficialmente logorata, e il logoramento inoltrandosi su pel fuso della colonna forma una fascia orizzontale scabrosa, e diseguale, larga oltre due piedi, quando il rimanente del marmo è liscio e pulito. Cotesta fascia è per ogni dove bucherata da' mitili, litofagi: e alcuni fori richiudono anche adesso i loro gusci o intieri, o in frammenti." Spallanzani, *Viaggi alle Due Sicilie*, 1:136.

34. That is, "animalucci marini." Spallanzani, *Viaggi alle Due Sicilie*, 1:136.

35. On the role played by the Temple in understanding the movements of the

earth's crust, see Rudwick, *Worlds Before Adam*, 106–13. The term "bradyseism" was not actually coined until 1883, by Arturo Issel.

36. "Mi si obbjetterà forse che sembra strano, che quelle colonne ritte in piedi sieno state a lungo bagnate dall'acque marine in quella fascia, e non già nelle parti sottostanti ad essa. Ma non può darsi che prima di destinarle a quella fabbrica, fossero state nel fondo del mare sepolte in modo, che quel solo anello, ricco di spoglie marine, toccasse l'acqua? E quando anche non piacesse questa ipotesi, e non se ne trovasse altra appagante, io mi riporterò sempre al fatto, poco premendomi di non saperlo spiegare." Spallanzani, *Viaggi alle Due Sicilie*, 1:137.

37. For Lyell, the issue of gradual movements in the earth's crust evidenced by the eroded bands on the columns of the Temple confirmed his uniformitarian theories about geological change. The principle of uniformitarianism maintained that natural laws are constant in space and time. It was opposed to catastrophism, which stated that the Earth's surface formed as a result of catastrophic natural disasters. See Rudwick, "Lyell and the *Principles of Geology,*" *Geological Society, London, Special Publications* 143 (1998): 1–15 and Rudwick, "The Strategy of Lyell's *Principles of Geology*," *Isis* 61, no. 1 (Spring 1970): 5–33.

38. Jean-André de Luc, *Letters on the Physical History of the Earth Addressed to Professor Blumenbach, Containing Geological and Historical Proofs of the Divine Mission of Moses*, trans. Henry De La Fite (London, 1831), 228. "Or la place que ces *monumens* des *Romains* occupent dans des amas de matières *transportées*, amas qui n'ont pu *commencer* qu'à la *naissance* de nos *continens*, transforme ces *documens historiques* en *monumens géologiques*; ils sont des exemples des *échelles chronométriques* qu'on peut trouver le long de toutes les *rivières*, d'accord entr'elles et avec toutes celles qui sont fournies par des opérations d'autre genre . . ." De Luc, Letter 5, section 55, in *Lettres sur l'histoire de la terre, addressées à M. le professeur Blumenbach; renfermant de nouvelles preuves géologiques et historiques de la mission divine de Moyse* (Paris, 1798), 284–85. Italics belong to the original text.

39. On uniformitarianism, see note 37 above.

40. On the connection between Lyell's uniformitarian theories and his choice of an image of the "Temple" of Serapis as frontispiece of his *Principles of Geology*, see Brian P. Dolan, "Representing Novelty: Charles Babbage, Charles Lyell, and Experiments in Early Victorian Geology," *History of Science* 36, part 3, No. 113 (Sept. 1998): 299–327.

41. Rudwick, "Lyell and the *Principles of Geology*," 8.

42. The complex urban landscape of the area contributed to the confusion about the exact location of Homer's Troy, which was actually located on Hisarlik. In 700 B.C. New Ilium was founded nearby. Around 300 B.C., however, Alexandria Troas was built in the south of New Ilium, along the coast, and would eventually come to be confused with both the actual Troy and New Ilium. By the eighteenth century only a few travelers believed that Alexandria Troas was the actual Troy, but many thought that Alexandria Troas was New Ilium. For a survey on the subject of the search for Troy, see Michael Wood, *In Search of the Trojan War*, 2nd ed. (Berkeley: University of California Press, 1996) and the exhibition catalogue by

A.C. Lascarides, *The Search for Troy 1553–1874* (Bloomington: The Lilly Library, Indiana University, 1977), which covers the topic from the Renaissance though Schliemann's excavations. Troy had been an important travel destination since antiquity; for its significance in Greco-Roman antiquity, see Andrew Erskine, T*roy between Greece and Rome* (Oxford: Oxford University Press, 2001). On travels to the Troad and on the development of archaeological knowledge about the area until Schliemann, see Justus Cobet, Emre Madran, and Nimet Özgünel, "From Saewulf to Schliemann: A Preliminary Bibliography of Travel Books about Troy and the Troad," *Studia Troica* 1 (1991): 101–9; and Donald F. Easton, "Troy before Schliemann," *Studia Troica* 1 (1991): 111–29.

43. "Est in conspectu Tenedos, notissima fama / insula, dives opum Priami dum regna manebant." Vergil, *Aeneid*, II.21–22, in *Opera*, ed. Roger A.B. Mynors (Oxford: Oxford University Press, 1969).

44. In 1761, Boscovich was sent to Turkey by the British Royal Society to observe the transit of Venus in front of the Sun. On the occasion of the trip, he visited the supposed ruins of Troy. He later published an account of his tour together with the travel journal of his journey from Constantinople to Poland: *Giornale di un viaggio da Costantinopoli in Polonia dell'Abate R.G. Boscovich, con una sua Relazione delle rovine di Troia* (Bassano, 1784).

45. Robert Wood, *An Essay on the Original Genius and Writings of Homer* (1769), qtd. in M. Wood, *In Search of the Trojan War*, 19. On R. Wood's archaeological exploration of the Troad, see David Constantine, *In the Footsteps of the Gods: Travelers to Greece and the Quest for the Hellenic Ideal*, rev. ed. (London: Tauris Park, 2011), 66–84 and T.J.B. Spencer, "Robert Wood and the Problem of Troy in the Eighteenth Century," *Journal of the Warburg and Courtauld Institutes* 20, nos. 1–2 (1957): 75–105.

46. On Lechevalier's theory and its impact, besides M. Wood, *In Search of the Trojan War*, 40–41, and Lascarides, *The Search for Troy*, 29–48, see John V. Luce, *Celebrating Homer's Landscapes: Troy and Ithaca revisited* (New Haven: Yale University Press, 1998), esp. 64–70. On Lechevalier's relevance for later archaeologists, see Susan Heuck Allen, *Finding the Walls of Troy: Frank Calvert and Heinrich Schliemann at Hisarlik* (Berkeley: University of California Press, 1999), 41–46, 72–73, and 81–83.

47. Jean Baptiste Lechevalier, *Description of the Plain of Troy*, trans. and ed. Andrew Dalzel (Edinburgh, 1791), 1–2. "Cet Ambassadeur [. . .] avoit aussi reçu dans son vaisseau le célèbre Docteur Spallanzani, l'un des plus ingénieux naturalistes de ce siècle, que l'Empereur Joseph II envoyoit dans le Levant, pour enrichir la science de la nature de découvertes nouvelles. Je ne tardai pas à appercevoir dans mes respectables compagnons de voyage, parmi les brillantes qualités qui les distinguent, la même passion que j'avois moi-même pour les monuments de l'antiquité [. . .]." Lechevalier, "Tableau de la Plaine de Troye: Accompagné d'une Carte, levée géométriquement, en 1785 et 1786," *Transactions of the Royal Society of Edinburgh*, Vol. 3, Part 2, *Papers of the Literary Class* (1794), 3–92 (3–4).

48. On Spallanzani's interest in the exploration of archaeological sites during his journey to Constantinople, see Mazzarello, "Spallanzani in Oriente," 18–19.

49. "La famosa isola di Tenedo, e le più famose ruine di Troia sono due oggetti che lasciar non doveva senza esame, non però facendola da antiquario intorno a quella distrutta città dell'Asia, ma da semplice naturalista col considerare la qualità de' marmi, de' graniti, e dell'altre pietre che compongono quelle ruine." Spallanzani, "Spallanzani a Landriani, Vienna [metà] Dicembre 1786," in *Carteggi*, 5:280.

50. "Ma i due fenomeni, a mio avviso, più difficili a comprendersi, più sorprendenti e più strani sono gli osservati da me; l'uno anni addietro nella Riviera di Ponente di Genova [. . .] l'altro fenomeno veduto ultimamente in Troia, e a Costantinopoli, giacché le immense ruine della prima città, e le strade, gli acquedotti, e la massima parte delle fabbriche della seconda constano d'un marmo biancheggiante, non d'altro generato che di sole telline petrificate. Maraviglia non piccola ella è senza fallo che queste tre grandiose ed illustri città sieno state fabbricate di spoglie animali . . ." Spallanzani, *Viaggio a Costantinopoli*, ed. Bottazzi and Patrizi, 52.

51. "Questi graniti sono esternamente, ed anche alcun poco nel loro interno, patentemente bruciati. Io adunque inclinerei forse a credere che questi fossero alcuni verissimi avanzi dell'antica Troja arsa da' Greci, su quali è stata in tempi assai posteriori fabbricata la Troja romana, essendo troppo chiaro, come anche ne avvisano i citati Autori [Lycon, Martiniere, Boscovich], che gli edifizi tuttavia esistenti sono troppo grandiosi, d'architettura, e di lavorio troppo nobili, e troppo fini per potersi dire opera trojana." Spallanzani, *Viaggio a Costantinopoli*, ed. Bottazzi and Patrizi, 68.

52. From the reference to the "Troja romana," one can infer that, although Spallanzani had understood that he was not on the actual site of Homer's Troy, he thought that Alexandria Troas was New Ilium. For a discussion of Troy's location, see note 42 above.

53. As a student, Spallanzani had acquired a profound knowledge of ancient Greek language and literature. One of his first academic posts was as professor of Greek at the *Collegio del Seminario* in Reggio-Emilia. In 1760, he published an essay in which he criticized a translation of the *Iliad* by well-known Greek scholar, Antonio Maria Salvini (1653–1729): *Riflessioni intorno alla traduzione dell'Iliade del Salvini*. It is no surprise, then, if he often cites Homer throughout his travelogues. On Spallanzani's knowledge of Greek, see Giovanni Garuti, "Spallanzani grecista," *Mem. Accad. S.L.A. di Modena*, series VI, vol. 21 (1979): 91–99 and, more recently, Agnese G. Barbieri and Veronica Padovani, "Lazzaro Spallanzani grecista," *Atti e Memorie dell'Accademia Nazionale di Scienze, Lettere ed Arti di Modena*, series 8, vol. 2 (2000): 267–77.

54. The critical literature on Schliemann and Troy is vast. I have found especially helpful, however, Allen, *Finding the Walls of Troy*.

55. "Chi detto avrebbe che una sì nobile e spaziosa città non d'altro fosse composta che di sostanze animali?" Spallanzani, *Viaggio a Costantinopoli*, ed. Bottazzi and Patrizi, 69.

56. "Chi avrebbe detto che Troia fosse stata composta di gusci di testacei, anzi d'un solo testaceo!" Spallanzani, *Viaggio a Costantinopoli*, ed. Bottazzi and Patrizi, 64.

57. "Dopo tante e sì lunghe dispute siam tuttavia nell'umiliante incertezza, se una generale agente cagione seppellito abbia sotterra, a quasi ad un tempo, questa prodigiosa quantità d'uomini, di quadrupedi, di pesci, e d'altri acquatici e terrestri animali; o più veramente se a produrre sì memorabili effetti concorse sieno più cause particolari, in diversi tempi, e in diversi modi operanti. Sappiamo solamente, perché l'esperienza cel mostra chiaro, che questo od unico, o molteplice principio ha cagionato nel nostro pianeta i maggiori sconvolgimenti [. . .] Ma se queste rivoluzioni, se questi violenti trasporti di animali in regioni straniere, sieno state l'effetto o di qualche universal cataclisma, o di tremuoti, o di vulcani, o di altrettali tumultuarj agenti, dobbiam confessarlo senza rossore, che da noi totalmente s'ignora." Spallanzani, *Viaggio a Costantinopoli*, ed. Bottazzi and Patrizi, 52.

58. Michael Shanks, "Archaeology and the Forms of History," in I*nterpreting Archaeology: Finding Meaning in the Past*, ed. Ian Hodder, M. Shanks, Alexandra Alexandri, et al. (London: Routledge, 1995), 169–174 (170).

59. Serres and Latour, *Conversations on Science, Culture, and Time*, 60.

60. Spallanzani's approach to ruins shows a tension between Serres's conception of time as chaotic and non-linear and the stratigraphic model of geology and archaeology. Stratigraphy implies a notion of time as a chronologically ordered succession, in that it is based on the idea that in a given series of successive strata, the lower stratum must be older than the deposits above it. Both models, however, share the notion of multitemporality and are cumulative in the sense that they imply the accretion and co-presence of different temporal layers. Spallanzani's archaeological and stratigraphic conception, which is evident in the second quote on page 14, is a direct answer to what is perceived as a chaotic reality: i.e. Alexandria Troas as a site of collapsed temporality. Serres's notion of time is useful to describe theoretically the reality of these sites as Spallanzani viewed them. In fact, the fossil accumulation within the ruins of Troy is a concrete example of Serres's pleated time: The ruins resist purification and chronological layering since one temporality is inserted within another. The use of Serres's model, finally, with its attention to how time affects and shapes objects concretely, helps us understand the way in which Spallanzani thinks about time in its material manifestations.

61. Zucker and Simmel are but two examples of such an aesthetic approach to ruins. Another key figure in ruins and aesthetic theory is, of course, Jean Starobinski; see, e.g., his essays, "Le rovine" and "Melancholy Among the Ruins."

Delicately Corrected and Constantly Befriended: Arthur Murphy's Female Characters

BARBARA MACKEY KING

Imagine this scene: a young woman stands on George's Quay in Dublin in 1729, looking out to sea. Her three year-old son, James, clings to her skirts, while one-and-a-half-year-old Arthur is held in her arms. Day after day she waits for the return of her merchant husband who has set off for Philadelphia in one of his ships, but she is destined never to see him again. All trace of him and his vessel have disappeared, she will learn, presumably lost in a storm. Jane Murphy remains in the house on George's Quay until the boys are eight and ten years old. Then, having exhausted her resources, she sells her property and moves to Boulogne-sur-mer, across the English Channel from Dover, to live with one of her sisters and her sister's children. There the future playwright and barrister resides until the age of ten, when he is sent to school.[1] Murphy would remain devoted to his mother and retain a connection to his aunts and female cousins until their deaths.[2] Did this early experience of a female-dominated household influence Murphy to be particularly fond of women's company throughout his life? Did the early conditions of his life later influence his creation of intelligent and strong-minded female characters in his journals and plays?

Through his two careers—in literature and in the law—Murphy had professional and personal relationships with many of the most important people in the political and literary worlds of eighteenth-century London. He wrote roles for the leading actresses of the period, instructing them in their performances and acting as their legal representative. He particularly fashioned five leading roles for the talents of his mistress, Ann Elliot. He had a 42-year relationship with Hester Thrale Piozzi, and, unlike Dr. Johnson, was one of the few people who did not abandon her when she married her second husband, Gabriel Piozzi. Jesse Foot, Murphy's close friend, executor, and first biographer, tells us that Murphy enjoyed the company of women: "He was fond of their society and delighted in giving them instruction."[3] Foot also felt that one of Murphy's outstanding abilities as a playwright was his creation of admirable and striking female characters:

> The study of the female character seems to have been his particular choice, and his *darling dramatic passion*: in all his scenes, women are *delicately corrected*, studiously cautioned, and *constantly befriended*. [4] (Italics mine.)

Among Murphy's three twentieth-century biographers,[5] only Howard Hunter Dunbar mentions this gift, and he dwells on it briefly:

> [Murphy's] forte was his capacity to depict sprightly ladies such as the Widow Bellmour, Maria, and Lady Bell. No author of the period equalled him in the presentation of this type of character.[6]

Modern critics have discussed Murphy's tempestuous relationship with David Garrick, his use of dramatic sources, his position as a laughing rather than a sentimental playwright, the brilliance and naturalness of his dialogue, and his use of specific male friends and family members as models for satiric portraits, but an exploration of his female characters is long overdue. Surveying those women whom Murphy "delicately corrects," as Foot puts it, shows that he criticizes those who have wasted their minds on trivialities, such as fads and gambling. In contrast, he "constantly befriends," as Foot continues, those who are intelligent, witty, confident, and vivacious.

Delicately Corrected

In his *Gray's Inn Journal*, written at first during 1753–54 and revised for his collected works in 1786, Murphy devotes a third[7] of his articles wholly or in part to criticisms of women's fashions, to their lack of intelligent conversation, and to similar trifles. Scholars who have commented on this fact[8] have agreed that Murphy spends more space on women than other contemporary journalists. More of Murphy's satire against women is directed toward shifting vogues in dress than toward anything else. In the second essay, for example, he rails against "artificial embellishments," especially when they "luxuriantly wanton into fantastic extravagances."[9] And in the following excerpt from essay no. 103, he criticizes extremes in fashion, hairdos, make-up and immodesty:

> The hoop has of late spread to a wider circumference, and fenced, as it is, with formidable rows of steel, no beau can approach, without the danger of a broken shin [...]. The [Amazons] of old advanced with only one breast exerted, but the modern fair comes forward with both displayed to view. The head is built up several stories higher than usual, and the art of painting is so well understood, that every woman has now as many faces as tippets, fans, or gloves. [10]

Fashions and fads are superficial and passing fancies, the preoccupations, Murphy feels, of trivial, rather than intelligent minds. In essay no. 33, Ranger, Murphy's *persona* in these essays, feels that he must pay his debt to society and go visiting. He says he is "not a little fatigued with the successive repetition of the same flimsy chit-chat in every company where I was admitted, and quite disgusted with so trifling a manner of spending my time."[11] Murphy gives us a witty example of what he means when Ranger appears at the home of Mr. and Mrs. Discount and their two daughters. During the conversation, Ranger mentions that Mrs. Brilliant is quite happy since her recent marriage:

> "O indeed," says Miss Discount, "I believe she is very happy, for she has got a very handsome equipage and a sweet pair of earrings; and then she sees a vast deal of company: there were ninety persons at her last rout. She plays crown whist."
>
> I could not forbear observing, that I was a little surprized [sic], so discerning a young lady should estimate Mrs. Brilliant's happiness from the stake she played at whist, when to me it appeared, that she possessed a more certain source of felicity, in the amiable qualities of her husband. "O law! That's true," replied the ladies, "they say her husband too is a pretty man." [12]

Murphy continues in this essay to criticize women for dressing competitively in order to excel other women, for going to the playhouse only for the purpose of being seen there, for perpetually playing cards, and for marrying only in order to have a husband to support them in these activities. In an essay written for *The Entertainer*,[13] Murphy creates another superficial character, "Mary Midnight." Neglecting her family, she rises late and plays cards until 3 a.m. She says:

> [M]y peculiar qualifications consist in the art of painting my face, and dropping my fan; I have acquired the most engaging motion of the eyes and lips; I can cheat at cards tolerably well, and in one word, I am possessed of all the qualifications that make up an accomplished woman; I beat my husband one hundred times every day, and spend twice the rent of his estate every year.[14]

A trivial mind occupies itself with scandal and gossip, rather than with intellectual pleasures. In *Gray's Inn Journal* no. 11, Murphy portrays an "elegant gentleman" who wishes to take revenge on a certain lord by spreading lies about his faultless and admirable wife. Swiftly he runs to Lady Tattleaid's toilette to convey his fabrications, when

> away flies my Lady Tattleaid, on the wings of malice, to all parts of town […]. The gossips at Garraways have it in a moment: at once it is buzzed on [the Ex]change, and the circling whisper in the boxes interrupts the play at night. At my Lady Trumpabout's assembly, the ladies are all in a titter […]. Pleased with these ideas, the ladies retire home from the rout, sink into a comfortable repose, dream of divorces, separations, and unhappy beauties.[15]

Murphy expresses an absolute passion against gambling, and a sizable percentage, more than a tenth, of his essays are about it. He is especially severe on women gamblers. In essay no. 70, gambling has cost Elisabeth Gayless not only to lose her beauty and all desire for her home and husband, but this addiction has also caused her to stake the money she was given to pay household bills, to "venture a daughter's portion upon the turning of a die," and even to have been "tempted by Lord Trumpabout, who offered to remit a considerable gaming debt, for so small a consideration as cuckolding her husband."[16]

If Murphy's satiric thrust in his *Gray's Inn Journal* is directed toward women in society, the focus in his comedies and farces is on individual character flaws, such as vanity and pretensions to learning. The role of the maid, Termagant, in *The Upholsterer* (1757), was written for Kitty Clive when her acting career was at its peak. The character is in the stage tradition of ladies who vainly seek to improve their powers of verbal expression while betraying their questionable education, with Fielding's Mrs. Slipslop as an antecedent and Sheridan's Mrs. Malaprop as a descendant. One of Termagant's choice passages is a page and a half monologue in which she reads the newspaper and comments on it, ending with a reference to a current politician:

> If, instead of his *policies*, he would *manure* his mind like me, and read good *altars*, and improve himself in fine *langidge*, and *bombast*, and *polite accollishments*— (Exit).[17]

Her part is actually longer than that of the romantic heroine, since she is onstage fully one-third of the play. *The Critical Review* of April 1758 says: "The character of Termagant, a foolish, prating chambermaid, ridiculously fond of hard words, will not fail to raise the laughter of an audience,"[18] and Murphy's modern biographers also praise the characterization. John Pike Emery says that the making of language errors seems more natural on the part of a servant who is trying to improve herself.[19] And Howard Hunter Dunbar prefers Termagant to many of her predecessors:

> Certainly Termagant flourishes her parts of speech with more grace and humor than Fielding's Slipslop, Smollett's Winifred Jenkins, or any of the numerous forerunners of Sheridan's incomparable gentlewoman.[20]

The farcical afterpiece, *The Old Maid* (1761), is Murphy's most brutal attack on women's vanity, and indeed, one modern critic has called his satiric portrayal of the leading character "cruel" and excessive.[21] The plot is one of mistaken identity: Miss Harlow is a 43-year old spinster who lives with her brother and his beautiful young wife. When the Harlow ladies are introduced to 22-year old Clerimont as "Miss and Mrs. Harlow," he assumes the younger lady is the unmarried one. As it unfolds, the farce is rife with scenes of false impressions and mistaken dialogue—a technique in which Murphy was an acknowledged master. Thinking herself to be desired by a man young enough to be her son, Miss Harlow says to her sister-in-law:

> These features are still regular and blooming [...] the love-darting eye has not quite forsook me; and [...] I have made a conquest which your boasted youth might be vain of [...] . Some faces retain their bloom and beauty longer than you may imagine, my dear sister.[22]

Miss Harlow is even self-deceived enough to dismiss the middle-aged beau who has been her faithful suitor for three years. In the end, when the mistake is revealed, Miss Harlow is laughed off the stage because of her vanity and arrogance. Her sister-in-law, Mrs. Harlow, remains to close the farce by saying:

> I cautioned my sister sufficiently about this matter, but vanity got the better of her, and leaves her now a whimsical instance of folly and affectation.
>
> In vain the Faded Toast her mirror tries,
> And counts the cruel murders of her eyes;
> For Ridicule, sly-peeping o'er her head,
> Will point the roses and the lilies dead;
> And while, fond soul! she weaves her myrtle chain,
> She proves a subject of the comic strain. [23]

Only one of the contemporary reviewers thought Murphy was too harsh in his treatment of Miss Harlow,[24] while other reviewers were quite favourable, and *The Old Maid* became "an extremely popular afterpiece"[25] until the mid-nineteenth century. There also developed a tradition of having Miss Harlow played by a man in drag,[26] which would obviously exaggerate the farcical elements of the character. Today the story of a middle-aged woman who tries to pass herself off as still young and desirable is no longer a fit subject for ridicule. Howard Hunter Dunbar says: "Miss Harlow's conduct justifies the ridicule to which she is subjected, but even a reader feels some pity for her as she stands confused and humbled in the final scene."[27] In no other play does Murphy focus his satire on a female character this strongly. For the twentieth-century audience, it may go beyond *delicate correction*.

Constantly Befriended

We have seen how Murphy satirizes and corrects women in his *Gray's Inn Journal*, a publication that he also uses to illustrate the characteristic he most admires in women: their intelligence. In issue no. 98, Murphy urges his female readers to leave trivial pursuits and instead cultivate their minds by reading.

> I must [...] beg leave to inform my pretty readers, that they are highly mistaken, if they imagine, that, by dedicating a few hours to literary amusements, they endanger their lovely features, or run a risk of dimming the sparkling lustre of their eyes. On the contrary, a page or two in the morning may serve to adjust the countenance: the acquisition of a new idea may give a more engaging ornament to the head, than a new Paris cap; and the eye will beam with brighter lustre, when directed by an active principle within, then swimming round the room in pretty, giddy, vain, senseless, affectation [...]. How much more eligible to employ some portion of our time in a way that may enlarge the mind, and increase its stock of ideas? [28]

After one cultivates her mind, "the manner of talking agreeably" will naturally result:

> We are pleased to see a beautiful pair of lips in motion, when everything that comes from them administers to the pleasures of conversation. The spirits of the fair are awakened by the exercise of their thinking faculties, and the eye beams with double lustre; the tongue confirms, what the countenance had before indicated, that all within is cheerful, gay, spirited, and sensible. [29]

Indeed, Murphy's preference for intelligent women may be found everywhere in his writings. He ends *The School for Guardians* by telling women they can maintain their relationship with their lover only through cultivating their minds: "Beauty, ye fair, may forge the lover's chain; / But the mind's charms your empire must maintain."[30]

Of all Murphy's tragic heroines, Euphrasia, the heroine of *The Grecian Daughter* (1769/1772)[31] has to be the one the most *constantly befriended.* First, Euphrasia drives the plot, being onstage close to two-thirds of the time. Murphy's four tragedies all deal with tyrannical usurpation; however, in this play it is the aging king's daughter who takes premeditated action to solve the dilemma. Her most memorable action appears in Act II where she gains entrance to see her father, sentenced to starve to death in a cave, and she nurses him with her own infant's milk. Looking in the (offstage) cave, the guard see her and says:

> O! I can hold no more; at such a sight
> Ev'n the hard heart of tyranny would melt
> To infant softness [...]

....

> Behold that unexampled goodness; see
> Th'expedient sharp necessity has taught her;
> The father foster'd at his daughter's breast!
> O! filial piety! — the milk design'd
> For her own offspring, on the parent's lip
> Allays the parching fever. [32]

She takes decisive means to save her kingdom, not only by suckling her father, but also by convincing the guards to assist her by acting as spies in the tyrant's court. She watches the progress of the battles with rapt attention, shouting in victory as she sees rival soldiers perish in the sea. She taunts the usurper to his face without backing down, and finally, she stabs him in his heart with as much firmness as any masculine hero, gloating over the blood on her dagger's point. The play ends with the restored king giving his crown, not to Euphrasia's husband, who is fighting in the army, but to Euphrasia herself, saying that he hopes that she may become "A parent to her people."[33]

Like Murphy's three previous tragic heroines,[34] Euphrasia does not fit the classic mould of the Shakespearean or Aristotelian tragic heroes, but rather, follows the example of Dryden's heroic plays which typically contain exemplary characters as moral paradigms for the audience to follow. Thus Euphrasia is the embodiment of what it means to be the perfect daughter. It is clear that Murphy's eighteenth century audience caught this message, since *The Critical Review* for March, 1772, reported that spectators were more interested in the relationship between father and daughter than in the theme of tyrannical usurpation:

> The fate of Evander and Euphrasia interests us through the whole play[…]. The incident on which this tragedy is founded[35] is one of the most singular examples of filial affection that we meet with in all history, and the author has improved it with all the lively force of description that words can possibly convey.[36]

Euphrasia not only drives the plot, but presents a remarkably rounded character by portraying different aspects of her personality to different people. She is heroically strong and militant to the invaders, tender and loving to her family, reverent to the gods, and in despair when falsely told her father has been executed. Her masterful persuasion in the scene in Act II in which she begs the guard to allow her to see her father, covers five pages of text, and illustrates a wide variety of moods and approaches. First she begs the guard, throwing herself at his feet, and when that is unsuccessful, she tries a patriotic plea: "Thou, like me,/ Wert born in Greece." Next she appeals to his filial sense: "You have a father, too." After that she raves in excess: "Here will I dwell, and rave, and shriek, and give/ These scattered locks to all the passing winds." She finally succeeds by shaming the guard's manhood. When he says he dare not let her see her father or else he will be punished, she replies:

> And if you dare!—Is that
> The voice of manhood? Honest, if you dare!
> 'Tis the slave's virtue! 'tis the utmost limit
> Of the base coward's honour. [37]

This ploy succeeds; the guard leaves the tyrant and, as one of Euphrasia's followers, becomes a spy in the enemy's camp.

When David Garrick first read the manuscript, he exclaimed, "The part of the daughter is one of the finest for an actress in all the dramatic circle."[38] According to Dunbar, the opening night reviews were "rapturous [. . .]. The enthusiastic approval of *The Grecian Daughter* [...] was almost wholly free from adverse comments."[39] Mrs. Thrale held it to be her favorite tragedy, and she wrote in her journal for March/April 1778: "Mr. Murphy's Grecian Daughter [sic] is I think unquestionably the best of all our modern tragedies, and all its merit is the power it has over our passions."[40] *The Grecian Daughter* outshone all other tragedies of the period and held the boards for seven decades,[41] continuing in stock until 1848.[42] Only four other tragedies were acted more frequently—*Hamlet, Macbeth, Romeo and Juliet*, and *Jane Shore*.[43] The role of Euphrasia was Sarah Siddons' favorite role and the one she used as her farewell piece.[44] As late as 1831, the role of Euphrasia was one young actresses felt they had to perform in order to establish their reputations,[45] much as young men today still feel they must perform *Hamlet*. As Murphy wrote his four tragedies, the role of the tragic heroine grew in length and plot significance in each succeeding play. Euphrasia, Murphy's ultimate tragic woman, is strong minded, action taking, multi-dimensional, and morally exemplary.

Unusual for the period, Murphy's comedy *The Way to Keep Him* (1758/1761) does not contain a young woman who wishes to marry against her father's will. Rather the play boasts three outstanding mature women, all of whom take part in directing the action, achieving dominance over the male characters, showing intelligence and complexity in their characterizations, and embodying the theme of the play, which is: how a wife is to keep the attention and love of her husband.

The audience does not meet the Widow Bellmour until the beginning of the third act, but by then their curiosity has been piqued, because diverse remarks have been made about her. Mrs. Lovemore, who needs to learn how to retain the love of her husband, sees her as a *femme fatale* who is taking her husband from her. Yet Lady Constant defends her, and Sir Brilliant Fashion describes her as: "amiable [...] young, gay, rich, handsome [...] . Her manner so entertaining! [...] That round of variety! And every new attitude does so become her."[46] Act III opens with Mrs. Bellmour's maid describing her mistress to the audience and stressing her intelligence: "They must rise early who can outwit her."[47] The widow enters reading "Of the Characters of Women" from Pope's *Moral Essays*. The section she chooses is significant and prophetic: Pope describes his ideal woman as one who retains solidarity with other women and who rules men with subtlety:

> She who can own a sister's charms, and hear
> Sighs for a daughter with unwounded ear;
> That never answers till a husband cools,
> And if she rules him, never shows she rules.[48]

The Widow is giddily in love with Lord Ethridge, not realizing he is really married Mr. Lovemore in disguise. Although she is cast in the role of the *other woman*, we realize from her ignorance of Mr. Lovemore's married state, that she is really virtuous.

The turning point of the play occurs in Act III when Mrs. Lovemore comes to confront the widow, Lovemore's ruse is revealed, and Mrs. Bellmour determines to help Mrs. Lovemore outwit her husband. The women's actions in this significant scene deserve to be studied in detail. Mrs. Bellmour is eagerly awaiting a visit from Lord Ethridge, yet when Mrs. Lovemore—a stranger to her—enters in distress, she asks her to stay and gives her her full attention. Hearing Mrs. Lovemore's story, but not understanding that she, herself, is the *other woman*, the widow instructs Mrs. Lovemore in the art of pleasing:

> It is the wife's business to bait the hook for her husband with variety. Virtue alone will not do it. Vice puts on allurements: why should not truth and innocence do the same? [. . .]. After the fatal words "for better, for worse," women in general relax into indolence, and while they are guilty of no infidelity, they think everything is right. But they are mistaken: a great deal is wanting; an address, vivacity, a desire to please.

While she is talking to Mrs. Lovemore, Mr. Lovemore, disguised as Lord Ethridge, is announced. It is significant that even though the Widow Bellmour had previously been eagerly awaiting his arrival, now she feels that helping a sister in distress is paramount, and she tells her servants to send Lord Ethridge away. When Mrs. Lovemore says she does not wish to inconvenience a pre-arranged meeting, the widow tells her to wait in an adjoining room and she will make the interview with Lord Ethridge short. In the meantime, Mrs. Lovemore can watch how the widow handles an admirer. The following scene exemplifies the instruction the Widow has just given Mrs. Lovemore. Thinking that Lord Ethridge is a single man who has come to ask for her hand, Mrs. Bellmour engages in witty badinage in the style of a Congreve proviso-scene. Comparing herself to "an old house in the country that wants a tenant," the Widow asks Lord Ethridge if he knows "a single gentleman . . . whom these conditions will suit?" However, as marriage is not Lovemore's aim, he evades her questions with some embarrassment. The Widow then continues with a bravura monologue in which she describes an evening at Ranelegh, mimicking the ladies of fashion there, and in particular singling out for her disdain those "insipid things that have features without a mind." [49] We are reminded of Murphy's advice on intelligence in his *Gray's Inn Journal*.

However, Mrs. Lovemore, peeking in and seeing her husband in disguise, has fainted in the next room. Upon being informed of this fact by her maid, the Widow Bellmour gets rid of Lord Ethridge immediately. Helping Mrs. Lovemore is more important to her than even a prospective proposal. When Mrs. Lovemore informs the widow that Lord Ethridge is really her husband, the widow becomes enraged at this deception and indignantly drops her interest in him, promising she will never allow him in her house again. Then she takes the lead in planning an hilarious discovery scene in which Lovemore's disguise is unmasked in the presence of his friends. Thus the Widow Bellmour is shown to be not only vivacious and witty, but also a wise and caring counsellor to Mrs. Lovemore. In contrast to the sentimental heroines who achieved their purposes through virtue and tears, Mrs. Lovemore is taught to keep her husband "through the way of wit, cleverness, and intrigue."[50]

Audiences of the time found it a novelty to have a virtuous *other woman*.[51] *The London Chronicle* for January 24–26, 1760, mentioned the complexity of the role: "The character of the Widow is very well-drawn; the giddy thoughtlessness of her conduct is mixed with a sufficiently apparent share of real worth."[52] Fanny Burney thought the widow was a "first-rate character."[53] And Robert Donald Spector, in his biography of Murphy for the Twayne's English Authors series, sees her as

> The embodiment of a [...] vision of commonsensicality. She knows how to deal with men and women. She maintains her dignity through adversity. With genuine understanding, she advises Mrs. Lovemore [...]. She is Murphy's heroine, whose voice of common sense speaks for the needed balance in a civilized society. [54]

Murphy's characterizations in this play—both male and female—have been highly praised by both eighteenth century and modern critics. The critic for the *Public Ledger* for January 12, 1761, found "the characters in general strongly pointed and their colouring closely copied from nature."[55] *The Monthly Review* agreed, noting that "[T]he characters are drawn from life."[56] After seeing a performance in 1811, Jesse Foot felt that "This is a play which will never go out of fashion."[57] It was so well known that Mrs. Thrale was able to quote lines from it at a party.[58] The play had a continuous stage history until late in the nineteenth century[59] and was revived by Allardyce Nicoll in 1926.[60] In 1929, Ashley Thorndike recognized the strength of the female roles in the play:

> It is perhaps indicative of the growing power of women in the theatre that at the end of the play, the ladies are triumphant and award forgiveness to their repentant husbands and lovers.[61]

Finally, London's Orange Street Theatre produced it in 1988. *The London Times* wrote of this production: "Where the piece is at its most interesting and original is in its taking of the female point of view."[62]

In addition to the Widow Bellmour and Mrs. Lovemore, there is a third major woman's role in *The Way to Keep Him*. Lady Bashful Constant is seeking a divorce from a husband who is constantly argumentative because he is too shy to express his true love for her. Beginning in the third act, all three women take over the direction of the plot and conclude the play by first exposing the male characters and then forgiving them and re-integrating them into society. These women are some of the most complex roles to come from Murphy's pen. Although the women are individually characterized, they also share certain similarities. All three are not only intelligent, they are also not afraid of displaying their intelligence in men's company. All are, or can be, witty and spirited. All the women remain virtuous, repulsing the two rakes, Lovemore and Sir Brilliant Fashion. And they all have strength of character: Mrs. Lovemore goes to face the *other woman* directly, and she is willing to develop and grow. Lady Bashful Constant has taken steps to arrange a divorce, and the Widow is capable of handling the plot situation with confidence and ease. None of them are simpering or long-suffering; instead, each takes the initiative. Their actions and dialogue are central to the play's theme of the improvement of conjugal love, and critics from both the eighteenth and twentieth centuries have continually praised them.

In general Murphy tailored his roles for the talents of the actresses he found upon the Drury Lane and Covent Garden stages. But according to several contemporary accounts, the role of Maria in his farcical afterpiece *The Citizen* (1761/1761), was created to utilize the personality of a particular actress.[63] Ann Elliot was a country girl who came to London to work in domestic service and was probably forced into prostitution. Murphy discovered her, felt she had natural dramatic talent, and took her to live with him in his cottage near Richmond where he coached her for the stage.[64] Maria's aim in *The Citizen* is to influence George, whom she is to marry, to break off the match so that she can marry her true love, Beaufort. She does this by outwitting George twice. In her first scene with him, she pretends to be a country bumpkin, mistaking the meaning of words like "burletta," "connoisseur," and "virtuoso." Unfortunately, George merely says: "I'll marry her and lock her up."[65] Thus in her second scene with him, Maria reverses the tactic and appears as a knowledgeable bluestocking. Where she had previously mistaken words, now she uses words for George to mistake. When she asks for a verse "extempore," George says, "I never have one about me." When she talks of Croesus' river, Pactolus, George thinks she speaks of a city merchant. And when she rattles off a list of poets she has read, George can only say: "Her tongue goes like a water-mill."[66] George could have tolerated a stupid wife, but he will not endure one smarter than he, and so he breaks off the match.

Maria's character is developed with variety and complexity. She enters the first scene in a lively manner, singing, teasing Beaufort, sparring with her brother, and mimicking both her father and miserly Philpot, her perspective father-in-law. In her first scene with George, she shows what a consummate actress she is by playing the fool and wailing like a child when she thinks she has been insulted. In her second scene with him, she is not afraid to show her intelligence, letting the audience know that she has lately come from a boarding-school and describing how she will deal with her suitor: "I have all the materials of an impertinent wit, and I will now twirl him about the room, like a boy setting up his top with his finger and thumb."[67] She is charming, vivacious, intelligent, self-confident, and strong-willed enough to defy both her father and convention. As Jesse Foot tells us, the role of Maria was specifically tailored to Ann Elliot's talents:

> Miss Elliot, in the character of Maria, was doing no more on the stage than she was doing every day off it: she had an uncommon flow of spirits, and had been instructed by Mr. Murphy to do the very same with her city lover on the stage, that she would have done with a similar offer from one at Tunbridge, at Deptford, or anywhere else. The character of Maria [...] only wanted ease, confidence, youth, volubility, seductive smiles, and attractive charms [...]; all these Miss Elliot had by nature. She tripped about the stage as light as a wood-nymph: everything about her was sylphic and enchanting: she talked in a sweet and clear voice: she bore so hard upon young Philpot that she confounded even Harry Woodward [the actor of young Philpot], and she played the fool with more *non-chalance* than can be described.[68]

Jesse Foot's opinion was corroborated by other contemporaries, for the words *lively*, *vivacious*, and *high-spirited* constantly recur in the reviews. Tobias Smollet described her as "a young spirited coquette, gay, giddy, arch, and frolicksome" [sic.][69] John Taylor said: "By all accounts she was one of the most original and spirited actresses that ever appeared on the stage."[70]

Like many of Murphy's afterpieces, *The Citizen* became a stock piece in London and the provincial theatres. From the time of its opening in 1761 until 1830, the piece was constantly being presented to London audiences. Actors and actresses frequently used it for their benefit nights, and it was still occasionally revived into the late nineteenth century.[71] In 1807, critic Leigh Hunt stated that Murphy "will be forever remembered as the author of the first farce in the English language, *The Citizen*.[72, 73]

Nonetheless, of all Murphy's female characters, critics have preferred Lady Bell in *Know Your Own Mind* (1760/1777), the fifth and last role written for Ann Elliot. The person of the title is Millamour, an indecisive man who cannot decide which of four ladies to marry. The first four acts are an elaborate dance in which four couples switch and mix combinations. Even though the audience can easily see who is best suited to whom, the fun is in watching how they sort themselves out. Each of the four eligible ladies has a distinct personality and is distinguishable from the rest. Of the four, Lady Bell easily dominates the audience's attention because of the brilliance of her wit and the variety of her moods. Before she enters, Millamour says of her, "the most amiable of her sex. She romps about the room like one of the graces; and deals about her wit with such a happy negligence."[74] Her sister, Lady Jane, describes her as "the veriest madcap,"[75] and Miss Neville, a cousin, speaks of her "overflowing gaiety and good humour."[76]

Although Lady Bell cannot be said to direct the whole plot, she does achieve her goal in the play, which is to capture Millamour. Her strategy is to show Millamour that she is just as volatile as he is by baiting her trap with a variety of moods. In Act II, Millamour has just been speaking to "demure and sober" Lady Jane[77] and has been captivated by her quiet charms, when he encounters Lady Bell:

> Lady Bell: My sister, I suppose, has given you some hope. Ay! That's her way: She moves by settled rules, and shines with equal light. Now I——I am a mere comet, I blaze of a sudden; dazzle for a while, then wheel away, and am thought of no more.
>
> Millamour: (aside) *That gaiety of hers is charming*. The impression your ladyship makes—
>
> Lady Bell: Words, mere words;—No, I am a strange piece of wild nature; never the same for two minutes together. Now, my sister, she is a Prussian blue, holds her colour, and is always the same.—I—I am a more changeable silk— I shift about, and display my wit and my folly, so curiously blended, that no body can tell where one begins, or the other ends. I am not worth your notice. (Walks and hums a tune.)
>
> Millamour: (aside) *She has described herself admirably; without variety, a woman is a downright piece of insipidity.*
>
> Lady Bell: Yes; I have my whims. Never the same for two minutes together. Now I love to give a scope to folly . . . . Then good sense is the word; and the next moment I can't bear the fatigue of thinking [...]. Then all spirit, and I long to lead up the ball [...]. (sings and walks about)
>
> Millamour: (aside) *Lady Jane is mere mediocrity compared to her*.
>
> Lady Bell: Lord! I run on at a strange rate. Yours, Mr. Millamour; *au revoir*. (going)
>
> Millamour: A moment longer: you must not leave me. You possess my heart: possess it without a rival.[78]

This scene does not end the matter however, as Millamour continues to change his mind, and Lady Bell continues to tease and intrigue him, often flinging pertinent asides to the audience to let them know how the affair is progressing, as:

> "Rivall'd, outwitted by my sister! Insupportable! This begins to grow serious."[79]
>
> "How Millamour follows me up and down! Charming! Here he comes."[80]
>
> And finally: "He is mine against the world!"[81]

Lady Bell has the final word when Millamour finally asks for her hand. She holds up both hands, saying: "Which will you have? Puzzle about it, and know your own mind if you can." [82]

Garrick liked the character from his first reading of the manuscript.[83] In 1929, Ashley Thorndike said: "Lady Bell is a capital heroine […] . Her gaiety, coquetry, and teasing recall the best madcaps of the old comedy."[84] Earnest Bernbaum (1958) says:

> Lady Bell is the most vivacious young woman (Goldsmith's Miss Hardcastle not excepted) that had appeared on the stage for at least one generation. In comparison with her, Sheridan's young women are tiresome.[85]

Robert Donald Spector says that "Lady Bell is one of the most attractive heroines in British stage history,"[86] and he agrees with Emery, Dunbar and other critics that Lady Bell surpasses any character created by Sheridan.[87] Thus Lady Bell seems to be the culmination of Murphy's ideal woman: intelligent, confident, witty, playful, lively, and vivacious.

Know Your Own Mind did not gain the instant success of some of Murphy's other plays, notably because it fell prey to quarrels between Garrick and Murphy and was delayed seventeen years in production. During that time, Ann Elliot and Harry Woodward, two of the actors for whom it was written, had died, and its eventual debut was at Covent Garden—not at Garrick's Drury Lane—where it was given an inadequate cast. However, it was revived at least once nearly every year in London until 1824 and was also played in the provinces and in America.[88] Today's critics feel the play is Murphy's best, and they laud in particular his characterizations. Dunbar says, "In some respects it is the best comedy of manners since Congreve […]. The characters are excellent and accurately delineated."[89] He praises Murphy's women in particular: "Murphy's greatest superiority lies in his female characters."[90]

Jesse Foot's contemporary biography of Arthur Murphy (1811) reports that the author both enjoyed the company of women and that he was particularly adept at creating female characters, some of whom he *delicately corrects* and others whom he *constantly befriends*.[91] Women with whom Murphy had close relationships range from intellectuals like Hester Thrale Piozzi to actresses such as Margaret Woffington and Katherine Clive, all of whom could be said to have had the intelligence, confidence, and vivacity Murphy demonstrated that he desired in a woman. Yet in one case only is there incontrovertible evidence that a particular woman influenced the creation of Murphy's stage characters – that of his mistress, Anne Elliot. For her he designed five roles that utilized her personality traits and illustrated what he most preferred in a woman.

Murphy liked intelligent women, and hence one of the traits he particularly criticizes in his *Gray's Inn Journal* essays is women who neglect their minds. For Murphy, an unimproved mind wastes itself in fads and trivialities. In his comedies, Murphy's satire is most harsh in *The Old Maid.* Miss Harlow's vanity and lack of self-knowledge lead her to become the butt of ridicule. Mrs. Bromley in *Know Your Own Mind* is also led by her vanity to mistake the advances of a young man, however she is more *delicately* satirized and is accepted back into society rather than evicted. Mrs. Woodvil in *The Choice* is simple-minded in her gullibility, but she remains an enjoyable gossip. Termagant in *The Upholsterer* is gently criticized in her pretensions to learning, as is Mrs. Drugget in her pretensions to society in *Three Weeks After Marriage*. In his Gray's Inn Journal, Murphy satirized gambling harshly and repeatedly. *Three Weeks after Marriage* illustrates the deleterious effects on marriage of gambling and arguing over trifles. In *Know Your Own Mind* the villain, Mavil, tries to persuade Millamour not to marry Lady Bell by misrepresenting her character as superficial, unintelligent, vain, and gambling addicted. These are all traits that Murphy, as well as Millamour, dislikes.

Looking at the characteristics that Murphy likes, it is clear that intelligence must be on the top of the list. Murphy encourages the female readers of the *Gray's Inn Journal* to read so as to improve their minds and conversation. Most of Murphy's female roles are not only intelligent, they are also not afraid to show their intelligence before men. Maria in *The Citizen* mentions her boarding school education twice and displays her vast knowledge of literature before her suitor. The Widow Bellmour enters reading Pope's essays, and Lady Bell's spirited repartee clearly demonstrates her intellect.

As well as intelligence, readers are impressed with the strength of many of Murphy's leading female characters. They show confidence in making decisions and display single-mindedness in the pursuit of their objectives. Euphrasia (*The Grecian Daughter*) is undoubtedly Murphy's strongest female character, saving both her father and her kingdom. Murphy's comic heroines, on the other hand, are occupied with family, not national, concerns, and in most cases their goal is simply to capture the appropriate husband. But they approach this goal as actively as Euphrasia does hers. Lady Bell in *Know Your Own Mind* describes her battle plan to her sister, saying that she will capture Millamour by appearing as volatile as he. Lucinda in *No One's Enemy But His Own*, likewise captures her spouse with wit, besting two men in metaphoric duels using images from war and hunting. Maria in *The Citizen* casts off an unwanted lover by manipulating him in two strategically planned scenes. The Widow Bellmour's strength of character in *The Way to Keep Him* lies in immediately discarding a deceitful lover and then, rather than brooding over the situation, unselfishly helping another woman to achieve her objective.

Although one can find stereotypes typical of the period in Murphy's plays, his leading women are often realized in more depth. Contemporary critics speak of the lifelikeness of Murphy's characters. Euphrasia is multi-dimensional and shows emotions as diverse as tenderness and militancy. Both the widow Bellmour and Lady Bell speak of attracting a man by displaying a variety of moods and emotions. This last role was one Murphy wrote for the talents and personality of Ann Elliot, who was famously adept at swiftly moving from one mood to another. As Lady Restless in *Three Weeks After Marriage*, Ann Elliot was able to move with great rapidity from affection toward her husband, to teasing, to pique, to distance, to fury, and then to regret.[92] Lastly, Murphy's women often carry the moral lesson of the play. As Euphrasia teaches the audience what it means to be the perfect Grecian daughter, the widow Bellmour teaches women how to hold onto their lovers.

This examination of some of Arthur Murphy's plays and expository works illustrates, as his friend and biographer, Jesse Foot, said, that Murphy wrote admirable and striking female characters, delicately correcting some but befriending most. We would do well to put the best of Murphy's works back in the curriculum and in the stage repertory.

NOTES

1. Jesse Foot, *The Life of Arthur Murphy* (London: J. Faulder, 1811), 7.
2. Arthur Murphy letter to Hester Thrale Piozzi, March 16, 1795. The Thrale

Piozzi and Related Manuscripts, John Rylands University Library, Manchester, England, MMS 548:12.

3. Foot, *Murphy*, 372.

4. Foot, *Murphy*, 309.

5. The other two of Murphy's biographers are John Pike Emery, *Arthur Murphy: an Eminent English Dramatist of the Eighteenth Century* (Philadelphia: University of Pennsylvania Press, 1946) and Robert Donald Spector, *Arthur Murphy* (Boston: Twayne, 1979).

6. Howard Hunter Dunbar, *The Dramatic Career of Arthur Murphy* (New York: Modern Language Association, 1946) 297.

7. Women are the primary or single topic in 11 of the 104 articles; they are the secondary topic in 24. With a total of 35 essays mentioning women, the result is 34%.

8. Emery, *Murphy*, 20; Spector, *Murphy*, 25.

9. Arthur Murphy, *The Works of Arthur Murphy, esq*., 7 vols. (London: T. Cadell, 1786) 5:13

10. Murphy, *Works*, 6:444–45.

11. Murphy, *Works*, 5:278–79.

12. Murphy, *Works*, 5:283

13. In *New Essays by Arthur Murphy*, (Lansing, Michigan: Michigan State University Press, 1963), Arthur Sherbo assigned about 30 essays, previously unattributed, to Arthur Murphy.

14. Quoted in Sherbo (ed.), *New Essays by Arthur Murphy*, 72.

15. Murphy, *Works*, 5: 96–97.

16. Murphy, *Works*, 6: 161–65.

17. Murphy, *Works*, 2:130.

18. Unsigned review of *The Upholsterer or What News*? by Arthur Murphy, *The Critical Review of Annals of Literature*, April 1758, 5:330.

19. Emery, *Murphy*, 38.

20. Dunbar, *Murphy*, 46.

21. Willard Austin Kinne, *Revivals and Importations of French Comedies in England, 1749–1800* (New York: Columbia University Press, 1939) 82–83.

22. Murphy, *Works*, 2:163–64.

23. Murphy, *Works*, 2:214

24. Unsigned review of *The Old Maid*, by Arthur Murphy, *The Monthly Review or Literary Journal* 25 (December 1761) 473.

25. Dunbar, *Murphy*, 134.

26. Harry Woodward in 1766, W. Farren in 1820. Dunbar, *Murphy*, 134.

27. Dunbar, *Murphy*, 135.

28. Murphy, *Works*, 6:400–01.

29. Murphy, *Works*, 5:16.

30. Murphy, *Works*, 4:298.

31. Two dates indicate date of writing and date of first production.

32. Murphy, *Works*, 1:242–43

33. Murphy, *Works*, 1:304.

34. Mandane in *The Orphan of China*, Orazia in *Alzuma*, and Zenobia in *Zenobia*.
35. Murphy found this story in Valerius Maximus..
36. Unsigned review of *The Grecian Daughter*, by Arthur Murphy, *The Critical Review of Annals of Literature*, March 1772, 33:226–27.
37. Murphy, *Works*, 1:230–35.
38. Quoted in Foot, *Murphy*, 222.
39. Dunbar, *Murphy*, 295.
40. Hester Lynch Thrale (Mrs. Piozzi), *Thraliana*, ed. Katherine Balderston, 2nd ed. 2 vols (Oxford: Clarendon Press, 1951) 1:248.
41. Richard W. Bevis, ed. *English Drama: Restoration and Eighteenth Century, 1600–1789* (London: Longman, 1988) 207.
42. Spector, *Murphy*, 149.
43. M. Victor Alper. *Arthur Murphy, Tragedian: A Critical Edition of "The Grecian Daughter*." (Dissertation, New York University, 1973) 1–li.
44. James Boaden, *The Memoirs of Mrs. Siddons: Interspersed with Anecdotes of Authors and Actors* (London: Henry Colburn 1827) 2:97.
45. John Galt, *The Lives of the Players* Vol. 2 (London: Henry Colburn and Richard Bentley, 1831) 2: 125.
46. Murphy, *Works*, 3:41.
47. Murphy, *Works*, 3:90.
48. Murphy, *Works*, 3:90.
49. Murphy, *Works*, 3:104–12.
50. J. Homer Caskey, "Arthur Murphy and the War on Sentimental Comedy," *Journal of English and German Philology* 30 (1931): 571.
51. Richard W. Bevis, *The Laughing Tradition: Stage Comedy in Garrick's Day* (Athens: University of Georgia Press, 1980) 193.
52. C. G. Comus, review of *The Way to Keep Him* by Arthur Murphy, *The London Chronicle*, January 24–26, 1760, 7:95.
53. Fanny Burney, *The Early Journals and Letters of Fanny Burney*, ed. Lars E. Troide (Kingston: McGill-Queen University Press, 1990) 2:241.
54. Spector, *Murphy*, 104.
55. Quoted in Charles Harold Gray, *Theatrical Criticism in London to 1795* (New York: Benjamin Bloom, 1971), 162.
56. Unsigned review of *The Way to Keep Him* by Arthur Murphy, *The Monthly Review, or Literary Journal*, February 1760, 22:144.
57. Foot, *Murphy*, 165.
58. James L. Clifford, *Hester Lynch Piozzi (Mrs. Thrale)* (Oxford: Clarendon Press, 1941), 172.
59. John Pike Emery, ed. "*The Way to Keep Him" and Five Other Plays by Arthur Murphy* (New York: New York University Press, 1956), 127.
60. Dunbar, *Murphy*, 98–101.
61. Ashley H. Thorndike, *English Comedy* (New York: Macmillan Press, 1929), 424.
62. Unsigned review of *The Way to Keep Him* by Arthur Murphy, Orange Street Theatre, London, *The London Times*, September 13, 1988, 18g.

63. See for instance Foot, *Murphy*, 188.
64. Emery, *Murphy*, 63
65. Murphy, *Works*, 2:256.
66. Murphy, *Works*, 2:290–91, 288.
67. Murphy, *Works*, 2:286.
68. Foot, *Murphy*, 188.
69. *Critical Review*, February 1763 15:118.
70. Taylor, *Records*, 1:205.
71. Dunbar, *Murphy*, 148; Emery, *Murphy*, 75.
72. Quoted in Dunbar, *Murphy*, 149
73. I revived it at Bowling Green State University in 1996.
74. Murphy, *Works*, 4:31.
75. Murphy, *Works*, 4:55.
76. Murphy, *Works*, 4:56.
77. Murphy, *Works*, 4:58.
78. Murphy, *Works*, 4:70–71.
79. Murphy, *Works*, 4:103.
80. Murphy, *Works*, 4:142.
81. Murphy, *Works*, 4: 171.
82. Murphy, *Works*, 4: 178.
83. Foot, *Murphy*, 292.
84. Thorndike, *English Comedy*, 423.
85. Ernest Bernbaum, *The Drama of Sensibility: A Sketch of the History of English Sentimental Comedy and Domestic Tragedy,* 1696–1780, Harvard Studies in English 3 (Gloucester: Peter Smith, 1958) 256.
86. Spector, *Murphy*, 122.
87. Spector, *Murphy*, 126; Emery, *Murphy*, 334.
88. Dunbar, *Murphy*, 281.
89. Dunbar, *Murphy*, 283.
90. Dunbar, *Murphy*, 287–88.
91. Foot, *Murphy*, 372, 309.
92. The other two roles not mentioned are Lucinda in *No One's Enemy But His Own* and Mary Ann in *School for Guardians*.

Tidying as We Go: Constructing the Eighteenth Century through Adaptation in *Becoming Jane*, *Gulliver's Travels*, and *Crusoe*

KAREN GEVIRTZ

What exactly does a film adaptation do, and how does it go about doing it? For one set of critics, adaptations offer a retrospective insight into the workings of a source text.[1] In this view adaptations are dependent or ancillary texts without full meaning in their own right that provide insight retrospectively into an originary text. The adaptation helps an audience to uncover a meaning for, and by extension a relevance of, the source text.[2] Recently, this approach has essentially given way to an intertextual one that regards an adaptation as a valuable text in its own right, and that sees the relationship between it and its source as dialogic, so that each affects the meaning of the other.[3] The time is right to complicate this intertextual approach still further by recognizing that the contexts of adaptation and source are also part of the interaction between these works. Texts inevitably interact with their contexts, whether the context of their creation or the context of their consumption or both, and texts have long been used to create or recreate an understanding not just of the present but also of the past. An adaptation can be used to construct an interpretation of a source text, but it can also construct a cultural function for the source in the source's original moment, in the adaptation's moment, or in any moment in between. The three adaptations discussed in this article—*Becoming Jane* (2007), *Gulliver's Travels* (2010), and *Crusoe* (2008–9)—demonstrate how adaptation can function inter-contextually as well as intertextually. Each of these recent adaptations constructs a narrative of the Anglo-American past by erasing historical conflicts involving gender, race, and empire, a maneuver with consequences for constructions of the eighteenth century, of history, and of the present.

A key difference between earlier forms of adaptation theory and recent versions is the role that history or context plays in understanding the relationship between the texts. Traditional approaches assume a one-way connection between past and present. In this formulation, the past or the original text has a certain stability against which or with which the adaptation and the present moment can react or engage: there is Daniel Defoe's *Robinson Crusoe*, for example, and then there are responses to it such as J. M. Coetzee's novel *Foe* or Derek Walcott's poem "Crusoe's Journal." The intertextual approach on the other hand refuses to privilege chronological order. As Linda Hutcheon says: "One lesson is that to be second is not to be secondary or inferior; likewise, to be first is not to be originary or authoritative."[4] Such an egalitarian relationship has a powerful impact on the understanding and cultural capital of both texts.[5] Hutcheon points out that adaptations are "haunted at all times by their adapted texts" so that when we know a prior text well, "we always feel its presence shadowing the one we are experiencing directly."[6] Currently, intertextual adaptation theory generally considers this impact in a positive light: Deborah Cartmell and Imelda Whelehan see film adaptations "increasing" or "enhancing" an original text or author's "cultural capital," for example. Critics who are less sanguine about intertextuality express concern about these interactions, particularly about the function of ideology in the relationship between source text and adaptation. Martine Voiret and Sara Maza, for instance, show how adaptations can use source texts and authors to support conservative, even misogynist, classist, and racist ideologies, ideologies that can in turn reduce the quantity or quality of the text or author's cultural capital.[7]

In addition to the ideological aspects of the connection between source and adaptation, there are the contextual aspects of this connection. An adaptation not only interacts with a source text and with that text's historical context but also with the notion of history itself, an interaction with potentially profound implications. Adaptations influence the present cultural moment through their effect on the interpretation and cultural standing of the source text and, by extension, through a construction of the source text's original cultural moment. The impact on context is particularly evident in a type of adaptation that draws on the eighteenth century as its originary moment. *Becoming Jane*, *Gulliver's Travels*, and *Crusoe*, for example, attempt to use old, perhaps hallowed or sanctified cultural objects to rewrite history and thereby rewrite the current historical moment. Remaking the past in order to remake the present betrays a considerable anxiety about that present as well as about history. It also assumes the relevance and the usefulness of the past, assumes the power of the past to shape the present moment, and assumes the cultural value of objects from the past. While the films discussed here may use different strategies for this project, they all invariably use adaptation to construct a narrative about the twenty-first century's origins in the long eighteenth century that encourages a vision of the present moment considerably less conflicted than it would appear in light of historical narratives more willing to include discord, injustice, and error as part of past action and ideology.

As Rachel Brownstein points out in *Why Jane Austen?*, the last twenty years have seen "an effective dismissal, or at least a high-handed under-reading and condescending rewriting, of what [Austen] wrote" as well as an erasure of "Austen's critique of selfishness and greed and a society that measured human worth and human relationships in terms of land and money" through a fascination bordering on an "obsession" with Austen's personal experience of "romance" in its most simplified sense. Crucially, Brownstein notes that our insistence on recasting Austen, and on using these terms to do it, reveals more about our current cultural moment than it does about Austen.[8] In fact, what Brownstein calls "Jane-o-mania," the explosion of Austen-related material from the 1990s, is part of a larger phenomenon that includes other film responses to works of literature.[9] Such film responses to "classic" works of literature reveal an anxiety about the past and an eagerness not only to control or limit the relationship between past and present, but also to redefine the past as part of that controlling and limiting effort. They serve to limit through redefinition the relationship between past and present in order to facilitate a vision or version of the current moment. It is revisionism with all that term's connotations in play. *Becoming Jane* is a case study; together, the films discussed here mark a trend.

Austen's conversion from a "great author" to a fortunately jilted woman is a key symptom of this enterprise. Recent film responses to Austen and her work, primarily *The Real Jane Austen* (2002), *Becoming Jane* (2007), *Miss Austen Regrets* (2008), *The Jane Austen Trilogy* (2010), and Gillian Anderson's introductions to the Austen series on PBS in 2008, draw a direct connection between certain aspects of Austen's personal history, some more speculative than others, and her novels in order to provide both an interpretation of the work and an explanation for the fact of Austen writing.[10] Anderson's statements that "Jane Austen is obviously making up for what's missing in her own life and putting it in her fiction" or "Who taught Jane Austen to recognize and understand these feelings? Was it a young man called Tom Lefroy?" or the trailer for *Becoming Jane* that invites viewers to

"Discover Jane Austen's untold romance, that would become the inspiration for her greatest love stories," insist on reading the fiction as encoded autobiography.[11] This approach is an extension of Jon Spence's thesis in *Becoming Jane Austen* that if Austen's relationship with Lefroy continued as late as 1796, then readers must conclude that the disappointment shaped her writerly choices until nearly the end of her life, thirty years later.[12] *Becoming Jane* therefore is ostensibly a film adaptation of the speculative narrative that Spence crafts based on the 1796 letter. As Spence points out, however, while his biography may have provided a hypothesis, the screenwriters provided what is presented as biography or history: "The scriptwriters of *Becoming Jane* have imagined what might have happened during this time," he writes, adding that "the plot and incidents of the film are fictional." This claim differs from that made by the film's publicity, which declares that "Jane Austen's Most Extraordinary Romance Was Her Own."[13]

While feminist critics from the 1980s pioneered the use of biography as literary criticism, the insistence on using *only* the life of the author to explain the meaning and existence of the author's productions in this form limits the opportunity for reading the work as socio-political critique or viewing the author as a critical force.[14] Tom Lefroy's assertion in *Becoming Jane* that "your horizons must be—widened. By an extraordinary young man" in order for Jane Austen to become a great writer is the primary claim of the film: that Austen has been introduced to ideas and to experience by a man, that he has "author-ized" and "authored" the author, as it were.[15] Martha Nell Smith points out that contemporary culture has a "limited range of story lines for scripting poetic influence and erotic devotions." The use of any of these storylines to script a life that does not actually fit them, she argues, has profound implications for the understanding of that author's work, and for the construction of that author as a literary and cultural presence.[16] In particular, the "near-hegemonic prevalence of conscriptive heterosexual story lines render inscrutable" literary practices outside this narrative formula, as the determined inscription of Austen's life within the bounds of familiar, conventional, and subjugating romance attests.[17]

In rewriting Austen's personal history, the film shapes current literary culture. With her artistry the result of a male gift, Austen's place in the canon changes, arguably diminishes, and so do the positions of other women writers who now may be judged on how their lives, rather than their skills, shaped their work. It is hardly a phenomenon limited to Austen; as Madeleine Dobie points out: "The problem of the recent Austen adaptations in this regard may perhaps be seen as a reflection of the continuing problem of women writers' place in the literary canon. Austen has long been accepted as a key figure in the history of English literature, yet like many other women writers, she occupies within this circle of prestige a circumscribed, distinctly feminine position, which at worst amounts to qualified acceptance, or to recognition as a woman writer."[18] This phenomenon can be understood as part of a larger trend of "screening the author"—using a film to present the author behind the source material.[19] This interest in attributing Shakespeare's work to his life experience produced *Shakespeare in Love* (1998), for example, and the Bard has recently come under renewed scrutiny in the film *Anonymous* (2011). *Becoming Jane Austen* has inspired the title of Robert Douglas-Fairhurst's biography, *Becoming Dickens* (2011).

There are important differences within this trend, however: "screening the author" does not occur the same way for all authors nor are the consequences the same. Shakespeare's ill-starred love affair with Viola de Lesseps in *Shakespeare in Love* did not make him a playwright; the film opens when he is established in that career. Furthermore, while the affair with her may have helped break his writer's block, Viola herself did not. As for *Anonymous*, few viewers, film critics, or scholars took it all that seriously, although The Shakespeare Birthplace Trust did organize a protest throughout Warwickshire.[20] The press called the film "revisionist," an adjective with disreputable connotations but not one applied to any of the so-called "biopics" of Jane Austen. In contrast, when Kathryn Sutherland attributed Austen's writing style to Austen's editor, she provoked a storm of discussion. Significantly, the defense of Austen received much less attention than Sutherland's initial claim.[21] Spence's *Becoming Jane Austen* is subtitled "A Life," while Douglas-Fairhurst's *Becoming Dickens* is subtitled "The Invention of a Novelist." This difference in title indicates a difference in approach: Jane Austen becomes a person, whereas Charles Dickens was already a person but becomes a professional writer. In the same vein, the title of Spence's biography uses Austen's full name but Douglas-Fairhurst's uses only the last: referring to someone by their last name is generally a mark of respect and distance— think, "Are you trying to seduce me, Mrs. Robinson?"—and in literary circles, an author is identified by the last name, not the first. Furthermore, Spence's title is shortened to *Becoming Jane* for the film version, establishing an intimacy between audience and subject that the title *Becoming Dickens* cannot. This intimacy appears in other materials taking a biographical approach to Austen and her work, such as *Sundays with Jane*, the supplemental website PBS launched to accompany their Austen film series in 2008.[22] The fact is that "screening the author" for Austen changes her cultural capital, with implications for Austen's place in the canon. As Smith observes, "Stories of romantic thralldom with men or of relationships with a male mentor are proliferatively familiar."[23] Alternative life narratives are not. When Austen's personal history is rewritten to fit a "proliferatively familiar" narrative, literary history is rewritten as well; in this case, revised to remove the phenomenon of a woman who was not contained within the usual constructions of femininity—unmarried yet unforlorn, keenly and clearsightedly critical of not just people, but institutions and systems around her.

While the consequences of these maneuvers are significant and symptomatic of a familiar effort to reduce or negate women's contributions to the public sphere,[24] they also constitute one aspect of a larger project to cleanse the past of conflict and challenge, and thereby justify aspects of the historical present. Further examples of how adaptations can serve this purpose are the 2010 film version of *Gulliver's Travels* starring Jack Black and *Crusoe*, a television series from 2008–2009.[25] In the hands of screenwriters Joe Stillman and Nicholas Stoller, Jonathan Swift's satire becomes the story of Lemuel Gulliver, the mailroom clerk at a large New York newspaper who lies to the travel editor, Darcy Silverman, about being a travel writer, gets an assignment to the Bermuda Triangle and winds up on Lilliput. There he defeats the Blefuscians, as they are called in the film, becomes the hero of Lilliput, is eventually unmasked as a fraud when he allows Lilliput to fall to Blefuscu, and is exiled to Brobingnag. Rescued by his Lilliputian friend Horatio, Gulliver liberates the Lilliputians, ends the war, and returns to New York to assume a career at the newspaper as a travel writer and as the boyfriend of Darcy Silverman, who he also has rescued after she followed him to the Bermuda Triangle and was captured in Lilliput by Blefuscian troops.[26]

In Stillman and Stoller's *Gulliver's Travels*, the past and its narratives must be rejected. This adaptation argues that history can have a direct and restricting influence on the present, and should therefore be treated with skepticism if not outright dismissal. The film makes this point in part by simplifying and homogenizing history.[27] Lilliput becomes "the past" in material form, but "the past" is invoked by conventional symbols such as speeches in which every word ends in –eth, eighteenth-century English architecture, Dickensian children in the street, and even the villainous general's full name, Edward Edwardian. The Blefuscians use nineteenth-century diving gear, sail ships from Golden Age Spain, and wear uniforms from Bismarck's Germany. As Dianne F. Sadoff and John Kucich note about a different film adaptation, Amy Heckerling's *Clueless* (1995), the film "flaunts a manic historical insouciance."[28] Lilliput becomes a museum, and as in a museum, as Umberto Eco or Susan Stewart would point out, by displaying objects from different periods all together, Lilliput collapses time and space into one display; in collections, Stewart notes, "all time is made simultaneous or synchronous within the collection's world."[29] None of it has independent meaning, and the collection as a whole is by definition "a fake," in Eco's words.[30]

A more sinister view of the past is expressed through the character of General Edward. His slavish adherence to restrictive Lilliputian traditions embodies the danger of tradition and the threat that the past poses to the potential of the new. Violence makes him happy—he excuses himself from Princess Mary's company with a cheerful "Must go. Those villages won't pillage themselves"—and he is overtly misogynist. He announces, "I can't be expected to take orders from a gargantuan fool. I would rather take orders from a woman," tells the Princess that he wants to marry her because of her breasts, interrupts her tender memories of her grandmother with stories about himself, and repeatedly and sinisterly invades her bedroom uninvited. (Twenty-first-century American male Gulliver, however, has no difficulty accepting a woman in authority: the film concludes with his reporting to Darcy upon his return from an assignment). The happy ending for Lilliput requires General Edward's literal overthrow, first by the team of Gulliver and Horatio, and then by Princess Mary, who coldcocks him when he attempts to kidnap her.[31] For this adaptation, history is a foreign country with a tendency to violence and misogyny.

History is also comprised of what General Edward calls "silly, silly, silly stories." Gulliver uses such stories to invent himself, once when he tells Darcy Silverman that he travels and writes travel pieces, the other when he invents himself as "President the Awesome" of Manhattan for the Lilliputians. In both instances, Gulliver fabricates a present identity by constructing a past out of others' narratives, whether plagiarized from travel websites or from blockbuster films including *Titanic* (tellingly, he does not use history but James Cameron's film fiction about the event), the *Star Wars* series, *X-Men*, *Avatar*, *Pirates of the Caribbean*, and *24*. His improbable and badly-written amalgam is indeed "silly, silly, silly." Unlike Swift's narrative, which draws on different contemporary genres both to establish itself and often to satirize them, the film rejects the use of stories by making fiction the key to Gulliver's failure. Once he stops constructing himself out of narratives, particularly narratives from and about the past, he is permitted to succeed, and the future he succeeds to is certainly rosy: he is a respected authority on transient experience, i.e., a travel writer, and he is romantically involved with Darcy.

Given this attitude toward history and especially narratives from the past, it is not surprising that the film would have an ambivalent attitude toward its own identity as an adaptation, a narrative depending on a text from the past for its existence. The film mildly acknowledges cinematic predecessors in its borrowing of certain conventions, such as Gulliver's love interest (originally appearing in *The Three Worlds of Gulliver* [1960] and the 1996 *Gulliver's Travels*) and a pair of star-crossed Lilliputian lovers (introduced in Max and Dave Fleischer's 1939 animated *Gulliver's Travels* and recycled in *The Three Worlds of Gulliver*). The film's handling of "classic" literature is less ambiguous, if only because it is more overt. For Stillman and Stoller, such texts undeservedly occupy sacred cultural space thanks to the uncritical acceptance of "readers" like the Lilliputians.[32] But it is not just uncritical acceptance that is a problem, according to Stillman and Stoller: the original texts are equally undeserving. They revise *Cyrano de Bergerac*'s famous ventriloquism scene, for example, so the Lilliputian Horatio, prompted by Gulliver crouched behind the palace, woos Princess Mary with the lyrics to Prince's *Kiss* as she stands on a balcony. Edmond Rostand's original scene is poignant and sharply critical. Stillman and Stoller's scene is shallow, comic, and conventionally romantic.

This conversion of satire and criticism into romance is the key tactic for the film's rejection of the past on one hand, and its sanitizing it on the other. Swift's narrative brilliantly and brutally exposes the problems of the socio-economic and political forces of its day, including the pettiness and corruption of the English government, the barbarity of war, and the cruel exploitation of the agricultural and imperialist systems. Stillman and Stoller instead use the cover of the older narrative to promote the corporate values that have origins in the institutions and systems that Swift attacked. Although like Swift's *Gulliver's Travels*, Stillman and Stoller's *Gulliver's Travels* critiques war, for example, their film uses a Hollywood-musical scene of Lilliputians and Blefuscians, led by Gulliver, singing and dancing to "War! (What is it good for?)" In converting satire into comedy, the film diffuses critique. Similarly, Times Square becomes a touchstone of a positive present, portrayed with a lively, upbeat soundtrack in the opening credits. This location marks the apogee of success for Gulliver. When he is at the height of his popularity in Lilliput, he remakes the capital into Times Square and hosts a public music festival there (with the aid of his iPod, which also gets screentime), thus converting one of the most famous sites of western capitalism into a locus of altruism. Gulliver's triumphant ending is a literal return to Times Square and corporate work. Furthermore, his boss is a woman, suggesting that there is no glass ceiling here, at least not if you are a beautiful, single woman who needs rescuing by your male subordinates. *Gulliver's Travels* thus is adapted to affirm limited contemporary values: success means becoming a corporate cog; war is bad (but individuals fighting each other is good entertainment); women in authority are acceptable (as long as they are also sexy and use their authority to elevate men);[33] and so forth. Pretending to tell Swift's story, Stillman and Stoller really tell contemporary western capitalism's favorite narratives about "reinventing the individual" and "corporate life is the ultimate in happiness," sanitizing history of the violence, heartlessness, and exploitation targeted by Swift. Without a past to connect the present to, whatever narratives are in circulation to explain the present face considerably less challenge.

At first glance, Stillman and Stoller's cleansing and rejection of the past seems opposite to the approach taken by the television series *Crusoe* that ran on NBC in the United States during 2008–2009. For *Crusoe*'s writers, history's influence is inescapable and necessary. Through the frequent use of flashbacks, the series emphasizes the importance of Robinson's personal history as well as his place in actual history. Scenes like these explain how Robinson got to this point by defining Dissenters, or showing Robinson unwittingly aiding soldiers fighting for Monmouth and being tried for treason by Judge Jeffries. Here, history is considered very relevant for the present. Because of this influence, however, it becomes imperative for the health of the present that the past be remade. *Crusoe* uses the premise of the original narrative—in this case, a determined, resourceful man stranded on an island with a companion named Friday who wants to escape this isolation—to present a highly heterosexualized, anti-imperialist, racially-harmonized, technophilic vision not just of the past, but also of the present in which the show was viewed.[34]

The homosocial and homosexual underpinnings of Defoe's original narrative have been well-explored elsewhere.[35] The writers for the television series have assiduously attempted to erase any traces of queerness, however. Their Robinson is determinedly heterosexual, which they reinforce with flashbacks of his sexual relationship with Suzanna and a collection of nubile young women who are attracted to him; Friday calls it "the Crusoe effect." But Crusoe is also virtuous and thoroughly housebroken: he resists all the women by averring his fidelity to and love for his wife, and with frequent articulations of his desire to return to her and their two children. One subplot of episode two, "Sacrifice," involves the loss of Robinson's wedding ring, which he is desperate to retrieve and finally does, to the romantic strains of a harp and oboe on the soundtrack. Friday, for his part, has family issues of his own, with a recurring subplot about tensions with his father. He, too, is resolutely heterosexual, being the recipient of a warrior princess's attentions in episode ten, "The Hunting Party." Friday and Robinson also call each other "brother," using a sibling vocabulary to further diffuse the possibility of queerness. In episode eight, "Name of the Game," the two men repeatedly discuss what they learned from their fathers and the ways in which they fear that they have let down those fathers. Friday and Robinson live in comfortable domesticity on their deserted island, far removed from either man's civilization; episodes repeatedly open or close, and sometimes do both, with a scene of cooking and sharing food at their treehouse. Nevertheless, each man is seeking emotionally and physically to leave this home for heterosexual family life.

DeeAnn DeLuna has complicated some of the most overt of the queer readings of Defoe's novel to argue that "Crusoe's sexual identity is aligned with the novel's focus on his mercantile exertions and their Christianization by Defoe, but in a way which bears no logic of correspondence with an alleged representation of homosexual desire."[36] Similarly, the writers for the series *Crusoe* have used his domestic heterosexuality to cleanse Robinson's commercial ambitions. Like Defoe's, their Crusoe wants to make money, but unlike Defoe's, their Crusoe does so in order to support his family. Throughout the episodes, flashbacks show how Robinson has been driven to colonialism by social, political, and economic oppression in England, which prevented him from providing for his beloved wife and children. In "The Name of the Game," a flashback reveals that Robinson exchanged a profitable coffee plantation for passage to England on the next tide when he learned that his family is in danger. Laura Brown argues that women often served to justify British imperialism: in order to provide for the little woman at home, countries must be conquered and elephants killed. Certainly, Brown notes, Defoe justified imperialism on this count.[37] Television's Crusoe performs the same maneuver, legitimating Robinson's mercantilism as a means of supporting his wife and children. Robinson's desire to return to his family converts the "solitary man" narrative central to Defoe's work as well as its associations with wealth for wealth's sake into a social, romantic, selfless, and heterosexual narrative thoroughly familiar and palatable to television viewers. Hence, his domestic heterosexuality is not only used to avoid even the notion of homosexuality, but also to legitimate British imperialism and with it, the global capitalism that ultimately arose from these beginnings.

Other fraught elements of the Anglo-American present are cleaned up and justified by *Crusoe*, as well. Crusoe and Friday's brotherhood rewrites the history of race in the Americas just as it rewrites the relationship those characters experience in Defoe's *Robinson Crusoe*. The racial element of Defoe's *Robinson Crusoe* has proved uncomfortable for filmmakers for the last few decades, so there is nothing new in *Crusoe*'s handling of this element of the original.[38] At least there is a Friday at all; as Robert Mayer points out, in *Cast Away* (2000), the human, dark-skinned, independent Friday becomes a volleyball called "Wilson" by the Crusoe character (named Chuck Noland, played by Tom Hanks).[39] Although in the television series, Robinson does liberate Friday from cannibals, Friday immediately becomes his partner, his "brother." They share household chores and nurture each other by cooking, caring for pets and livestock, and nursing each other through sickness and injury.[40] In episode five, "Long Pig," Robinson tells Friday that they are safe from cannibals because "We have traps near the beach and a home we can defend," using the key image of the defended home to confirm both the domesticity and the first-person plural of their situation.

The two men also share a rivalry of equals. Unlike in the novel, Friday acquires impeccable English, which he adds to the roster of languages he already speaks; develops a taste for Milton's sonnets; and memorizes *Paradise Lost*. Robinson, on the other hand, never learns to pronounce Friday's language, as he admits early in the pilot episode. In addition, a current of competition runs through the series. Although Robinson consistently supplies the engineering and scientific knowledge and skill, the episode "Name of the Game" is based on Friday's efforts to match Robinson's feats. On the other hand, Friday repeatedly bests Robinson in feats of physical skill. The men roughhouse and "play games," as Robinson calls them in the episode "Bad Blood," attacking each other with weapons and fighting both to compete and to keep themselves ready for the inevitable attack by outsiders. In the pilot episode, Friday rescues Robinson from pirates who are pursuing him through the jungle:

> Friday: Friday wonders what kind of idiot builds all those traps, then runs yelling to the beach without a weapon.
> Crusoe: You knew I was at the beach?
> Friday: I could guess it, from the beacons.
> Crusoe: Well, in that case, Crusoe wonders, why Friday didn't join in sooner?
> Friday: I was enjoying the Idiot Show.

In the concluding episode of the series, Friday shoots arrows to frighten off rather than kill sailors trying to kill them, because Robinson wishes those sailors to summon their superiors. "It offends me to miss deliberately," Friday says waspishly to Robinson, and Robinson apologizes for asking it of him. In scenes like this one, the imbalance between Defoe's Friday and Crusoe is not only adjusted, but tipped in the other direction: Robinson does not command Friday's help but asks it, which means that he depends upon Friday and owes him gratitude, an inferiority of position thoroughly unfamiliar to Defoe's Crusoe. As scholars have pointed out, Defoe's narrative is deeply implicated not just in imperialism and colonialism, but specifically in the slave trade and the racism that was developed to sustain and justify it.[41] Interaction between the races in the seventeenth-century Americas is thus reconstructed to provide a fluidity of power dynamics, a respect, and a mutuality that actual history does not generally indicate. It is an ideal of the past and an ideal of the present, not unlike the claims following the election of Barack Obama in 2008 that the United States is a "post-race" society.[42] According to *Crusoe*, virtuous people yearn for and actively seek a brotherhood of men, hence the presumed audience satisfaction when it appears on the small screen.

While *Crusoe* idealizes heterosexual norms and justifies capitalism expressed through domesticity and racial equality, its most overt object of adoration is technology. In Defoe's narrative, Crusoe struggles with the basics of subsistence, as he already lives in a world where the consumer does not produce his own goods. In *Robinson Crusoe*, Crusoe is delighted to make raisins by accident, struggles to discover how to make bread, and learns the hard way how to build a sheep pen and a canoe. These are not technologically advanced objects; perhaps the most complicated undertaking is his umbrella, which takes him years to accomplish. In *Crusoe*, however, Robinson, and Friday to a more limited extent, are brilliant engineers. Food, clothing? The boxes washed up from Robinson's shipwreck and their own ingenuity with indigenous materials suffice. In the pilot episode, deprived of their gunpowder, Friday improvises a weapon by dismantling an umbrella (surely no accidental reference to the original novel) while Robinson makes throwing stars from coins. In other episodes Robinson forges a skeleton key, a compass, a telescope, and a tranquilizer dart. Defoe's Crusoe lives in a cave. Robinson and Friday occupy a multileveled tree house not only balanced through the canopy of several trees and cantilevered over the edge of a cliff, but also complete with wind power, running water, and a juicer. Crusoe has two walls of spiky poles and a ladder to get over them. Robinson and Friday have a ladder bridge over a bottomless swamp, a giant wheel in which they walk like bipedal hamsters to cross a chasm and when that is destroyed, a rope bridge over it. From the base of the main tree, they ascend to their house by elevator. Robinson "becomes a seventeenth-century *MacGyver*," says one of the program's art directors proudly.[43]

Their technological ingenuity is emphasized in the visual vocabulary and emphasis of the series, such as lingering camera shots of their work and the recurring image of the airy tree house as the visual shorthand of their domestic base. Director Duane Clark states, "The fact [is] that the whole show opens up with this rather clever device that he has: this spyglass that he's fashioned out of some lenses and some brass salvaged from the ship."[44] As Robinson puts it succinctly in episode four, "High Water," "What's the point of making tools if it doesn't make the job easier?" Villains, on the other hand, are marked by their scientific ignorance or crudeness. Pirates have a map etched into the skin on the back of a prisoner. A mutinous ship's doctor cannot tell one medicine from another. In the final episode, Robinson's antagonists steadily destroy Robinson and Friday's technological marvels and repeatedly struggle to comprehend the principles underlying those marvels. At the end, Robinson's superior knowledge of science and medicine, like his superior grasp of engineering and physics, enables him to recognize the signs of plague on the captain of the British ship. While his leaping off the ship with Friday seems inexplicable and practically suicidal to the villains on board, the final moments of the series show another plague-infested mariner exiting his prison to infect the rest of the ship. *Crusoe* thus converts Defoe's recognition of the alienation of seventeenth-century people from the basics of survival into a technophilic past, one that looks familiar and that justifies a technophilic present.[45]

Recently, Raymond Malewitz has argued that behaviors like Friday and Robinson's belong to "new archetypes in contemporary American culture—rugged consumers" who "repurpose[. . .] the objects in their environments" and "ennoble such actions by viewing them through the intertwined American myths of primal nature and rugged individualism."[46] Although Malewitz invites "others to determine" whether "such behaviors subvert or in fact support the conditions of late capitalism," he inadvertently answers the question, at least in part, by noting that the "literary imagination" in such moments is "reflecting the current repurposing culture but also asking us to reimagine the creative relations between humans and all objects that populate our worlds."[47] Behaviors like repurposing may affect the relationship between human and object, that is, but they do not in and of themselves necessarily change the system within which that relationship is constituted and conducted. Friday and Robinson repeatedly repurpose what they find in order to resist the commodification of Friday by intruders on the island, who inevitably wish to kill Robinson and sell Friday, but they do not ultimately resist capitalism any more than Gulliver does in Stillman and Stoller's film.

In his review of Stillman and Stoller's *Gulliver's Travels* for *The New York Times*, A. O. Scott, taking the persona of Swift, writes, "Surely I state what can only be apparent to any man not a Jackass when I observe that it bears little relation to my original Work. Perhaps you construe that my intent in this epistle is to thunder against a grievous misappropriation of my Book, but please be assured that I have no such complaint. An Apple is but an Apple, while an Orange is some other thing."[48] Classifications of fruit notwithstanding, Scott is missing a central issue to *Gulliver's Travels* and the other films discussed here, which is that as Hutcheon points out, an adaptation cannot by its nature be "some other thing" entirely: "We experience adaptations (*as adaptations*) as palimpsests through our memory of other works that resonate through repetition with variation," as she explains.[49] But as these adaptations suggest, the palimpsest itself can change if the adaptation works to revise the construction of that source's original moment.

Why should this be news to us? Shakespeare attempted such a maneuver with his history plays, after all. Mary Favret notes that the Victorians undertook a similar project with Austen, even if they were more interested with containing her through domesticity than through romance.[50] When we seek to understand adaptations as adaptations, and not as separate or "stand-alone" texts—and that certainly can be done, as literary history testifies on numerous occasions—then we ought to consider how the relationship between contexts is inter-contextual, just as the relationship between adaptation and source is intertextual. Inter-contextuality is unlikely to be the same for all relationships, any more than the relationship between texts is always the same, but as adaptation studies continues to flourish, we might now begin to consider other pieces in the puzzle. Furthermore, the role of ideology in the construction of source, adaptation, and context makes the function of adaptation in any given historical moment particularly significant. Eco points out that the Middle Ages "have always been messed up in order to meet the vital requirements of different periods," and he describes "at least ten types of Middle Ages, to warn readers that every time one speaks of a dream of the Middle Ages, one should first ask which Middle Ages one is dreaming of."[51] In changing the nature of the value of historical products, our own moment changes profoundly and the possibilities and powers of that moment change, as well. The very real relationship between the source and adaptation has, in turn, very real ideological consequences here and now. For Eco, the answer to this question—"what kind of Middle Ages are we talking about"— reveals if, in his words, "we are supporting, perhaps without realizing it, some new reactionary plot."[52] We should examine what long eighteenth century we are dreaming of with such adaptations, and with it, what present we are dreaming, as well.

NOTES

The author would like to acknowledge the support of Angela Weisl, Donovan Sherman, Jonathan Farina, and Aleksondra Hultquist in writing this article.

1. The term "adaptation" is often used to refer to any text based on a textual forebear; as Linda Hutcheon defines them, "adaptations have an overt and defining relationship to prior texts." In this sense, film versions of *Gulliver's Travels* and *Sense and Sensibility* are adaptations in the way that *Foe* and *Clueless* are adaptations. "Adaptation" is often used as a catch-all phrase for works with different relationships to originals: *Becoming Jane*, for example, is not an adaptation of Jon Spence's *Becoming Jane Austen* in the same way that the 1995 A&E/BBC production of *Pride and Prejudice* is an adaptation of Austen's novel, but it is an adaptation of the story that Spence hypothesizes. In this article, "adaptation" refers to a text that claims to be a transposition of an original in one medium into another medium, such as the film *Gulliver's Travels* and television series *Crusoe* discussed here. Linda Hutcheon, *A Theory of Adaptation* (New York: Routledge, 2006), 7; Jon Spence, *Becoming Jane Austen: A Life* (London: Hambledon Continuum, 2003).

2. Writing about contemporary Robinsonades, for example, Charles W. Pollard concludes, "[T]eaching these contemporary works helps students see how Crusoe's world is still a place that they have both lived in and come out of, a place that remains useful because it helps them understand themselves by understanding their past." See his "Teaching Contemporary Responses to *Robinson Crusoe*: Coetzee, Walcott, and Others in a World Literature Survey," in *Approaches to Teaching Defoe's Robinson Crusoe*, ed. Maximillian E. Novak and Carl Fisher (New York: The Modern Language Association, 2005), 168.

3. See for example Hutcheon, *Adaptation*; Imelda Whelehan, "Adaptations: The Contemporary Dilemmas," in *Adaptations: From Text to Screen, from Screen to Text*, ed. Deborah Cartmell and Imelda Whelehan (New York: Routledge, 1999), 3–19; Brian McFarlane, "Reading Film and Literature," in *The Cambridge Companion to Literature on Screen*, ed. Deborah Cartmell and Imelda Whelehan (Cambridge: Cambridge University Press, 2007), 15–28; Deborah Cartmell and Imelda Whelehan, "Introduction—Literature on Screen: A Synoptic View," in Cartmell and Whelehan, *Cambridge Companion*, 1–12; Thomas M. Leitch, "Literature vs. Literacy: Two Futures for Adaptation Studies," in *The Literature/Film Reader: Issues of Adaptation*, ed. James M. Welsh and Peter Lev (Lanham, MD: Scarecrow Press, 2007), 15–34; Gina Macdonald and Andrew Macdonald, Introduction to *Jane Austen on Screen*, ed. Gina Macdonald and Andrew Macdonald (Cambridge: Cambridge University Press, 2003), 1–8.

4. Hutcheon, *Adaptation*, xiii.

5. The popular use of "cultural capital" often equates the term with "cultural cachet," but Pierre Bourdieu formulated "cultural capital" as the fusion of a linguistic value and a social value that is signaled by how a text is treated by systems and institutions of dissemination and propagation, such as the university and print culture. It is not simply a matter of "how much" cultural capital a text possesses

or is assigned, but "what kind" of cultural capital: as John Guillory puts it, "the canonical *form* in its social and institutional contexts." Pierre Bourdieu, *Distinction: A Social Critique of the Judgement of Taste*, trans. Richard Nice (Cambridge, MA: Harvard University Press, 1984); John Guillory, *Cultural Capital: The Problem of Literary Canon Formation* (Chicago: The University of Chicago Press, 1993), ix, xiii, original emphasis.

6. Hutcheon, *Adaptation*, 6.

7. Cartmell and Whelehan, "Introduction," 6; Martine Voiret, "Books to Movies: Gender and Desire in Jane Austen's Adaptations," in Pucci and Thompson, *Jane Austen and Co.*, 229–45; Sarah Maza, "'It Can't Go on Like This': *Dangerous Liaisons* in the Reagan-Thatcher Years," in *Jane Austen and Co.: Remaking the Past in Contemporary Culture*, ed. Suzanna R. Pucci and James Thompson (Albany: SUNY Press, 2003), 93–110. See also Walter C. Metz, "The Cold War's 'Undigested Apple-Dumpling': Imaging *Moby-Dick* in 1956 and 2001," in Welsh and Lev, *Literature/Film Reader*, 65–76; Jessica Durgan, "Framing Heritage: The Role of Cinematography in *Pride & Prejudice*," *Persuasions On-Line* 27, no. 2 (Summer 2007): np., http://www.jasna.org/persuasions/on-line/vol27no2/durgan.htm; Ruth Perry, "Sleeping with Mr. Collins," in Pucci and Thompson, *Jane Austen and Co.*, 213–28; Joyce Goggin, "*Pride and Prejudice* Reloaded: Navigating the Space of Pemberley," *Persuasions On-Line* 27, no. 2 (Summer 2007): np., http://www.jasna.org/persuasions/on-line/vol27no2/goggin.htm; Madeleine Dobie, "Gender and the Heritage Culture: Popular Feminism Turns to History," in Pucci and Thompson, *Jane Austen and Co.*, 247–59. See also Linda Troost and Sayre Greenfield, eds. *Jane Austen in Hollywood*, 2nd ed. (Lexington: University Press of Kentucky, 2001).

8. Brownstein, *Why Jane Austen?* (New York: Columbia University Press, 2011), 4, 7, 247. Mary Favret points out that the Victorians undertook a similar project with Austen, constructing Jane Austen to fulfill wishful thinking about their own cultural moment and to satisfy a nostalgia for a lost, better past. Mary Favret, "Being True to Jane Austen," in *Victorian Afterlife: Postmodern Culture Rewrites the Nineteenth Century*, ed. John Kucich and Dianne F. Sadoff (Minneapolis: University of Minnesota Press, 2000), 66.

9. Brownstein, *Why Jane Austen?*, 6. See also Suzanne R. Pucci and James Thompson, "Introduction: The Jane Austen Phenomenon: Remaking the Past at the Millennium," in Pucci and Thompson, *Jane Austen and Co.*, 1; John Kucich and Dianne F. Sadoff, eds. *Victorian Afterlife*.

10. Brownstein, *Why Jane Austen*?; Karen B. Gevirtz, "(De)Constructing Jane: Converting 'Austen' in Film Adaptations," *Persuasions On-Line* 31, no. 1 (December 2010): np., http://www.jasna.org/persuasions/on-line/vol31no1/gevirtz.html.

11. "Introduction to *Mansfield Park*," from a performance televised by PBS on January 27, 2008; "Introduction to *Sense and Sensibility*, part 1," from a performance televised by PBS on February 1, 2008; "Becoming Jane," *Miramax*, 2007, http://www.imdb.com/title/tt0416508/.

12. Spence, *Becoming Jane Austen*.

13. Spence, *Becoming Jane Austen*, ix; advertisement for *Becoming Jane*, Miramax, 2007.

14. Brownstein, *Why Jane Austen?*, 7.

15. *Becoming Jane*, directed by Julian Jerrold (Santa Monica, CA: Miramax Films, 2007), DVD.

16. Martha Nell Smith, "Suppressing the Books of Susan in Emily Dickinson," in *Epistolary Histories*, ed. Amanda Gilroy and W. M. Verhoeven (Charlottesville: University Press of Virginia, 2000), 101, 104.

17. Smith, "Books of Susan," 104.

18. Dobie, "Gender and the Heritage Culture," 257.

19. Cartmell and Whelehan, "Introduction," 8.

20. Donovan Sherman, "Stages of Revision: Textuality, Performance, and History in *Anonymous*," *Literature/Film Quarterly* 41, no. 2 (2013) (forthcoming). The author thanks Dr. Sherman for sharing his analysis in advance of publication. A. O. Scott writes, "'Anonymous,' a costume spectacle directed by Roland Emmerich, from a script by John Orloff, is a vulgar prank on the English literary tradition, a travesty of British history and a brutal insult to the human imagination. Apart from that, it's not bad." A. O. Scott, "How Could a Commoner Write Such Great Plays?" *The New York Times*, October 27, 2011, http://movies.nytimes.com/2011/10/28/ movies/ anonymous-by-roland-emmerichreview. html. For a report of The Shakespeare Birthplace Trust's response, see Ben Child, "Shakespeare film *Anonymous* has lost plot, says Stratford," *The Guardian*, October 25, 2011, http://www.guardian.co.uk/ film/2011/oct/25/shakespeare-filmanonymous-stratford.

21. For a comprehensive summary of the reaction to Sutherland's claims and a practical refutation of them, see Geoff Nunberg, "Was Jane Austen Edited? Does It Matter?" *Fresh Air*, November 17, 2010, NPR.org, http://www.npr. org/2010/11/15/131335890/was-jane-austen-edited-does-it-matter.

22. This website is no longer available.

23. Smith, "Books of Susan," 102.

24. For further discussion of how recent adaptations constitute a backlash against women, see for example Dobie, 247–59; and Voiret, 229–45.

25. For a more detailed examination of the relationship between Jonathan Swift's *Gulliver's Travels* and this adaptation, see Karen Gevirtz, review of *Gulliver's Travels, Eighteenth-Century Studies* 44, no. 4 (2011): 559–64.

26. *Gulliver's Travels*, directed by Rob Letterman (Beverly Hills, CA: Twentieth Century Fox Home Entertainment, 2011), DVD.

27. Similarly, the film collapses all islands with a colonial history into one homogenized locale. Although Gulliver goes to Bermuda, his guide has a Jamaican accent and the soundtrack during this part of the film is Reggae, which originated in Jamaica, not Bermuda.

28. Dianne F. Sadoff and John Kucich, "Introduction: Histories of the Present," in Sadoff and Kucich, *Victorian Afterlife*, ix.

29. Umberto Eco, *Travels in Hyperreality*, trans. William Weaver (New York: Harcourt Brace Jovanovich, 1986), 3–58; Susan Stewart, *On Longing: Narratives of the Miniature, the Gigantic, the Souvenir, the Collection* (Baltimore: The Johns Hopkins University Press, 1984), 151–62. Eco considers this behavior particularly American: "The American imagination demands the real thing and, to attain it, must

fabricate the absolute fake" (8). Eco's allusions to the German Wunderkammer (5, 6) connect this tendency back to the seventeenth- and eighteenth-century cabinets of curiosity popular in Europe and in England, where the British Museum was founded on the collection amassed by Sir Hans Sloane. For a discussion of collecting and miscellanies in England, see for example Barbara M. Benedict, "Collecting Trouble: Sir Hans Sloane's Literary Reputation in Eighteenth-Century Britain," *Eighteenth-Century Life* 36, no. 2 (Spring 2012): 111–42; Stacey Sloboda, "Displaying Materials: Porcelain and Natural History in the Duchess of Portland's Museum," *ECS* 43, no. 4 (Summer 2010): 455–72.

30. Eco, *Hyperreality*, 8.

31. It is worth noting that the film retains its unexamined representation of the past in the clothes and architecture at its end, however. While ideology, behavior, and speech have been reformed to suit contemporary ideals, the Lilliputians retain their eighteenth-century wardrobe, including the corsets. Evidently some ways of restricting women are permitted to remain.

32. Favret points out that in Emma Thompson's adaptation of *Sense and Sensibility*, the "avid consumerism promoted by the film" is supported by a rejection of reading in favor of viewing (80).

33. In addition to Darcy Silverman's hiring and sleeping with Gulliver, Princess Mary elevates Horatio by marrying him. In both cases, women in authority are contained at the end of the film within a romantic narrative, not unlike the conversion of Jane Austen into a romantic heroine discussed earlier in the paper. Women who use their power for other purposes, however, are not just frightening but, in the parlance of this *Gulliver's Travels*, downright dangerous, as in the case of the temperamental, violent Glumdalclitch, who seems to have been constructed out of a multifaceted castration anxiety.

34. Stephen Gallagher et al, *Crusoe*, directed by Duane Clark (Universal City, CA: Universal Studios Home Entertainment, 2009), DVD. All further references to episodes will be to this DVD.

35. See for example Hans Turley, *Rum, Sodomy, and the Lash: Piracy, Sexuality, and Masculine Identity* (New York: NYU Press, 1999); Srinivas Aravamudan, *Tropicopolitans: Colonialism and Agency, 1688–1804* (Durham: Duke University Press, 1999); DeeAnn DeLuna, "Robinson Crusoe, Virginal Hero of the Commercial North," *Eighteenth-Century Life* 28, no. 1 (2004): 69–91; George E. Haggerty, "Thank God It's Friday: The Construction of Masculinity in *Robinson Crusoe*," in Novak and Fisher, *Approaches to Teaching Defoe's* Robinson Crusoe, 84–85.

36. DeLuna, "Robinson Crusoe," 70.

37. Laura Brown, *The Ends of Empire: Women and Ideology in Early Eighteenth-Century English Literature* (Ithaca: Cornell University Press, 1993), 14–19, 113.

38. Robert Mayer, "*Robinson Crusoe* in Hollywood," in Novak and Fischer, *Approaches*, 169–74.

39. For a thoughtful reading of the significance of Wilson in terms of race, see Mayer, "*Robinson Crusoe* in Hollywood," 172–73.

40. "Theoretically fraternal" because the amount of effort that the series puts into affirming Robinson's heterosexuality suggests the degree to which the relationship,

particularly when it involves keeping house even if the men have separate bedrooms, has queer undertones.

41. Pollard, *Approaches*, 163–64; Haggerty, "Thank God It's Friday," in Novak and Fischer, *Approaches*, 79–81; Roxann Wheeler, "*Robinson Crusoe* and Early-Eighteenth-Century Racial Ideology," in Novak and Fisher, *Approaches*, 88–95; Abby A. Johnson, "Old Bones Uncovered: A Reconsideration of *Robinson Crusoe*," *CLA Journal* 17 (1973): 71–78. Wheeler points out that "reading for racial multiplicity" in texts like *Robinson Crusoe* reveals how race was an "emergent, rather than stable concept in the eighteenth century." Roxann Wheeler, "'My Savage,' 'My Man': Racial Multiplicity in Defoe's *Robinson Crusoe,*" *ELH* 62, no. 4 (Winter 1995): 821, http://www.jstor.org/stable/30030104.

42. See for example Gwen Ifill, *The Breakthrough: Politics and Race in the Age of Obama* (New York: Doubleday, 2009); Roy L. Brooks, *Racial Justice in the Age of Obama* (Princeton: Princeton University Press, 2009). Brooks uses the term "post-civil rights," arguing that "The Age of Obama is not, in my view, postracial. It is racial," but that the civil rights movement has ended (xiii).

43. Unknown, "Weapons, Gadgets, and Traps."

44. Unknown, "Weapons, Gadgets, and Traps."

45. Robinson and Friday also have a highly ecologically responsible approach to technology. In the final episode, for example, when Robinson's enemy Josiah Blackthorn says admiringly, "You've tamed the wilderness," Robinson replies, "Hardly. I've adapted to it." Similarly, in "The Hunting Party," Friday delivers a monologue to their dog about the necessity for living in harmony with nature.

46. Raymond Malewitz, "Regeneration through Misuses: Rugged Consumerism in Contemporary American Culture," *PMLA* 127, no. 3 (2012): 527. For some reason Malewitz views "rugged consumers" as more than one archetype, but of course the "rugged consumer" can only be one archetype, although it may appear in many forms, just as the "hero" can only be one archetype, even if it takes many forms.

47. Malewitz, "Regeneration," 532, 539.

48. A. O. Scott, "A Gut Visible All the Way from the Eighteenth Century," *The New York Times*, December 24, 2010 C: 6 (late edition), http://www.lexisnexis.com.ezproxy.shu.edu/hottopics/lnacademic/?shr=t&sfi=AC00NBGenSrch&csi=6742.

49. Hutcheon, *Adaptation*, 8; original emphasis.

50. Favret, *Afterlives*, 66.

51. Eco, *Hyperreality*, 68, 68–72.

52. Eco, *Hyperreality,* 72.

Contributors to Volume 43

Paula R. Backscheider is Philpott-Stevens Eminent Scholar at Auburn University and a former president of ASECS. Author of several books and many articles, her most recent book is *Elizabeth Singer Rowe and the Development of the English Novel* (Johns Hopkins UP, 2013). She is writing "The Transforming Imagination," a study of the relationships between novels and drama.

Rori Bloom is Associate Professor of French at the University of Florida. She has published a book on the abbé Prévost as well as essays on Crébillon fils and Restif de la Bretonne. She is currently pursuing a new project on aesthetic issues in the tales of Mme d'Aulnoy.

Ann Campbell is Associate Professor of Restoration and Eighteenth-Century British literature at Boise State University. Her research focuses on eighteenth-century novels. She has published articles in *The Shandean*, *Eighteenth-Century Women*, and *Eighteenth-Century Life*. At present, she is writing a monograph focusing on surrogate families in the eighteenth-century British novel. Her article is a part of this larger project.

Patricia Comitini is an Associate Professor of English at Quinnipiac University. She is author of *Vocational Philanthropy and British Women's Writing* (Ashgate, 2006), as well as articles on nineteenth-century British literature. Her current scholarly work includes a manuscript that investigates the intersection between aesthetics, ideology and addiction in the long eighteenth century.

Sabrina Ferri is Assistant Professor of Italian at the University of Notre Dame, where she is also a fellow at the Nanovic Institute for European Studies. She has recently enjoyed a stint as a fellow at Notre Dame's Institute for Advanced Studies and also as visiting scholar at Stanford University. Her work on Giacomo Casanova, Giambattista Vico, and Vittorio Alfieri has appeared in *Sincronie*, *New Vico Studies*, and *European Romantic Review*. She is currently completing a book manuscript on ruins in eighteenth- and nineteenth-century Italian literature and culture, entitled *Temporal Ruinations: A History of Time in Italy, 1744–1836.*

Rebecca Dowd Geoffroy-Schwinden is a Ph.D. candidate in musicology at Duke University, where she earned the M. A. in 2011. During 2012-13 she conducted archival research for the present *SECC* article in Paris, and also worked on her dissertation treating of music performance and discourse in revolutionary France. In addition to her work on French musicology 1600-1900, she is interested in music composed for the cinema and also teaches courses in music and politics from the Enlightenment to the present.

Karen Gevirtz *is* Associate Professor of English at Seton Hall University and Executive President of the Aphra Behn Society for Women in the Arts, 1660–1830. Her current research examines film adaptations of eighteenth-century texts and authors, and the role of natural philosophy in women's contributions to the emerging novel. She has published *Life After Death: Widows and the English Novel, Defoe to Austen* (University of Delaware Press, 2005) and co-edited *Gender and Space in British Literature, 1660–1820* (Ashgate, forthcoming in 2014) with Mona Narain.

Barbara Mackey King received her Ph.D. in theatre history from Bowling Green State University focusing on the eighteenth century. She also studied at the University of Michigan and Penn State University. Now retired, she has taught at Southern University of Louisiana, Penn State University, Shippensburg State University, the University of Toledo, Owens Community College, and was a visiting professor at Kolej Damamsara Utama in Kuala Lumpur, Malaysia. She has published in T*heatre Journal, Restoration and Eighteenth Century Theatre Research*, and *Text and Performance Quarterly*, among others.

April London is Professor of English at the University of Ottawa. She is the author of numerous articles on eighteenth-century and Romantic topics and of *Women and Property in the Eighteenth-Century Novel* (Cambridge University Press, 1999), *Literary History Writing, 1770–1820* (Palgrave Macmillan, 2010), and *The Cambridge Introduction to the Eighteenth-Century Novel* (Cambridge University Press, 2012). She is currently working on anecdotal writing in the long eighteenth century.

Joanne E. Myers is Assistant Professor of English at Gettysburg College and her research focuses on the relative secularity of eighteenth-century Britain. She has published articles about the role of enthusiasm in the work of Daniel Defoe, Mary Astell, and Damaris Masham, about the role of the body in sentimental culture, and about the place of Catholicism in the career of Catharine Trotter Cockburn. She is currently working on a project about walking and other forms of embodied knowledge.

Sarah B. Stein is a Visiting Assistant Professor of English at St. Olaf College. She has articles on John Denham, Isaac Watts, and the influence of Hebrew script on the work of William Blake forthcoming. Her book manuscript, A *Hebraic Modernity: Poetry, Prayer, and Translation in the Long Eighteenth Century*, investigates the central role play by translations of the Hebrew Psalms in British literature of the long eighteenth century.

ASECS Executive Board 2013–2014

For information about the
American Society for Eighteenth-Century Studies, please contact:
ASECS
P.O. Box 7867
Wake Forest University
Winston-Salem, NC 27109-7867
Telephone: (336) 727-4694
Fax: (336) 727-4697
E-mail: asecs@wfu.edu
Web Site: http://asecs.press.jhu.edu

American Society for Eighteenth-Century Studies

Patron Members 2013–2014

Hans Adler
Richard Shane Agin
Stephen Ahern
Stanford Anderson
Mark S. Auburn
Paula Backscheider
Eve T. Bannet
Joseph F. Bartolomeo
James G. Basker
Denise Baxter
Barbara Benedict
Oliver Berghof
Kevin Binfield
Martha F. Bowden
Theodore E.D. Braun
Fritz Breithaupt
Peter M. Briggs
Jane K. Brown
Marshall Brown
Michael Burden
Joseph A. Byrnes
Ann Campbell
Susan Carlile
Vincent Carretta
Jeng-Guo Chen
Julie Choi
Brian A. Connery
E. Heckendorn Cook
Kevin L. Cope
Brian Cowan
Margaret Mary Daley
Marlies K. Danziger
Jenny Davidson
Joan DeJean
Robert DeMaria, Jr.
Julia Douthwaite
William F. Edmiston
Roger J. Fechner
Frances Ferguson
Riikka Forsstrom
Bernadette Fort
Patsy Fowler
Christopher Fox
Jennifer E. Frangos
Gorden Fulton
Robert Glen
Charles E. Gobin
Scott Gordon
Sayre Greenfield
Monika Greenleaf
Loyd Grossman
Anita Guerrini
Phyllis Guskin
Susan Gustafson
Basil Guy
Knud Haakonssen
Wolfgang Haase
Martha Hamilton-Phillips
Corrine Harol
Phillip Harth
Donald M. Hassler
Julie C. Hayes
Charles Hinnant
Robert D. Hume
Lynn A. Hunt
J. Paul Hunter
Sheila M. Hwang
Catherine Ingrassia
Malcolm Jack
Margaret C. Jacob
Regina Mary Janes
Alessa Johns
Sandro Jung
George Justice
Sarah Kareem
Gary Kates
Michael Keevak
Shirley Strum Kenny
Thomas Keymer
Heather King
Charles A. Knight
Jocelyne Kolb
Scott Krawczyk
Thomas W. Krise
Susan Lanser
Meredith Lee
Elizabeth Liebman
Devoney K. Looser
Aino Makikalli
Elizabeth Mansfield
Robert Markley
Jean I. Marsden
Marie E. McAllister
Christie McDonald
Paula McDowell
Dennis McEnnerney
George C. McElroy
Alan T. McKenzie
James C. McKusick
Heather McPherson
Donald C. Mell Jr.
Eun Kyung Min
Dennis Moore
Anja Mueller-Muth
Yvonne Noble
Felicity Nussbaum
Mary Ann O'Donnell
Frank Palmeri
Virginia J. Peacock
Ruth Perry
Jane Perry-Camp
Stuart Peterfreund
R.G. Peterson
George W. Poe
John Valdimir Price
Ruben D. Quintero
John Radner
Bryant T. Ragan
Tilottama Rajan
Paul Rich

Patron Members 2013–2014 (Con't)

Joseph Roach
James Rosenheim
Laura Rosenthal
Roseann Runte
Elizabeth Samet
Carole Fungaroli Sargent
Steven D. Scherwatzky
Harold Schiffman
Volker Schroder
Norbert Schurer
Richard Sher
Eleanor F. Shevlin
John C. Shields
Craig A. Simmons
Robert Louis Smith
G.A. Starr
Kristina Straub
Susan Staves
Masashi Suzuki
Mika Suzuki
Astrida Tantillo
Ruud N.W.M. Teeuwen
Linda V. Troost
Randolph Trumbach
Bertil Van Boer
David F. Venturo
Joachim Von der Thusen
Cynthia S. Wall
Howard D. Weinbrot
Byron R. Wells
Betty E. White
J. Edmund White
Lance Wilcox
Annie Williams
Karin E. Wolfe
Larry Wolff
Servanne Woodward
James Woolley
Karin Wurst
Myron D. Yeager
Janet E. Aikins Yount
William J. Zachs
Lisa M. Zeitz

Sponsoring Members 2013–2014

Paul Alkon
Misty G. Anderson
Robert Bernasconi
Thomas F. Bonnell
Leo Braudy
Daniel Brewer
Charles Burroughs
Samara Cahill
Michael J. Conlon
Brian Corman
Joyce East
Clarissa C. Erwin
Daniel Timothy Erwin
David Fairer
Jan Fergus
Lisa Freeman
Jack Fruchtman
Michael Genovese
George Haggerty
Daniel Heartz
Deborah Kennedy
Issac Kramnick
Joan Landes
R.W. McHenry
Maureen E. Mulvihill
Melvyn New
John C. O'Neal
David Oakleaf
Douglas Lane Patey
Adam Potkay
Suzanne R. Pucci
Larry L. Reynolds
John Richetti
Albert J. Rivero
Wendy W. Roworth
Treadwell Ruml II
Peter Sabor
Laura Schattschneider
Barbara B. Schnorrenberg
William C. Schrader
Julia Simon
John Sitter
Jeffrey Smitten
Ann T. Straulman
Astrida Tantillo
Dennis Todd
Raymond D. Tumbleson
Ann Van Allen-Russell
Kenneth Winkler

Institutional Members 2013-14

American Antiquarian Society
Colonial Williamsburg Foundation, *John D. Rockefeller, Jr. Library*
Folger Institute
Fordham University
Newberry Library
Ohio State University Libraries, *Thompson Library*
Omohundro Institute for Early American History, *Kellock Library*
Princeton University
Smithsonian Institute, AAPG Library
Stanford University, *Green Library*
UCLA, *William Andrews Clark Memorial Library*
University of California, Santa Barbara, *Division of Humanities and Fine Arts*
University of Kentucky, *Young Library*
University of North Carolina, *Davis Library*
University of Pennsylvania Library
University of Rochester Library
University of Victoria, *McPherson Library*
Yale University Library

Index

Every effort has been made to include references to all identifiable persons living before or during the long eighteenth century, as well as to often cited contemporary critics and commentators, and to provide a selective listing of relevant concepts and keywords. Readers may also wish to consult the endnotes of each essay for more comprehensive information.